REFORM IN THE MAKING

REFORM IN THE MAKING

THE IMPLEMENTATION
OF SOCIAL POLICY IN PRISON

Ann Chih Lin

PRINCETON UNIVERSITY PRESS   PRINCETON, NEW JERSEY

Copyright © 2000 by Princeton University Press
Published by Princeton University Press, 41 William Street
Princeton, New Jersey 08540
In the United Kingdom: Princeton University Press
Chichester, West Sussex
All Rights Reserved

Library of Congress Cataloging-in-Publication Data
Lin, Ann Chih.
Reform in the making: the implementation of social policy
in prison / Ann Chih Lin
    p.   cm.
Includes bibliographical references and index.
ISBN 0-691-00984-8 (cloth : alk. paper)
1. Prisons—Government policy—United States.
2. Criminals—Rehabilitation—United States.
3. Prisoners—United States—Social conditions.
I. Title.   II. Title: Implementation of social policy in prison.
HV9304.L56 2000
365'.7'09573 21—dc21   99-045173

This book has been composed in Sabon

The paper used in this publication meets the minimum
requirements of ANSI/NISO Z39.48-1992 (R 1997)
(*Permanence of Paper*)

http://pup.princeton.edu

Printed in the United States of America

10 9 8 7 6 5 4 3 2 1

To my grandparents ─────────────────────

YUEN-CHING CHANG LIN AND WEI-MIN LIN

EDITH SHU-MIN WANG MA AND DR. YUEN-CHEUNG MA

Contents

List of Tables

Acknowledgments

IN MARCH 1992, I stepped off a plane in a state I had never visited, got into the first car that I had ever driven solo, and made my shaky way down miles of country roads to a prison I call Antelope Valley. It was the first of five prisons I visited in a year-long odyssey that gave me an enormous respect for the men and women who work and live within the dangers, the isolation, and the absurdities of the American prison system. Seven years later, this book and this formal expression of gratitude to them are long overdue. The staff and prisoners I met did more than just sit for interviews: they answered hundreds of informal questions, interrupted their routines to accommodate mine, took me aside to tell me how things "really" worked, included me in their social gatherings, and, not the least, fretted about my safety. Their generosity, and their honesty, made my work possible.

The people who introduced me to the prison field were also an extraordinarily welcoming group. Without Norval Morris, who corrected an untold number of mistakes and still made me feel as if I had something to say, I would have had neither this project nor this book. John DiIulio gave me the benefit of his warm enthusiasm, early letters of introduction, careful readings of preliminary drafts, and an introduction to Princeton University Press. Charles Logan and Charlotte Rausch listened to my initial hypotheses and volunteered their extensive knowledge and resources to help in formulating more. Gerry Gaes, Harriet Lebowitz, Bernadette Pelissier, and their colleagues at the Office of Research and Evaluation at the Federal Bureau of Prisons read numerous drafts of my research proposal and convinced their colleagues to give me the opportunity to carry it out. J. Michael Quinlan, director of the Federal Bureau of Prisons, and Howard Gray and Michael O'Leary, director and assistant director of the Illinois Department of Corrections, gave my request to enter their institutions their personal attention and favor. Ike Eichenlaub provided random lists of interview subjects and endless pages of data.

Turning all those trips, all that data, and all that help into a dissertation and a book has been another, and longer, odyssey. My first debt there is to the teachers who taught me how to do it. Gary Orfield, Norval Morris, Russell Hardin, and Mark Hansen took my unconventional topic in stride and never, even when it was obvious, told me that I had bit off more than I could chew. They were generous with suggestions, some even helpful, for getting me into prison. They were also generous in spirit, encouraging me to challenge their opinions and find my own way back to their advice—and in this ungainly way, learn to become an independent scholar.

I have also had an exceptional amount of financial and emotional support along the way. While I had no "dissertation money" for this project, a graduate fellowship from the National Science Foundation supported my education and gave me the margin of financial safety that first allowed me to contemplate traveling to five prisons in five different states. The Mellon Foundation provided a predissertation research grant that allowed me to make the initial contacts at the Bureau of Prisons and finance my first research trip. Charles and Synthia Foskey opened their home and their hearts to me during my first prison visit. A Grodzins Lectureship at the University of Chicago financed another three prisons. The Brookings Institution provided a stipend, an office, and a wonderful research environment. The Department of Political Science and the Center for Research and Training on the Underclass, both at the University of Michigan, funded a semester to finish writing the dissertation. Under the direction of Sheldon Danziger, the Center also found course relief for me when I needed some extra time to write.

A very patient group of friends has accompanied me through this book; come to think of it, they probably feel as if they have been released from prison. Mark Brandon and Pradeep Chhibber found numerous excuses to get me to stop writing and go run (or stumble or gasp or walk) instead. Sheldon Danziger, Mary Corcoran, Mark Hansen, Dean Lin, Noga Morag-Levine, and Caroline Wang kept assuring me that I would finish. Bill and Sara Hacker, David and Linda Sung, Gene Lin, and TinhVan Diep let me whine in the way only family can. Diane DelGuercio and Elizabeth Wingrove listened to every lament about every awful phrase and loved me anyway.

My intellectual debts would leave me in debtor's jail were I ever to be arrested. The first Ph.D. seminar I taught at the University of Michigan gave me a group of fantastic students, who taught me much more about implementation than I had ever figured out on my own. Mark Brandon, Evelyn Brodkin, Pradeep Chhibber, Michael Cohen, Mary Corcoran, Sheldon Danziger, Martha Feldman, Richard Hall, Heather Hill, John Kingdon, Lawrence Mohr, Robert Pahre, Michael Ross, Michael Tonry, Jodi Sandfort, Kent Weaver, Margaret Weir, Janet Weiss, Elizabeth Wingrove, Patrick Wolf, and an anonymous reviewer for Princeton University Press read and commented on pieces of the text. Nancy Burns gave me the quote that opens Appendix 1. And I owe a particular debt of gratitude to Don Herzog, who not only read the dissertation, but wrote a twenty-page, single-spaced, cross-referenced commentary that is still an intellectual goad. Slow as I am on the uptake, I know that I could have made much better use of the advice I have gotten. Thus, gentle reader, forbear from blaming anyone but me for the mistakes that remain.

My parents, Otto C. C. and Ada Wen-Shung Ma Lin, taught me that personal inconvenience should never stand in the way of work that needs doing. That this particular work is mine still puzzles and distresses them, but they let it take me to prison just as their own work has taken them halfway across the world. The 1989–1990 Faith Community, staff, and kids of Covenant House New York taught me to take Matthew 25:44 seriously. I could ask for no better blessing. And four teachers—Marvin Bressler, Daniel Rodgers, Gary Orfield, and David Laitin—lent me their calling. Were it not for them, my work now would be perhaps more useful, but certainly less publishable.

REFORM IN THE MAKING

Introduction

"This Place Just by Being Here Is Not Going to Correct You"

THE REDISCOVERY OF REHABILITATION

> Once you in here—regardless of whether you're
> 16, 17, or 18—now you alone. You're cut off
> from everything out there, and you have to
> begin surviving. It's not an easy task . . . just
> because this place looks nice, it's still not a place
> to come to.
>
> This place just by being here is not going to
> correct you—I don't know why they call it the
> Department of Corrections.
>
> (*Prisoner*)

WHEN POLITICIANS compete to increase prison terms and prison time, their implicit promise is that they can keep criminals away from the rest of us. But while sentences get longer and time gets harder, most prisoners do eventually return to society. The average felony sentence imposed upon federal and state offenders in 1996 was sixty-two months, or just over five years. Those prisoners actually serve, on average, 45 percent of a state sentence for a mean prison stint of two years and four months, and 85 percent of a federal sentence for a stint of four years and five months.[1] Once prisoners are released, recidivism rates, though notoriously difficult to calculate, are high. In 1995, 19 percent of all parolees were returned to prison, before their parole was completed, for a new crime.[2] A 1989 study of recidivism showed that 40 percent of all released prisoners were rearrested for a felony or serious misdemeanor by the end of the first year, and 62.5 percent were rearrested within 3 years (Beck and Shipley 1989).

[1] Information taken or calculated from Table 5.58, "Average Sentence Length and Estimated Time to Be Served in State and Federal Prison," in Maguire and Pastore (1998: 431).

[2] Information calculated from Table 6.68, "Sentenced Prisoners Admitted to State and Federal Institutions for Violation of Parole or Other Conditional Releases," in Maguire and Pastore (1998: 520). Note that 40 percent of all parolees do not complete their parole successfully. More commonly, however, their parole is revoked for violations of the terms of release (for instance, failure to find a job), and not for a new crime.

In other words, incarceration, as it stands, does not prevent recidivism. Moreover, even if released prisoners do not reoffend, they do not necessarily become self-supporting. A study of federal prisoners from 1984 to 1987 showed that only 63 percent were employed a year after release; the percentage rose if they had vocational training or work experience in prison industries during prison, but only to 72 percent (Saylor and Gaes 1997). Such numbers suggest that simply avoiding recidivism does not assure that former prisoners do not become a problem for themselves or for the community—or, more positively, that former prisoners are able to contribute to society upon their return.

In the last decade, crime policies in the states and on the national level have focused on incarceration: longer sentences, "mandatory minimum sentencing," the reduction of time off for good behavior, and the abolition of parole. Such policies are expected to reduce the crime rate by keeping possible recidivists off the streets; they supposedly also deter prisoners from reoffending. The extent to which these policies succeed at achieving their goals is a subject of vociferous debate. But even assuming they do, they create new policy problems: the problem of ballooning prison populations and rampant overcrowding, and the problem of released prisoners, who for their sake as well as society's must be reintegrated into the community.

This last problem has gone almost unnoticed in the move toward longer sentences and more widespread sentencing. But larger prison populations result inevitably in more released prisoners. Their ability to return to society is the difference between regaining their contributions and restoring their lives as citizens, workers, and family members, or creating a permanent population of revolving-door prisoners. Yet increasing the ability of released prisoners to return to society is an inherently, and objectively, difficult dilemma. Even the most repentant, well-meaning, and well-prepared ex-prisoners face a world that is infinitely more complicated than the isolation and the structure that characterize prison. While the obvious place to help them readjust is a structured environment outside of the prison, there is neither a bureaucratic infrastructure nor a network of private charities and social-service providers to give that help. And, of course, even were they to get that help, ex-prisoners are not abundantly blessed with the resources to meet the challenges of life outside prison: 41 percent of the state prison population, and 23 percent of the federal, lacks even a high school diploma.[3] To the extent that ex-prisoners are to be at all prepared to return to society, therefore, that preparation must come in prison, at least for the foreseeable future.

[3] Information taken from Table 1, "Characteristics of Sentenced Federal and State Prison Inmates, 1991," in Harlow (1994: 2).

But it is not clear that prisons, as institutions, have the capacity to provide this kind of preparation. Prisons are not currently designed to be schools or factories; still less are they set up as places where trusted advisors can dispense either counseling or good counsel, or environments where family ties and family support can be nurtured. And the history of school, work, counseling, and family programs in prisons does not inspire confidence: while programs of these sorts are not uncommon in prisons, they are difficult to evaluate, often operated haphazardly, and plagued by skepticism about whether "rehabilitation" actually "works."

The skepticism about rehabilitation springs from three sets of concerns, all reasonable, yet all paralyzing if accepted without thought. The first reason for skepticism is the fear that people who have demonstrated their contempt for society's laws may continue to flout them, even after they are better prepared to survive as law-abiding citizens. Preparation cannot change the mind of someone committed to crime. Yet one might also argue that without the preparation—educational, emotional, psychological—to survive without crime, even someone committed to reform will have a hard time changing his life. Preparation is neither a panacea nor a guarantee, but it makes reform possible.

A second reason for skepticism is the adversarial environment of the prison. Prisoners are confined involuntarily, and prison staff are the ones keeping them there. The resulting bitterness, resentment, wariness, and contempt would seem to preclude the trust and mutual respect necessary for effective teaching, supervising, or counseling. Yet those who have studied prisons, or other social organizations, know that it is not impossible for opponents to work together for some mutual advantage, even if their mutual suspicion never quite disappears. If programs meant to prepare prisoners for release are beneficial to both staff and prisoners, one might see cooperation begin to develop.

A final reason for skepticism is the sense that programs have simply not worked in the past. Yet a closer look at the record does not justify that grimness. Programs never work for everybody, and they often work for very few. But reexamining the history of failed prison programs shows that they are often accompanied by garish mismanagement: internecine warfare between staff, outright subversion of programs by prisoners or administrators, untrained staff directed to run a program, or trained staff who are not given the latitude to act. One would not expect programs implemented—or misimplemented—in these ways to work. Understanding what prevents the successful implementation of programs is the first step in discovering whether prison programs can act as effective agents of correction.

In this book, I take up these three challenges to the reigning skepticism about rehabilitation. The management of programs in prisons, I argue, is

an implementation problem, of the kind that political scientists and public policy scholars have studied extensively in the last twenty-five years.
Reframing the failures of rehabilitation as implementation failures leads
us to see that staff and prisoners base their support for and participation
in programs on criteria different from what most policymakers or advocates might believe. Staff and prisoners work with and participate in programs not because of their long-term rehabilitative benefits, but because
programs can satisfy their immediate, prison-centered needs. Their interest is in programs that keep prisoners busy and interested, with incentives
that are valuable, given the context of a particular prison. They also look
for programs that are congruent with the values that staff use to govern
their interaction with prisoners and their understanding of their jobs.
Programs are part of a particular style of prison management: one that
encourages accommodation between staff and prisoners, as opposed to
group loyalty. In prisons where existing patterns of staff interaction em-
brace this kind of interaction, programs will be welcomed. But in prisons
that do not, staff will reject programs or attempt to subvert them.

The prison environment structures the extent to which staff understand policy and both staff and prisoners decide to cooperate with it.
Implementing programs successfully, therefore, requires an understanding of how the organizational context of each individual prison will
interact with the written policies and provisions that govern rehabilitation programs. This understanding recasts the debate about whether prisoners must first be "amenable" to rehabilitation before programs can
work. Stated in this way, the claim is true but somewhat trivial: the real
task is to create prison environments that encourage prisoners to rehabilitate themselves, and that encourage staff to help the prisoners along.

Rehabilitation on the Ground

Prison programs in the United States range from carefully designed, extensively monitored experiments for a handful of selected prisoners, to
the GED (General Equivalency Diploma) classes and trades programs
conducted as part of many prisons' normal offerings. With a few exceptions, most of the research on prison rehabilitation has focused on the
first type of program, with an emphasis on testing whether a particular
program design—"boot camps" or sex-offender treatment or the like—
have an effect upon recidivism rates. Yet most prisoners participate not in
such programs but, when at all, in routine literacy and educational programs: adult basic education, the GED, and some vocational training.
Seventy-five percent of all state and federal prisons provide adult basic
education, 80 percent offer the chance to get a high school diploma or

GED, 54 percent provide vocational training, 37 percent prison industries, and 33 percent college-level coursework. Over 21 percent of all prisoners participate in the educational programs offered.[4]

These programs are hard to evaluate, not only because they vary
widely in curriculum, requirements, and scope, but because they are often
an afterthought to the more pressing tasks of ensuring the safety of prison
staff and prisoners, and making sure that the day-to-day operational
tasks of the prison—food service, showers and exercise, building maintenance—get accomplished. Staff turnover, program consistency, bud-
geting, and resource availability all affect the quality of programs. Low
participation from prisoners and resentment from staff—and politicians—who feel that prisoners are getting "too much" prove to be common barriers.

The prison literature has documented numerous instances of problems
such as these with programs (Clemmer 1958; Sykes 1958; Cressey 1961;
Giallombardo 1966; Heffernan 1972; Irwin 1970, 1980; Jacobs 1977;
McKelvey 1977; Rothman 1980; Craig and Rogers 1993; Josi and
Sechrest 1996). Yet for the most part, it has assumed that such problems
are unavoidable, simply a consequence of the fact that programs will
never be a prison priority. Other scholars disagree, suggesting that programs can be an effective tool for helping to preserve prison order and, in
return, can even develop support within the prison (DiIulio 1987, 1991;
Fleisher 1989; Toch and Adams 1989; Useem and Kimball 1989; Wright
1993). But for these scholars, like their earlier counterparts, the chief concern is the orderly maintenance of the prison environment and the adaptation (or lack thereof) of prisoners to that order, rather than the quality
or the functioning of prison programs themselves.

The lack of attention to programs and how they can fit into the everyday prison environment reflects a more fundamental problem: the tendency of researchers and policymakers to see programs—prison rehabilitation, welfare reform, job training, education reform—separately
from the organizations—the prisons, the welfare offices, the job-training
centers, and the schools—in which they are housed.[5] Even the language
of analysis is different: programs are evaluated, but organizations are

---

[4] Information taken or calculated from Table 17, "Number of State and Federal Correctional Facilities Providing Work, Education, and Counseling Programs, and Number of
Inmates Participating, Midyear 1995," in Stephan (1997).

[5] A real exception to this is the classic *Organization for Treatment*, by David Street,
Robert Vinter, and Charles Perrow (1966). The task in this case is simplified because the
juvenile detention centers they examined were "organizations for treatment": the treatment
goal and strategy was an explicit part of each of the centers. But Street, Vinter, and Perrow
also spend a good deal of time talking about routine interactions that do not have anything
specifically to do with treatment, but which do affect the environment in which treatment
occurs.

described. As a result of this separation, evaluators tend to expect that organizations can be changed to accommodate programs, while organization theorists tend to explain that programs are inevitably changed by the organizations implementing them. Both sets of insights are useful and important. But apart, they talk past each other, their assumptions preventing an accurate assessment of how programs and organizations interact and mutually adjust.

In this study, I attempt to fill these gaps. This book presents the everyday world of programs in five prisons—programs established not as experiments with tightly controlled procedures, but as a routine fixture in the prison regime. All five of the prisons are medium-security, male prisons—the prisons that confine the largest number and the greatest variety of prisoners in the United States. Four of these prisons—known by pseudonyms in this book as Antelope Valley, Beaverton, Drake, and Evergreen—are federal prisons. One—Catawba State—is a state prison.

Like most state and all federal prisons, these five prisons all offer literacy and high-school-equivalency classes, some vocational-training options, and pay-for-performance assignments in prison industries. Three offer intensive drug-treatment programs; four allow inmates to work toward a college degree through in-prison classes; all make some type of work assignment mandatory. The four federal prisons operate under the same federal guidelines with respect to their programming effort; they receive funding under the same criteria, and all their personnel are required to take the same basic training course at a federal law enforcement training center and to meet standard minimum qualifications. While the state prison operates under very different administrative conditions, it is known for its programming options and its staff training, and is thus roughly comparable in programming to the federal prisons in the study. I give further information about research design and site selection in Appendix 1.

The five prisons also share an important organizational similarity: despite the many programs they offer, none would be mistaken for treatment centers or therapeutic communities. They are prisons, with programming to be sure, but prisons nonetheless. Staff and prisoners in these prisons describe very similar background conditions: a world in which an uneasy peace reigns, where staff care most about staying safe and avoiding trouble, and prisoners care most about getting through their sentence in safety and with sanity intact. Both groups have some common interest in maintaining order, minimizing tension, and finding constructive occupations for the prisoners. Consciously or no, they create strategies to achieve this; those strategies develop in response to formal prison regulations, to history, and to informal prison practices.

TABLE I.1
Characteristics of Prisons

	Antelope Valley	Beaverton	Drake	Evergreen	Catawba[b]
Prisoners' History of Violence					
None	62.3%	34.8%	52.1%	42.2%	(Drugs)[c] 18%
Minor	12.4%	17.3%	16.2%	17.4%	(Robbery) 29%
Major	25.5%	47.8%	31.8%	40.4%	(Violence) 53%
Percentage of prisoners w/disciplinary reports[a]	23%	25%	22%	23%	NA
Population	789	933	1061	1115	1777
Percentage over capacity	62%	63%	81%	57%	66%
Staff-inmate ratio	1 : 1.9	1 : 2.6	1 : 2.9	1 : 2.9	1 : 3.2
Custody staff-inmate ratio	1 : 5.1	1 : 5.9	1 : 6.8	1 : 6.9	1 : 4.4
Education staff-inmate ratio	1 : 78.9	1 : 71.8	1 : 66.3	1 : 69.7	NA
Black staff-inmate ratio	1 : 2.5	1 : 37.1	1 : 31.7	1 : 3.7	NA
White staff-inmate ratio	1 : 1.7	1 : 1.6	1 : 1.7	1 : 2.2	NA

[a] The numerator is the number of prisoners who committed one or more minor (300–400 level) infractions in the last year, or one or more moderate (200 level) offenses in the last two years. Serious disciplinary infractions (100 level) are summed over the last 10 years, and so have been left out of this table. The denominator is the number of prisoners for whom disciplinary data was available: 79% of the total population at Antelope Valley; 84% at Beaverton; 88% at Drake; and 85% at Evergreen.

[b] Much of the data in this table was unavailable for Catawba, the state prison.

[c] I did not have information for prisoners' history of violence in Catawba as a whole. The percentages shown here are from my interview sample, and reflect the major categories of crimes for which prisoners were convicted.

The five prisons, of course, are not identical, and Table I.1 summarizes many of these differences. The state prison, Catawba State Correctional Center, is nearly twice the size of the smallest prison, Antelope Valley, and it is one and two-thirds times the size of Evergreen, the largest federal prison. Catawba also has more violent prisoners than the federal prisons, reflecting a difference in the kinds of crimes that fall under state and federal statutes. Within the sample, therefore, one might expect Catawba to have a more difficult time implementing programs than would the federal prisons. Among the federal prisons, the differences are less stark. Beaverton has the highest proportion of prisoners with violent backgrounds; Drake, the most severe problem of overcrowding. Again, one's initial hypothesis would be that these prisons would find it harder to implement programs than either Evergreen or Antelope Valley.

Some of these hypotheses are in fact confirmed. Catawba State and Drake were both unable to implement their rehabilitative programs successfully. At Catawba State, scarce resources and rapidly increasing demands overwhelmed staff and prisoners, distracting them from any but the most basic coping tasks. At Drake, hostility between prisoners and staff made working and participating in programs seem irrelevant, even dangerous. Yet difficult external circumstances cannot be the entire story. Although implementation at both prisons failed, it failed in distinctive ways. At Drake, numerous programs existed on paper, but the teaching staff was embittered and isolated, and prisoners were unwilling to sign up for the programs or simply unaware of their existence. Essentially, program implementation was abandoned: while the federal system's guidelines required Drake to have programs, the programs were essentially a shell. By contrast, Catawba State, where one might expect implementation to be much more difficult than at Drake, presented a very different picture of failure. The teaching staff was enthusiastic; the programs of good quality; and all of the programs had long waiting lists. What was lacking at Catawba was support from staff other than the teaching staff, a lack of support that resulted from chronic resource and supervisory problems. Programs were not abandoned at Catawba, but they were neglected: marginal to the operations of the prison, they were relegated to the sidelines.

Thus similar problems at Catawba and Drake translated into different kinds of implementation experiences. The mystery deepens when one looks at the other prisons. Evergreen and Drake are similar in size; Evergreen is not as crowded, but its prisoners have a more serious history of violence and staff-inmate ratios are no higher than Drake's. However, at Evergreen, programs fill up and, in contrast to both Catawba and Drake, the correctional officers and other nonprogram staff get very involved in encouraging prisoners to participate in programs. A closer look at those programs makes the picture murkier: once enrolled, prisoners are asked to do very little, and staff cut corners in ways that make learning difficult, if not impossible. But despite—or perhaps because of—this problem with program quality, staff are enthusiastic about and supportive of programs in a way unimaginable at either Drake or Catawba. One can say that implementation is subverted at Evergreen: programs exist, but their rehabilitative purposes are vitiated in favor of other uses.

Programs at Catawba, Drake, and Evergreen illustrate the problems that arise when detractors of rehabilitation conclude that programs cannot or do not work. On paper, each of these prisons has a set of policies that should promote rehabilitation. In practice, the policies are never given a chance to work. Such programs make a mockery of the question, "What works?" Whether specific policies are effective at reintegrating prisoners into society is an important question. But no answer to it can be found if the policies in question are never implemented, do not function as designed, or are changed beyond recognition. Before it is possible to test "what works?," one must ensure that the conditions for a fair test exist.

Yet simply knowing that programs at these prisons were not implemented properly would not, in and of itself, improve the prospects for rehabilitation either. The distinctively different ways in which implementation failed at each of these three prisons suggest that there is no "cure-all" solution, no way to design programs differently to avoid all possible problems. Instead, the different kinds of failure at Catawba, Drake, and Evergreen suggest that it is important to see programs in conjunction with prisons: to examine how the context of programs affects their fate.

The importance of doing this is made more apparent when Beaverton and Antelope Valley's programs are compared. The two prisons are very different: Beaverton has more prisoners with violent histories than any other federal prison in the sample; Antelope Valley has the least.[6] They differ in staff education, prisoner background, racial mix, and staff culture. But staff and prisoners at both prisons believed that prison programs fulfill their institutional needs, and they identified the rehabilitative goals of the program with the prison's goals. Without deliberate design, these prisons managed to weave policy goals together with institutional practices, so that the two complement each other. Although not immune to the problems that plague the other prisons—staff hostility, institutional demands, scarce resources (note that teacher-inmate ratios are actually higher at these two prisons than at Drake or Evergreen)—these prisons did not allow such problems to derail the implementation of rehabilitative policies. Their example illustrates what must happen before programs can work.

Are there ways of thinking about organizational context that can systematize this wide variety of implementation experiences? In this book, I argue that there are. But doing so requires that easy statements about the incommensurability of treatment and custody, or the benefits that good programs bring to prisons, be put to one side. Instead, one must be willing to think of programs not as the focus of staff and prisoner interactions, but rather as a minor part of a different story. That story is about the more general needs and the values of prisoners and staff, their attempts to cope with the constraints and the scarcities of a difficult life, and the way that programs fit into those coping mechanisms. In this story,

---

[6] Antelope Valley has a particularly difficult mix of prisoners in another way: it houses a hospital and a psychiatric treatment facility for prisoners, and its higher staff-inmate ratios reflect in part the special problems of its population.

rehabilitation programs are something of an afterthought, their fate a byproduct of other struggles and accommodations. And yet taking the focus away from programs allows us to understand them better, and to develop a better sense of the conditions under which they can, or cannot, work.

Learning about Implementation

Detailed knowledge of program activities on the ground, and of the beliefs behind staff and prisoners' activity, cannot be discovered by looking at official statistics. It is even obscured if one talks only with wardens and administrators. Instead, it requires an examination of classrooms and lieutenants' offices, discussions with prisoners who have chosen or rejected rehabilitative programming, interaction with guards and maintenance workers as well as teachers and psychiatrists. Accordingly, as I discuss more fully in Appendix 2, I spent ten to twelve hours a day for three weeks in each of these five prisons. I was escorted by a staff member from place to place within the prison, but moved freely in each particular location—housing units, educational buildings, work sites. I also conducted 354 semistructured, open-ended interviews, each lasting forty-five to ninety minutes, with a list of randomly selected staff and inmates that I generated before going to each prison. I supplemented these interviews with in-person observation of various programs, staff meetings, and staff-inmate conferences, and with casual conversations in the prison.

In addition to the site work, I did informal interviewing at a federal jail, and at the Washington, D.C., headquarters of the Federal Bureau of Prisons, where I also gathered quantitative data and information on official policies and procedures. I gathered data on state inmates and state policies on-site at the state prison. Each prisoner interviewed was asked if he would be willing to release information from his personal file on his age, conviction, sentence, security level, and prior record. Seventy-two percent of the prisoners agreed, and conclusions involving these factors are based only upon this group.

All the interviews were conducted privately, and in the case of prisoners, in rooms where they could be sure that we would not be overheard. For staff the interviews were less likely to take place in a fixed location, but we also spoke only when we could not be overheard by others. Because of security and privacy considerations, none of the interviews were taped. Instead I took notes and transcribed all interviews in their entirety from those notes. I promised neither to name nor to identify anyone, from staff to prisoners to prison officials to the prisons themselves. This means that apart from the name of the then-director of the

Federal Bureau of Prisons, J. Michael Quinlan, all names I use are ficti-
tious. In particular cases, such as when naming the job title or special-
ization would identify the person I interviewed, I have changed the person's job description. I have also changed some details, particularly when
it comes to describing the subject area of particular classes: this is because correctly identifying the vocational training programs at the different prisons could lead to the identification of the prisons. Each interview has a unique identifier, which I have retained for the quotations used
in the book: a number from 1-5, indicating the prison (where Antelope
Valley = 1, Beaverton = 2, Catawba State = 3, Drake = 4, and Evergreen = 5), and a one- or two-letter code. Capital letter combinations
stand for prisoners; lowercase letters for staff. Thus an interview labeled
"1AB" is a prisoner from Antelope Valley, whereas an interview labeled "3fr" would be a staff member from Catawba State. No additional
meaning is attached to either the letter or the number-letter combinations.

I was not able to follow prisoners for long enough, or under conditions
that were closely enough controlled, to discover whether their participation in programs influenced their lives and choices upon release. But as I
discuss more fully in Appendix 1, controlling the implementation of programs carefully enough to establish their success or failure would first
require the kind of knowledge about implementation that this study provides. Instead, throughout this book I use a careful discussion of program
process, prison operations, and participant choices to establish how implementation works. And I argue that this kind of examination should be
standard before researchers attempt to reach any conclusions about program success and failure.

Chapter 1 introduces the reader to the longstanding argument over
programs in prisons, and explains why ignoring the organizational characteristics of prisons almost guarantees that prison reforms will fail.
Chapter 2 then explains how an implementation approach to programs
allows us to see how two critical aspects of the prison context—the institutional need for order, and the institutional values that govern the choice
of different strategies for maintaining it—structure the fate of rehabilitation programs. Chapter 3 turns to the prisons themselves, describing staff
and prisoner strategies in Catawba State, Drake, and Evergreen Correctional Centers that led, and so often lead, to implementation failure.
Chapter 4 then contrasts these prisons with Antelope Valley and Beaverton, two prisons that pursue very different strategies for maintaining
prison order, but which succeed at implementing rehabilitative programs
as well. With the empirical cases established, Chapter 5 examines the
major challenge to my theory of implementation: that my approach to
implementation, invoking as it does a set of prison-centered reasons for
participating in programs, might encourage insincere participation from

prisoners who have not made a commitment to change their criminal behavior. Although this argument is intuitively plausible, I argue that it falsely simplifies the lessons that research teaches us about the causes of crime, and provides excuses for prison administrators, staff, and prisoners to avoid serious efforts to improve implementation. Finally, I conclude the book with some reflections about how useful this framework might be to the study of implementation more generally. I argue that policymakers need to take seriously the role of staff and policy targets in making the reforms that are thrust upon them. Every grand idea and good wish that policymakers have lies in the hands of others. They require not clearer mandates or greater discretion, but to satisfy their needs and protect their values while implementing policy. Policymakers can make their task easier. Or they can unmake reform.

1

Revisiting Rehabilitation

WHY "WHAT WORKS" IS THE WRONG QUESTION

AT DRAKE Correctional Center—a prison built in the first half of the twentieth century, with cellblocks that still boast bars rather than doors—literacy classes are held in a room looking incongruously like an elementary school classroom. With the alphabet marching in cursive script around the walls and the date written on an otherwise pristine blackboard, about twenty functionally illiterate men sit facing their teacher. The men range in age from 20 to 55; some have the knitted caps of Black Muslims, others a host of religious medals dangling around their necks. Though you cannot tell from looking at them, their numbers include bank robbers, crack sellers, those who grow or transport pot; there are Marielitos from Cuban prisons, and Native Americans convicted of crimes on the reservation. Six or seven of the men are sitting, heads in hands, staring at workbooks; the rest are sleeping, talking, or doodling. The teacher reads a newspaper at her desk in front, looking up once in a while to restore order or answer a question when someone approaches her. Given the amount of sleeping and staring in the classroom, the occasions requiring her intervention are few.

Discussing the class with me later, she shrugs, frustrated and resigned. The men are in a mandatory literacy program, she explains, and most stay only because the alternative is time in solitary confinement, and a restricted choice of prison jobs. Their lack of motivation, and the vast differences in their aptitudes and knowledge, mean that individualized study is the only way to run a classroom. She assigns lessons and helps the ones who ask her for help; their preparation is so uneven that even doing this is a challenge. As for everyone else, she lets them sit as long as they don't cause trouble; it's their problem if they don't want to learn.

In a similar classroom, halfway across the country at Beaverton Correctional Center, the same mix of black, white, Hispanic, and Native American men are also studying math. Like the students at Drake, these men have long passed their schooldays; they are also mandatory students, condemned to class because of their low test scores. But instead of sleeping or staring, these men are out of their seats, clustered in groups of four around tables with sheets of scrap paper, animatedly arguing about math formulas. While a few students hang back, most are taking rulers to objects outlined with masking tape in the room and calling back measurements to the figurers at the table. Half of the blackboard is covered with formulas; the other half has the remnants of last hour's history lesson. The teacher rotates, hinting that one team should check an answer, encouraging another with a whoop of pleasure.

In which class is learning more likely to be occurring? One would certainly not want to say, from observation alone, that the men in the second classroom at Beaverton are all mastering basic math skills. Yet one could be confident in saying that, despite a few exceptions, the men at Drake are not likely to be learning much. At Beaverton, tests could be administered to determine the effectiveness of learning math in teams; the recidivism rates and future job prospects of the inmate graduates could also be monitored upon release, to see if their education made a difference. At Drake, however, tests to measure achievement would be beside the point; there is little reason to expect that sleeping in a classroom would have an effect on test scores or recidivism rates

The contrast between the quiet classroom at Drake and the lively classroom at Beaverton is the rock upon which prison rehabilitation programs founder. Literacy programs like the ones at Drake and Beaverton, or similar job training, drug treatment, and counseling programs, are available in numerous prisons. Yet their presence does not seem to lower recidivism rates, which studies estimate fall in the 40 to 60 percent range (Baumer 1997). Specific treatment programs in particular prisons also often disappoint the hopes of their proponents when evaluations find that they have little effect upon recidivism rates. Yet few investigate whether these programs actually operate in ways that would allow them to succeed. Instead, faced with little evidence of change, legislators, corrections officials, researchers, and the public come to the conclusion that rehabilitation "doesn't work." Like other social programs—compensatory education, job training, welfare—rehabilitation is easily dismissed as a soft-headed, idealistic effort, attempted during the social experimentation of the 1960s, ready for replacement by "tougher," "no-nonsense" policies.

Given widespread frustration with social programs, with the size and efficacy of government, and with the shocking crimes that so often turn up on the television news, such criticism of rehabilitation is understandable. It is also wrong. Research over the last fifteen years has shown that some programs, designed and administered carefully, can reduce recidivism rates. Unfortunately, the programs that are available to most prisoners, the education, job-training, drug treatment, and work programs mandated in the federal and in most state prison systems, are often carried out in ways that defeat their purpose. The result is cynicism, not only about prisoners and their chances for reform, but about our capacity as a society to do more than put prisoners away and hope they stay gone.

Why does the routine implementation of programs receive so little attention? In part, it is because the common explanations for implementation failure at prisons like Drake are taken for granted. Bad or burnt-out staff, unmotivated or irresponsible students—what more is there to know, and aren't both to be expected in a prison? In part, it is also because researchers and policymakers believe implementation to be a second-stage consideration, important only after they find a successful program to try. Cynicism about rehabilitation programs leads to disinterest in ways to run them better, since running programs better might still not lead to success.

Both of these premises are primarily habits of mind, habits that are seriously challenged by new research into how organizations operate and how policies are made. An understanding of people within organizations explains that they respond to incentives but also impart meaning to, or "make sense of," those responses. Applying this insight to prisons suggests that the right incentives, and encouragement to interpret those incentives in the right ways, can create prison environments that foster implementation as at Beaverton, or stunt it as at Drake. In other words, there is no reason to assume that staff will be burnt out or students unmotivated merely because they are in prison: the prison they are in matters.

Similarly, a new generation of work on policymaking suggests that early, linear models of policymaking—ideas lead to enactment, and enactment leads to implementation—oversimplify and mischaracterize the policy process. In the actual working-out of policy on the ground, the ideas that went into policymaking are reexamined and replaced, and the policy conflicts that first surfaced during enactment reappear. A policy with successful outcomes results not from getting first the ideas and then the implementation right, but from groping toward workable ideas as part of implementation. To put it another way, studying implementation is not second to studying policy success: it is a necessary part of understanding which policies can be successful.

Applying these insights into prisons as organizations and programs as policy implementation can lead us to a reevaluation of rehabilitation. The history of rehabilitation in prisons has been marked by two recurring patterns: new, intellectually plausible reforms that degenerate rapidly into excuses for prisoner abuse, administrative chaos, or both; and continual efforts to invent new forms of treatment, followed by equally dogged attempts to discredit the very possibility of reform. For critical theorists such as Michel Foucault, the implication is that prison reform is

not about reform at all, but rather about the continual creation and justification of new forms of social control. For prison experts and policymakers who see each successive wave of reform fail, the conclusion is to
abandon even the ideal of rehabilitation as simply unworkable in the context of prisons. But there is also a third interpretation: that reform will
never succeed as long as the emphasis is on discovering the right method
instead of creating the right organizational conditions. This does not
mean designing the ideal prison and superimposing it on the existing
penal system, with the assumption that the right ideas can create miracles.
Rather, it means starting from the prisons we have—the patterns of interaction that currently exist—and exploring how they are set, in ways that
bode good or ill for attempts at reform.

Explaining the Failures of Reform

As long as there have been prisons, there have been efforts to rehabilitate.[1] America's first prison, the Walnut Street Jail in Philadelphia, was
established by Quakers in the hope that isolation, religious counseling,
the Bible, and simple useful work would lead offenders to reform. The
famous Auburn "silent system" attempted to give prisoners discipline
and structure while keeping them from countervailing influences in the
form of conversation with other miscreants. The Progressive Era belief in
individualized treatment led to the practice of indeterminate sentencing
and parole review, in which different plans would supposedly be established for each prisoner, who would then be monitored and confined until
evaluations established his fitness for release. And fascination with the
possibilities of psychology led to experiments with behavioral modification, counseling, and other forms of psychiatric treatment in the 1960s
penitentiary.

   Yet each of these regimes has also been corrupted by a litany of abuses.
The solitary confinement of the Walnut Street Jail may have induced in-
sanity in its inmates (American Friends Service Committee 1971: 18). The
Auburn system was unable to maintain silence without whippings and
other physical punishments (McKelvey 1977: 28). At the Norfolk Prison
Colony, a model Progressive Era prison in Massachusetts, ditch digging,
necessary for the construction of the prison, was redefined as "rehabilitative" so that prisoners could be assigned to it. The warden justified this
somewhat novel theory of treatment by suggesting that "it will help to
teach them [the prisoners] to meet emergencies that are bound to arise in

---

[1] Histories of the American prison are numerous, but see in particular Cullen and Gilbert
(1982); Goodstein and MacKenzie (1989); McKelvey (1977); and Morris and Rothman
(1995).

their life outside." (Rothman 1980: 406). Indeterminate sentencing, originally designed to enable the release of prisoners in individually sensitive ways, became an excuse for longer and longer sentences and the slow torture of an uncertain release date (Allen 1981; Morris 1974). Psychiatric counseling and behavioral modification programs licensed new forms of prison discipline and control (Mitford 1973; Ross and Gendreau 1980).

Why do reform regimes, whether they are as extensive as Auburn's silent system or as targeted as a behavioral modification program, fail in such depressingly similar ways? One common answer is that prisons are meant, not to reform delinquents, but to create them. Michel Foucault's influential *Discipline and Punish* (1979) points out that recommendations for prison reform resemble each other throughout the ages and always entail more supervision, more control, more inculcation of moral habits to correct the failures of past supervision, control, and moral inculcation (264–72). But this perpetual failure does have a use. Prison creates delinquents: it brings prisoners together and encourages the creation of a criminal subculture, fails to give them real opportunities that could serve as an alternative to crime, serves as a reason to supervise their actions closely both before and after release, and essentially labels them as unfit to participate on an equal footing with others in society (281–82). This delinquency, "maintained by the pressure of controls on the fringes of society, reduced to precarious conditions of existence, lacking links with the population that would be able to sustain it," is at once recognizable and scorned, impotent to pose a real threat to the state (278). Delinquents prey on their fellow poor, dividing the working-class among itself and making unified rebellion against the state impossible. They provide an outlet for the delinquency of dominant groups—prostitutes for upper-class johns, alcohol and drugs for upper-class addicts, spies and informants upon organized-crime networks—and in doing so prevent this delinquency from threatening the dominant power structure (279–80). Through the prison and its sister institutions of control, the state thus manages to use its opposition, to regulate it, and to prevent it from posing any real danger.

More recent critics have extended this account by arguing that the latest movements in penology—classification of prisoners, the cost-benefit analysis of incarceration—create a type of risk management consistent with the claim that the state's primary interest is in managing rather than reducing crime (Feeley and Simon 1992). Certainly as description, accounts like these warn against the arrogant optimism of reformers who seek to end crime, as well as the fashionable cynicism of realists who, taking laws as invariably just, scoff at blaming anything or anyone but law-breakers for breaking them. But as an empirical story, Foucault's

critique lacks actors (Garland 1990). Neither the adminstrators who enforce the disciplinary function of the prison, nor the prisoners who suffer
it, appear as anything but illustrations. As such, it is impossible to ask
questions that compare how different groups of prisoners or staff experience, reduce, or resist the pains of imprisonment. The one account of
resistance is a passage on workers' newspapers, which tried to recast
criminality as a challenge to an unjust social order (Foucault 1979: 287).
Yet even this is isolated at the end of a chapter; Foucault gives no story of
how this resistance arises or how it is overcome.

Foucault's account makes no use of agency, because he intends to show
that the actions available to individuals within the penal system are actually first constructed by the categories of submission and resistance implicit in it. But this approach elides the possibility that different categories of submission and resistance may not be equal: different choices
about resistance might lead to different micro-outcomes for the individuals involved. Even if these differences in outcomes do not threaten the
logic of the penal system, they may nevertheless point to better and worse
policy choices or reform strategies, and to different spaces for the assertion of human dignity.

Historical research suggests that social theorists like Foucault are right
when they point to the way coercive practices follow upon, are justified
by, or sweep away reformist impulses. But it offers a different but equally
compelling story about the decline of reform, one that takes the prison
more seriously as an institution with distinctive security needs, tight resources, and a general fear of disorder. Control, in this formulation, is not
social but situational: the commitment to reform is present at the administrative level, but thwarted at the front lines when suspicious staff and
equally suspicious prisoners hijack programs for their own uses. Rather
than seeing staff as tools of social control and prisoners as its passive
objects, this account advances the possibility that reform is possible but
antithetical to the conditions of prison, where staff and prisoners struggle
to make their constrained and difficult circumstances slightly less difficult, in any way they can.

David Rothman's study of a Progressive prison in *Conscience and
Convenience* (1980) and Rose Giallombardo's study of a 1960s women's
prison in *Society of Women* (1966) tell this micro-story. Work programs
in these prisons were designed around the labor needs of the prison,
rather than around marketable skills. Education and counseling programs suffered from a severe lack of resources. Less familiar observers
might be led to blame incompetent staff or simple shortages for these
problems. But by developing an understanding of the prison environment, Rothman and Giallombardo were able to explain that in these prisons, rehabilitation was imperfectly understood and equated with permis-

siveness. Staff considered rehabilitation an "extra," incidental and clearly secondary to the more pressing needs of custody. Thus, everything from getting accurate counts to keeping prisoners orderly, from preventing escapes to clamping down on contraband, from maintaining the daily routine to instilling a healthy fear of guards, necessarily preceded any thoughts of treatment.

In both these cases rehabilitation enjoyed support from the wardens of the prison, as well as much of the administrative staff. But this support did not translate into a coherent understanding of how the demands of programming could be reconciled with the custodial functions of the prison. Thus, supervisors in each prison repeatedly emphasized rehabilitation in discussions with staff, but did not see the conflict that programs created with custody, and could not give their staff direction on how to handle it. Staff responded by fighting among themselves about the relative priority and importance of their jobs, or simply by insisting that the demands of everyday life in the prison required the modification of programs. In Rothman's Massachusetts prison, for instance, the counselors complained that guards revoked rewards that counselors had given inmates who showed improvement; guards responded by complaining that the inmates needed more discipline. Prisoners, quick to catch on to the situation, played off one set of staff against the other (Rothman 1980: 401).

A staff meeting on the education program at Giallombardo's prison illustrates well the progression from support to compromise. At the beginning of this passage, the warden is giving a pep talk to her staff about the advantages of prisoner education. Notice that she tries to frame the argument, not in terms of shaping or molding the minds of prisoners, but in terms of staff professionalization. Yet as the conversation progresses, her subordinate administrators turn that rhetoric back onto the programs. As professionals, they know what's best for them, for the prison, and even for the prisoners, and education simply is not it.

> *Warden*: An educational program in an institution like ours, or any institution, is very important. No more is the correctional officer looked upon as a jailer by society—as a guard with a key. . . . It's the job of everyone to support the program so that this can be done.
>
> *Supervisor of Education*: In setting up the education program, scheduling the inmates was difficult. . . . On Tuesday and Thursday evenings, classes will be given for inmates who work during the day . . . youth classes will be scheduled in the morning.
>
> *Associate Warden, Business*: We in Fiscal and Operations have a question. If you send all the main dish cooks off to school when you have to get out a meal, what are you going to do? . . . Warden, I'm Associate Warden here,

and this is the first time I've heard of it! People in Operations would like to be in on things so we can plan.

Correctional officer: Were rosters sent around? Some of the girls didn't know anything about it. And I had one that didn't want to go anymore.

Lieutenant: Were their [the prisoners'] names just put on the list? You know, if these girls don't want to take something, they won't unless they're interested. I tell you, *we've had a time* with all this. [Emphasis in original.]

Associate Warden, Treatment: Well, I know it's not easy. After all, we're dealing with the failures. These people are unintelligent, emotionally unstable, and insecure. . . . But we're supposed to do something with these people. We're supposed to have a treatment program, and we can't do it without everyone's cooperation.

Associate Warden, Business: Well, do they have to go during those hours? . . . Couldn't those people go from three to five or at another time? Or in the evening?

Supervisor of Education: Perhaps some shifts can be made as far as the courses are concerned. It will have to be worked out.

Warden: If you're really interested in an education, you'll go in the evening. After all, people outside take evening courses after work. And you officers take your course in the evening. And—I don't have to tell you about Abraham Lincoln.

Courses for the prisonsers, the warden argues, are about professionalization—"no longer is a correctional officer . . . a guard with a key." But her staff uses that argument against the warden. What about planning for the smooth operation of the prison—after all, the food has to be prepared and served on time. How about the prisoners?—the correctional officer suggests that prisoners need to be consulted, and the lieutenant implies that the administrators don't know much about what prisoners will and won't do. The associate warden for treatment, perhaps as a reflection of her own beliefs, perhaps hoping to curry favor with the officers, denigrates the prisoners' ability to learn. And soon the warden, who started out calling for everyone's cooperation in order to get the education program off the ground, is moralizing about how prisoners can make sacrifices to get an education if they really want to.[2]

The story told by this passage is not about prison administrators forcing education upon prisoners in order to make them easier to control, or about dangling education as a bribe in order to make prisoners more docile. Instead, it is about the staff's attachment to routines, about their unwillingness to disrupt their working relationships with the prisoners by making a new set of demands, and about the rationalizations they engage

[2] This passage is a heavily condensed version of the transcript of a staff meeting. The entire transcript is available in Giallombardo (1966: 68–72).

in to support their refusals to make any changes. Both Rothman and Gial-lombardo realized that seemingly small problems such as these revealed deeper problems with prison rehabilitation. "The prison," wrote Gial-lombardo, "faced with the practical concern of maintaining itself and the uncompromised claims of custodial security and internal order, views the treatment goals as an ideal to hold out as legitimate only when the pre-dominant tasks of maintenance, custody, and internal order are clearly in equilibrium" (Giallombardo 1966: 72). Rothman observes that "to join assistance to coercion is to create a tension that cannot persist indefinitely and will be far more likely to be resolved on the side of coercion" (Roth-man 1980: 419).

If one accepts this interpretation of the failure of prison reform, two possible consequences follow. One is to work within the ways prisons are structured, to reach an accommodation between the goals of mainte-nance, security, order, and treatment. Giallombardo alludes to this possi-bility when she writes that "the possibility of arriving at a solution to [the conflict between maintenance and treatment needs] by a reorganization of units at the maintenance and custodial levels was not considered." Yet she casts doubt upon the efficacy of this solution, calling it a "structural weakness of prisons" and concluding that "in the nature of the case, it could not be otherwise" (Giallombardo 1966: 72–73). Most commenta-tors take this to its logical conclusion. If the attempt to join assistance to an essentially coercive institution eventually negates that assistance or turns it into another instrument of coercion, better not to try at all. In-stead, this reasoning goes, prisons should be places of incapacitation and incapacitation only: their aim is to confine sentenced offenders and to confine them well—nothing more and nothing less.

Known variously as the "justice model" of imprisonment (Von Hirsch ed. 1976), as the rejection of "coerced cure" (Morris 1974), or as "hu-mane containment" (King and Morgan 1980), this critique of prison re-habilitation has assembled a varied cast of supporters. Many of these felt that rehabilitation, premised on the paternalistic belief that criminal be-havior was caused by a problem with offenders, was not an adequate response to the complex social and individual histories that led people to commit crimes (American Friends Service Committee 1971). They also pointed out that a rehabilitative rationale could be used to justify all sorts of abuses. Some prison staff attempted medical experiments on prisoners with the hope of changing their propensity to crime (Mitford 1973). Under indeterminate sentencing, parole boards could refuse to release prisoners until "rehabilitation" appeared (Allen 1981; Irwin 1980; Mor-ris 1974; Von Hirsch ed. 1976). This kind of rehabilitation, proponents of the justice model argued, was worse than simply leaving prisoners alone.

As one can surmise from this group of proponents, the justice model of imprisonment is often suggested as a way to make prisons more, not less, attentive to the needs of prisoners. As one of its proponents argues, "it was as well to recognize that all prison systems were in fact, and of necessity, human warehouses and that the point was to prevent them from becoming inhuman warehouses, whatever their lofty ideals" (King and McDermott 1995: 9). Proponents of this model often advocated for shorter sentences (as opposed to the longer ones felt necessary for treatment to take hold) (Von Hirsch ed. 1976); for an extensive array of educational, vocational, and counseling programs that prisoners would be free to choose or reject (Morris 1974); and for performance indicators that would hold prison officials accountable for maintaining humane standards of prison life and treatment (King and Morgan 1980).

But this model was also supported by another group of proponents for whom the consistent failure of prison reform suggested something else: the hopelessness of reforming most prisoners, who would continue to commit crimes if not deterred by their cost. Scholars like Gary Becker, James Q. Wilson, and Ernest Van den Haag were influential in promoting the idea that criminals knowingly committed crime because it paid, and would only be deterred by stricter and swifter punishments (Becker 1988; Wilson 1975, 1980; Van den Haag 1975; Van Dine, Conrad, and Dimitz 1979). Two research agendas in criminology also, indirectly, added support to this position. An influential body of work on criminal behavior argues that differences in criminality are primarily related to childhood antisocial behavior, and thus are stable across individuals. In other words, some people are predisposed by childhood experiences to commit crimes and others are not, even though they may suffer the same disadvantages or enjoy the same advantages later in life (Gottfredson and Hirschi 1990; West and Farrington 1977; Wilson and Herrnstein 1985; Wolfgang, Thornberry, and Figlio 1972, 1987). If this is the case, attempts to change prisoners are useless: the best hope is to keep prisoners in prison long enough so that they "age out" of their propensity to crime. Similarly, recent work on the benefits and costs of incarceration argues that imprisonment actually saves money when the cost of all the crimes criminals commit is considered. Based on data that show that prisoners commit many more crimes than they are arrested for, these studies argue that the social benefit of crime prevention is great enough to justify the continual expansion of both prison facilities and prison sentences (Piehl and DiIulio 1995; Marvell and Moody 1994; see Canela-Cacho, Blumstein, and Cohen 1997 for an alternative view).

The criminological studies that have most served to deprive rehabilitation of its legitimacy, however, have been studies of its ineffectiveness. Arguments that reformers should only concentrate on improving prison conditions, or that the most socially useful thing prisons can do is deter future crime, are harder to justify if there is evidence that prison programs can proactively assist prisoners to become productive citizens. But if programs are not effective, as research throughout the 1970s and 1980s suggested, there is no reason to try rehabilitation. A 1974 article by sociologist Robert Martinson, summarizing a review of 231 studies of correctional treatment programs, said it all: "With few and isolated exceptions, the rehabilitative efforts that have been reported so far have had no appreciable effect on recidivism" (Martinson 1974: 25). A later report by the National Academy of Sciences concurred, finding that if anything, the study (Lipton, Martinson, and Wilks 1975) Martinson summarized was too optimistic (Sechrest et al. 1979). A simple way of talking about the failure of rehabilitation became popular: "nothing works."

Research and politics have thus joined to suggest that the recurrent failure of attempts to reform prisons for rehabilitative purposes means that it is time to stop trying. But there is also a countervailing critique, which argues that the research on program effectiveness is not so bleak, the capacity of offenders to reform not so limited, and the failure of rehabilitation not quite so clear. This critique starts with recent evaluations that have reassessed program success. It draws strength from criminological work suggesting that criminal behavior does change with changes in life circumstances. And it returns to the history of prison programs to provide a different interpretation: one that focuses on how staff and prisoners interact around programs.

Re-viewing Rehabilitation

The defense of rehabilitation in the second half of the 1980s and 1990s has, in an odd way, been made easier by its thorough discrediting. In many ways expectations have changed: proponents no longer expect that most programs will work, and opponents have become the new orthodoxy, against whom any successful challenge seems a victory. This is, in fact, the tone taken by a set of new studies updating the original Lipton, Martinson, and Wilks (1975) review. Martinson himself withdrew his original conclusion in 1979, and by the late 1980s, meta-analyses—an analytical technique that recategorizes the variables in separate studies to allow for their reexamination en bloc—were beginning to show that rehabilitative programs did have an effect.[3] Evaluations showed that

[3] Martinson (1979) explains how his views changed. Palmer (1991) is a good review of the history of the changing debate and the meta-analyses that support the change; most notably Gendreau and Ross (1987) and Lipsey (1989). In addition, Gerber and Fritsch

programs incorporating behavioral, cognitive, life skills, multimodal, or family intervention offered promising strategies. More importantly, they suggested that combining different kinds of treatment within a program, and targeting certain approaches on certain offenders, should be tried (Ross and Gendreau 1980; Cullen and Gendreau 1989; Palmer 1991, 1995; Andrews et al. 1990a, 1990b). Other studies, more negative in their conclusions about treatment in general, also point out that some programs do show positive results despite the lack of an overall pattern of success (Lab and Whitehead 1990).

The cautious optimism of this return to behavioral approaches to rehabilitation is complemented by a parallel development in criminology: research that suggests that criminal careers are more variable than formerly thought. While acknowledging the importance of early childhood experience on delinquency, work such as Robert Sampson and John Laub's *Crime in the Making* also suggests that changes in life events—an increase in social ties and social stability, employment and marriage, positive school experience—have a significant impact on an individual's propensity to commit crimes (Sampson and Laub 1993; Horney et al. 1995; Paternoster and Brame 1997; Warr 1998). This implies that programs that could improve a prisoner's ties to institutions of informal social control—such as family, workplace, or school—could have an indirect impact upon recidivism. It also suggests that to the extent that programs can create self-control around criminogenic predictors such as alcohol use or deviancy, ex-prisoners will reduce their chances of becoming involved in more serious crime.

It is important to note that the research base for these two sets of studies is very different. The studies examined in meta-analyses of successful rehabilitation programs are usually small and often focus on juveniles: their power comes from the technique of isolating analytically similar relationships across multiple, separately conducted studies. Thus a result that shows success when services are targeted at higher-risk cases is based not on studies that show the same targeting method used in many different locations, but on multiple studies of different programs, all of which used some method of targeting services at higher-risk populations. By contrast, the research on criminal careers is based on studies of the same individuals repeated over time. It makes no claim about the effectiveness of particular programs or types of intervention and indeed, its focus is on life events after release, not treatment in prison. Thus their relevance is not in specifying how criminals can be reformed, but rather

---

(1995) and Saylor and Gaes (1987; 1992), focusing specifically on education and work programs, also find positive results.

in describing the conditions—social and familial stability—under which reform occurs.

Nevertheless, these two bodies of work taken together suggest that a more sober approach to rehabilitation is warranted: research that does not examine "whether" treatment is effective, but that uses theoretical guidance about individual behavior and lifecourse events to explore "how" and "when" treatment might be of assistance. Several studies taking a historical look at the turn away from rehabilitation (Cullen and Gilbert 1982; Rotman 1990; Hudson 1987) make the same point, arguing in particular that critics have been too quick to discard rehabilitation rather than its inappropriate link to other penal policies, such as indeterminate sentencing. Such studies point out, as well, that studies of rehabilitation programs are often inconclusive because the programs were badly implemented. Another "how" question for rehabilitation, in other words, is how treatment is actually carried out.

For researchers themselves, the lack of standards for program implementation, known in evaluation research as a lack of "treatment integrity," has always been an important, if unpublicized, factor in their conclusions. Lipton, Martinson, and Wilks (1975), the review of 231 studies of correctional rehabilitation whose pessimistic results set off this debate, was careful to point out that the biggest problem faced by evaluations of correctional rehabilitation was not the failure of techniques, but the lack of reliable reviews of those techniques. Many of the studies examined by the reviewers were of dubious scientific validity (Lipton, Martinson, and Wilks 1975: 604–5, 608, 627–28; Martinson 1974: 33–34). For example, improper measurements, the lack of controls, poor record keeping, and the lack of a similar theoretical framework made it difficult to compare the studies they reviewed, to generalize from a study to the general population of prison inmates, or even to place much confidence in any particular study's conclusions, positive or negative. And study reports seldom reported the information needed to determine if programs had actually been carried out as designed.[4]

A report commissioned by the National Academy of Sciences (Sechrest et al. 1979) later reiterated the importance of this finding. The lack of proper implementation, it pointed out, was both more widespread and more serious than was normally recognized. The researchers described one famous study, which found that group psychotherapy had no impact on recidivism. Upon closer examination, however, one researcher discovered that the counselors who led psychotherapy groups had not

---

[4] Sechrest et al. (1979: 37). Also note Martinson (1974: 11–12), on implementation problems with certain studies.

been trained, had little personal investment in the success or failure of their groups, were often moved from one group to another and were poorly supervised.[5] Whatever one's expectations of the effect of psychotherapy on recidivism, it is certainly not surprising that poorly administered psychotherapy has no positive effect! Sechrest and his colleagues concluded,

> It is not clear for how many rehabilitation studies interpretations are seriously jeopardized by failure to maintain integrity of treatment. That some of the more widely cited evaluation studies are flawed in this way implies that any conclusion that rehabilitation does not work would be premature. Mark Twain once observed that not only is the thirteenth chime of a clock in and of itself suspect, but it also casts doubt on the validity of the preceding twelve. (Sechrest et al. 1979: 42)

The newer studies of rehabilitation have begun to address these concerns. They show that "nonprogrammatic factors"—characteristics of the staff, of staff-offender interactions, of offenders themselves, of the setting in which the program took place, and of the rules, decision-making, and guidelines within the program—make a difference in the success of programs (Palmer 1995). In other words, a successful rehabilitative treatment incorporates not only a particular type of program, but also the conditions under which the program is carried out. Other scholars have begun to point out the importance of doing process evaluations before outcome evaluations: of getting researchers involved in programs early to provide the proper staff training, the appropriate data collection, and perhaps most importantly the discussions that will create understanding and support for programs (Hamm and Schrink 1989; Scarpitti, Inciardi, and Pottieger 1993; Wolk and Hartmann 1996; Harris and Smith 1996). Elliot Currie sums up this latter point well: "Whatever the specific technique used in treatment programs, the most important issue is whether it is implemented intensively, seriously, and for a reasonable length of time" (Currie 1985:239–40).

But why aren't programs "implemented intensively, seriously, and for a reasonable length of time"? Returning to Giallombardo's analysis of an abortive attempt to schedule education classes helps to answer this question. In principle, the warden supported the program and exhorted her staff to comply. In practice, each staff member, starting from the demands of her own position, wanted programs to accommodate those needs: the operations staff wanted to be able to get out a meal without changing work assignments, the officers wanted to avoid coaxing prisoners to do

---

[5] Sechrest et al. (1979: 40–41); see also the original study, Kassebaum et al. (1971) and Rossi and Freeman (1993: 158).

something they weren't interested in. Nor were staff simply raising a set of administrative concerns that might be settled with a little more compromise. They invoked beliefs about prisoner behavior—"If these girls don't want to take something, they won't unless they're interested"; professional obligation—"These people are unintelligent, emotionally unstable, and insecure. . . . But we're supposed to do something with these people"; and moral action—"If you're really interested in an education, you'll go in the evening. After all, people outside take evening courses after work. And you officers take your course in the evening." These rhetorical claims structured the kinds of action the staff took—or, in this case, refused to take. Perhaps the most revelatory detail in Giallombardo's account is the fact that the education supervisor actually started the conversation by announcing that evening classes had been scheduled for those prisoners who needed to work. Thus, the operations staff were complaining about the presumed lack of an accommodation that had *already* been made. Yet this did not keep the staff from protesting, nor, significantly, from winning the argument: the education supervisor promises to rethink the scheduling and the warden publicly agrees that classes should not interfere with work.

Taking this example seriously requires a thorough look at prison structures, and at program requirements, from the point of view of organizations and of policy. For even in this vignette, more is going on than simply a failure of scheduling—as is shown by the education supervisor's willingness to run evening classes. In that sense, a process evaluation might find that there was no real reason for education classes not to run as planned—except, of course, that the ensuing conversation convinced the education supervisor to back down, introduced persuasive rhetorical claims that could be used against programs, and set the stage for conflict over other programs, at other times. As Giallombardo recognized, coordinating a rehabilitation program with the prison's maintenance needs, security considerations, and strategies for keeping order is a task requiring structural changes: not simply exhortations or training, but a rethinking of the prison's needs and organization.

This is not to say that a prison should be changed from a place that confines prisoners to a place that treats them. That approach would simply re-create the Walnut Street Jail, Auburn, and indeterminate sentencing: turning confinement toward the purpose of rehabiltation usually ends by allowing rehabilitation to justify confinement. Instead, the task of coordinating treatment with the prison's other purposes first requires understanding confinement: understanding the maintenance and security needs of the prison, understanding how prisoner and staff interactions can create or destroy prison order, understanding the rhetorical claims that prisoners and staff find persuasive. Understanding confinement allows us to recognize when rehabilitation will be abandoned, implemented half-heartedly, or turned away from its original purposes. It also allows us to discover when rehabilitation will be implemented successfully.

Rehabilitating under Confinement

The prison environment is inescapably bound up with the problem of keeping order. This is hardly a new insight; nary a study of prisons, from classics such as Donald Clemmer (1940), Gerald Sykes (1958), and James Jacobs (1977) to recent works such as John DiIulio (1987), Mark Fleisher (1989), and Richard Sparks, Anthony Bottoms, and Will Hay's aptly named *Prisons and the Problem of Order* (1996) is not concerned with it. On its most basic level, order is about the absence of violence, both against staff and between prisoners. But below that surface, order is also about warding off violence: about routines that make behavior predictable, and thus less threatening; about displays of power that seek to deter violence before it might start; about communication, which can defuse disagreements before they escalate into violence; and about incentives and sanctions, which serve as a check on the behavior of both prisoners and staff.

Seen in this light, the problem caused by the education program at Giallombardo's prison is clearer. Education programs in and of themselves, of course, were hardly likely to cause violence. But they did disrupt routines that the other staff were used to. They introduced something new for prisoners to complain about and for staff to explain. They were not set up in quid pro quo fashion, thus eliminating the possibility that they could be used as an incentive—or a sanction—for violations of order. And they seemed to require a change in the definition of staff professionalism, away from what the warden dismissed as "a guard with a key," toward assisting in the treatment of prisoners—a change in definition that staff clearly rejected.

Programs in particular and reforms in general can threaten the sense of order in prisons, not so much because they breed disorder, but because they often represent a challenge to established ways of keeping order. They disturb routines, they introduce new ideas, and they do not compensate for the disruption they cause. Yet programs can also play a very different role. In a famous study of prison order, *Governing Prisons* (1987), and a later book on corrections policy, *No Escape* (1991), John DiIulio argues that prison programs can do the opposite: fit into routines, enhance professionalism in ways that staff support, and improve the communication between staff and prisoners. Treatment programs such as education, vocational training, and group counseling can be adapted so that they keep the prisoners occupied and the staff challenged—thus making the prison easier to manage (DiIulio 1991:118–21). DiIulio offers evidence that by providing professional challenges to staff, incentives for inmates to cooperate with the prison administration, and a forum for nonconfrontational inmate-staff communication, treatment programs can gain the support of the most conservative wardens and the most cynical staff (DiIulio 1991:113)

Whatever their rehabilitative value, then, it seems the first consequence of understanding confinement is that programs must fit into confinement purposes—must be incorporated into a prison's set of strategies for keeping order—if they are not to be abandoned or marginalized, as at Drake or at Giallombardo's prison. But aiding in the task of keeping order is only half of the problem. As the review of prison reform showed, prison programs have often been subverted—turned to purposes other than that of rehabilitation, in ways that actually keep them from being rehabilitative. From the prisoners ordered to dig ditches because it would help them learn to meet life's exigencies, to behavioral modification programs that merely provided covering for the prison's existing disciplinary structure, programs with rehabilitative ambitions can flourish on the ground without fostering any actual rehabilitative activity.

The message here is that it is not enough to integrate programs into the prison's set of strategies for keeping order. In fact, modifying programs and prison strategies so that they complement each other can inhibit rehabilitation as well as foster it. Because keeping order is such a central aim within prisons, its demands can crowd out any other functions that programs might have. Thus the second consequence of understanding confinement is the realization that while programs must help to keep order in prisons, they cannot exist solely to keep order. The multiple purposes that programs serve must be reconciled; one cannot overtake the other.

The picture of prison programs that emerges from understanding confinement first is quite different from the one that philosophers, historians, and program evaluators give us. Unlike Foucauldian accounts of the social functions of punishment, this account looks not at what prison programs mean as cultural representation, but at what they mean within specific sites and to the actors—staff and prisoners—who inhabit those sites. Unlike historical accounts of the failure of prison reform, this approach describes not the inevitable disappointment of noble ideals but the day-to-day imposition of local ideals—order, professionalism, communication, self-respect—upon programs that must absorb or resist them. And unlike evaluations of the success of prison programs, this approach examines not whether people change in response to an invariant treatment, but how context and treatment interact to create programs that vary in meaning and function across multiple sites.

Learning How Programs Work

In the historiography of prison programs, prisons like Drake are the rule. In the face of the importance of keeping order, and the multiple staff and prisoner concerns that spring from that goal, rehabilitation disappears or is subverted beyond recognition. The tale is so common, in fact, that both philosophers and criminologists have declared the failure of rehabilitation inevitable. The only exceptions to this tale of failure are the "new" programs that are proposed every so often, and their potential is conceded only because they are new. Given enough time to disappoint the expectations of their proponents, they provide yet more proof that "nothing works."

But this cycle of hope and disillusionment has an interpretation apart from that of inevitable failure. This alternative springs from the realization that Drake and Beaverton are not all that different. Programs at both prisons operate under the same constraints. Those constraints can block programs. But they also present opportunities for creating symbiosis between prisons and programs—a symbiosis whose specifics will differ from prison to prison, but, as the rest of this book will argue, a symbiosis whose essentials remain the same.

To accept this interpretation is to accept a fundamentally different approach to rehabilitation. If rehabilitation first starts with understanding confinement—the environment in which programs must operate—then a customary model of rehabilitation as first and foremost the identification of promising "treatments" also needs to change. Unlike chemical experiments, in which the environment surrounding a chemical reaction can be controlled, the utility of social treatments is inescapably bound up with their context. It is not that experimental and quasi-experimental techniques such as randomization or controls, informed and guided by appropriate theoretical work, cannot be used to identify promising interventions. But to translate those "treatments" into programs that can actually operate in existing social environments—in prisons, but also in schools, in welfare offices, in social service agencies or churches—the environment, the context of treatment itself, must also be examined as an integral part of a program.

The task of those who would rehabilitate rehabilitation is thus not primarily to discover "what works." Instead, the task—which the rest of this book takes up—is to discover "how programs work": to understand how the interaction between programs and their context redefines programs from prison to prison, and ultimately how it affects their success.

2

Keeping the Peace

INSTITUTIONAL NEEDS, INSTITUTIONAL VALUES, AND IMPLEMENTATION

> It is a responsibility of corrections in general—and
> it is certainly a responsibility for the Bureau of
> Prisons in particular—to provide a decent, safe,
> and humane environment and offer opportunities
> that society may not have provided before then to
> help some of its misfits improve their prospects for
> future success in the community.
> (*J. Michael Quinlan, Director,*
> *Federal Bureau of Prisons, 1987–1993*)

> No one believes in rehabilitation, but we should
> have the option for them. Also, it keeps
> them busy.
> (*Captain, Federal Bureau of Prisons*)

WITH THE warden, assistant wardens, and captain gone for the night, the evening shift lieutenant is the acting warden. As the highest ranking staff member available, the lieutenant gets everything from medical emergencies to questions about the availability of cleaning supplies, from prisoners who have gotten into a screaming match to the sudden outbreak of a fight. On one particular night, the shift lieutenant invited me to sit with him and fit in an interview between his phone calls and consultations. The phone rang constantly. He answered a question about getting bedding for a prisoner who had just been moved into the medical unit; promised to send an officer to look for a prisoner absent from his assigned literacy class; pacified a young correctional officer who came by, furious about what she considered a breach of security; dressed down the prisoner for refusing to go to his literacy class; monitored the nightly prisoner count. When we were finally finished, three hours after the hour-long interview had started, he summoned an officer to escort me through the gate, but warned me first that he would be doing so without a required clearance. "Let's see," he said, grinning, "if they're on their toes at the checkpoint tonight."

"Babysitting," "housekeeping," "I'm the Maytag man"—not terms that one automatically associates with prisons, and yet terms that I heard often as prison staff described their duties for me. None of the tasks the lieutenant did that night is at all odd in the context of running a housing complex for 1000 residents, and yet one doesn't think of a prison in quite that way. Prison movies and television exposés have taught most people to think of prisons as combat zones—sadistic staff beating up on vicious criminals, guns at the ready to face homemade but deadly knives and clubs. In reality, as one prison captain explained, "The secret of an institution is to keep them moving; if you can only give them one assignment, you have to find other ways of breaking the monotony. Here they see the same people every day, the same walls; they've got one store and one restaurant; they want a change, just like anyone else" (5nf). Danger is always present; the lieutenant's stratagem of sending me out without a clearance is an example of the way that supervisors remind their staff to stay on their toes. And yet, in many ways, danger is primarily a backdrop for the mundane daily tasks of checking passes, getting the food served, and making sure that prisoners are where they are supposed to be.

But mundane as these daily tasks are, the ways that prisoners and staff deal with them vary from prison to prison. In Antelope Valley, the prison where the interview described above took place, it was not at all uncommon for a lieutenant to dress down a prisoner for missing night classes. In other prisons, this would never happen; the prisoner would instead be called to account by the counselor, the case manager, or the unit manager in his housing unit.[1] The prisoner might miss numerous classes before any disciplinary action was taken at one prison, but be late fifteen minutes and find himself berated by the education supervisor at another. And of course, in some prisons the whole incident would be moot: there would be no classes in the evening for the prisoner to miss.

[1] In the Federal Bureau of Prisons, prisoners are assigned to a housing unit. Their counselor, case manager, and unit manager are all located within the same housing unit. In theory, the counselor handles the prisoner's in-prison needs: his work assignment, his adjustment to prison rules or customs, and any trouble with other prisoners. The case manager handles the prisoner's relationship to the prison system and to the criminal justice system: pending trials or arrest warrants, requests for a transfer to another prison or for placement in a halfway house. The unit manager supervises both the case manager and the counselor. There is often also a unit secretary who works with all three staff. In practice, however, the lines between counselor and case manager can blur, especially when the four staff, also known as the "unit team," work closely together—or when one of the members of the team is disliked or incompetent, and the others try to fill in.

The state system is a little different. At Catawba State Correctional Center, counselors are not assigned to housing units. Instead, they work in a central office and prisoners are assigned to them without reference to the unit they live in. These counselors handle both internal and external relations for the prisoners on their caseloads. Their caseloads also tend to be much larger: 200 to 400 prisoners per counselor, as opposed to 75 to 150 in the federal system.

Such distinctions may seem trivial. In fact, they are a window onto the tacit negotiations that not only determine how prisons keep peace, but govern the fate of rehabilitation programs in the process. What such distinctions reveal is different strategies for keeping order: some which prioritize programs and the staff-prisoner interaction that programs facilitate, others which prioritize staff solidarity and the staff-prisoner distance that solidarity requires. These differing priorities also reveal the ways in which the purposes of programs are shaped and reshaped by the characteristics of their implementing environment: it is not merely that rehabilitation programs receive different levels of support in different prisons, but that they are understood differently in different prisons as well.

If programs are implemented differently in different prisons, not merely because they are considered more or less relevant to the task of keeping order but because they are also understood as having different purposes in different places, then classic notions of implementation success must be reexamined. Implementation is not best measured by program outcomes, which say little about the process that produced them, but instead by program activities—the numerous little actions, like sleeping in class or being dressed down by correctional officers for missing class—that taken together *are* the substance of policy. These activities are produced by the interaction of a program's rules and resources with an environment that filters, interprets, and makes use of those rules and resources in different ways. Evaluated with respect to some desired state of affairs, these activities show when implementation has been successful, neglected, subverted, or absent—conditions under which program activities are plausibly related to some desired outcome, and conditions under which they are not.

Evaluating Implementation

An important strand of implementation theory has commonly presented implementation as a period when things go wrong: when a promising policy gets derailed because of actors with divergent interests, because the policy mandate is unclear, or because of a lack of resources or political support. This attitude has been with the field since the publication of the classic *Implementation*, whose subtitle blithely states that the book recounts "*How Great Expectations in Washington Are Dashed in Oakland; or Why It's Amazing that Federal Programs Work at All*" (Pressman and Wildavsky 1979). The apogee of this work is probably Daniel Mazmanian and Paul Sabatier's detailed and nuanced account of the implementation process (1989) in which they discuss six conditions, sixteen variables, and five stages that need to be present in order for implementation to be successful.

   Work like this, which focuses on the prerequisites for successful implementation, makes two important assumptions. First, it measures implementation by policy outcomes. If a program of loans and capital subsidies
to business is supposed to create jobs, or a state land-use program is supposed to provide recreational opportunities or protect wetlands, this
work looks for ways to assess the number of jobs, of new public beaches,
or of protected wetlands. Second, because of its emphasis on outcome
measures, this type of work emphasizes the importance of policy theory.
While having the right idea to solve a problem does not guarantee outcomes, research in this tradition insists that having an "adequate causal
theory" and a "tractable problem" (Mazmanian and Sabatier 1989:22)
are important elements of implementation success (see also Meier and
Licari 1997).
   Although these assumptions are appropriate for many types of policies, they are not appropriate for all. As Helen Ingram (1990) and Richard Matland (1995) have argued, many policy problems lack adequate
causal theories; they are problems with low information (Ingram 1990)
or high ambiguity (Matland 1995). In these cases, while outcome information is important in and of itself, it will not tell us very much about
the programs that produced them. Take recidivism, for instance: a finding that prisoners in a literacy program were just as likely as prisoners
without an education to commit crimes upon release could mean several things. The theory behind the policy—that education should increase
the availability of legitimate opportunities for ex-offenders—could be
wrong: people might commit crimes for reasons having nothing to do
with education. But it might also be that the amount of education, the
ability of the teachers to teach, or the kind of education delivered, was
wrong: in other words, that the wrong kind of education, delivered in-
competently, will not affect recidivism but the right kind, administered
competently, will. It might even be that some unanticipated but important factor intervened in the education-crime relationship: perhaps the
economy was so bad that there were no jobs for either educated or un-
educated ex-prisoners, forcing even educated prisoners back to crime.
There is no way to disentangle these different explanations by looking at
outcomes alone: in each case, the outcome is the same.
   One can do little to prevent or correct for the effect of unanticipated
factors on policy outcomes. However, it is possible to differentiate between correct and incorrect policy implementation by looking, not at
policy outcomes, but at policy activities—at the actions on the ground
that together constitute policy. Consider the math classes at Drake and
Beaverton, the two prisons introduced at the beginning of the last chapter. The enthusiastic students at Beaverton participated in an activity—
measuring geometric shapes and calculating their area—that has a plau-

sible relationship to learning; the teacher, by circulating, checking work, or suggesting steps, actively participated in the students' learning. By contrast, the classroom at Drake reveals the active participation of only a few students in activities, like reading a textbook, that are plausibly related to learning; the teacher is also largely disengaged from the class. Successful implementation, from this example, is active participation, by those who are implementing the policy and those at whom the policy is targeted, in activities consistent with some desired state of affairs—in this case, learning.

Note that this definition makes no judgments about either the type of activities used (as long as a plausible argument can be made for them) or the effect of those activities. In this example, for instance, the issue is not "team learning versus individual study." One could imagine a classroom in which prisoners were divided into teams and given assignments, but in which they used the time for passing contraband, gossiping, or fighting. That would be unsuccessful implementation of a team-learning concept; just as a classroom full of students, each working at his own pace, with a teacher who was grading assignments, helping students, or designing new curriculum, would be the successful implementation of an individualized study program.

This kind of evaluation is consistent with the aims of those who recommend process evaluations, also known as program monitoring. For instance, Peter Rossi and Howard Freeman's *Evaluation: A Systematic Approach* reminds students that "in a large proportion of programs that fail to show impacts, the real problem may be failure to deliver the interventions in the ways specified in the program design . . . monitoring the actual delivery of services to identify faults and deficiencies is essential" (Rossi and Freeman 1993: 188–89). Lawrence Mohr's *Impact Analysis for Program Evaluation* reminds readers that "it is essential that the activities be carried out, and done so properly—adequately—for all instrumental and inherently valued objectives to be achieved" (Mohr 1995: 39). Donald Campbell, a pioneer in research design and evaluation, has pointed out that evaluations too often take place before the right activities have been discovered and put into place. He suggests that social scientists "evaluate no program until it is proud" (Campbell 1987: 346–47). Other researchers, such as Carol Weiss and Robert Stake, champion the importance of process and practice-centered evaluation research (Shadish, Cook, and Leviton 1991). While these approaches cannot guarantee that program effects will be forthcoming, "a program that is established and operating at least has the potential to realize its objectives" (Peterson, Rabe, and Wong 1986: 30-31).

In this type of analysis, it is still possible to evaluate the success of implementation. But the phrase "successful implementation" must be understood as two concepts: "implementation," which suggests that program activities are present, and "successful with respect to x," which suggests that the program activities in question are plausibly related to some objective "x." Thus one should speak of successful implementation with respect to rehabilitation, successful implementation with respect to keeping order. And "successful implementation with respect to rehabilitation" does not mean "successful at rehabilitation." Rather, it establishes something prior: a knowledge of what is happening in the name of rehabilitation, and the intent to take it seriously. Far from being merely the study of "good implementation and bad results—or doing the inappropriate thing very effectively" (Ingram 1990: 465), this approach makes it easier to figure out what might create good results. It does so because the study of program activities is more than just monitoring: it is the study of what a policy actually is.

It is a fiction of policymakers and, perhaps, policy advocates, that programs can be easily described by what exists on paper in a law, a regulation, or an agency memo. Battles fought over enactment and design, compromises over language and resources, reoccur as soon as implementation begins (Brodkin 1990). These battles take place because different agencies and different interests fight over jurisdiction (Bardach 1977). They take place because what policymakers provide is often not what those targeted by policy, or the staff who work with them, need (Elmore 1979–80). But most of all, they take place because the administrative patrons, the staff, the target group or groups, and the many constituencies of a policy reinterpret what a policy means and, in how they choose to act or refrain from acting, reconstruct its form and functions (Yanow 1996). The knowledge that policy activities will differ from what the designers of policy expect, and that they will vary from site to site, can cause consternation and allegations of policy "capture" and private agendas (Wilson 1989; Melnick 1994). It can also, however, open up the "black box" of policy implementation (Palumbo and Calista 1990), draw attention to the expressive and symbolic functions of policy (Schneider and Ingram 1993), and reveal the activity of those excluded or absent from traditional fora of policymaking (Yanow 1996).

Seen in this light, an implementation experience that is not "successful," or is inconsistent with some desired state of affairs, does not immediately signal a need for better monitoring, simpler or clearer requirements, more carefully designed incentives or sanctions, or even more attention to the process. While any or all of these may eventually help to create more successful implementation, the absence of appropriate policy activities indicates something else first: a gap between the purposes and values supposedly embedded in a policy, and the purposes and values of those who implement it. This gap often does not reflect disagreement or opposition to policy. Instead, it may reflect a preoccupation with issues, concerns, and motivations that seem, at first glance, to be tangential to the policy the evaluator is trying to assess. Yet this is exactly the point: policies pick up new meanings, new concerns, and new purposes that their designers might not even have considered, much less intended. What a policy actually is, therefore, is as much about context as it is about original intent. And in prisons, the context is about keeping the peace.

Programs and Their Uses

Prison programs provide an excellent case with which to examine these claims. From the outside, rehabilitation is the obvious reason for the school and work programs now found in prisons around the country. Within prisons, however, the commitment to rehabilitation is greeted with much more skepticism. "Prison isn't about rehabilitation—it's a moneymaking thing" (5MM), sniffs one prisoner; and a counselor laughs when he is asked about programs. "I'm laughing because you always think of rehabilitation when that question is asked, but that's not where we're at—we're in the keeping business" (5mj). Their comments are particularly surprising in light of the wide variety of programs that these five prisons offer. As Table 2.1 suggests, both the quantity and the range of choices is impressive. In no prison are fewer than three trades courses offered; schooling from basic literacy through high school is offered everywhere, and four of the five prisons offer some sort of on-site college courses. Moreover, the federal system allows prisoners to apply for a transfer if they want to enroll in a program at another prison, and the programs themselves are monitored routinely by the central administrative office in each region and periodically through on-site inspections.

None of this is to suggest that the supply of programs is sufficient, or that programs are necessarily implemented well. But given what does exist, it may be surprising that prisoners and staff are so certain that it is not rehabilitation. Yet as the quotations that opened this chapter show, even the director of the Federal Bureau of Prisons (BOP), praising the "opportunities" that the BOP offers "to help some of its misfits improve their prospects for future success in the community," is careful to talk around the word "rehabilitation." And note the contradiction in the captain's words: "Nobody believes in rehabilitation," he says, "but we should have the opportunity for them." To make matters more confusing, he ends with a seeming *non sequitur*—"And it keeps them busy." (2ck).

TABLE 2.1
Program Offerings in Prisons

Program	Antelope Valley	Beaverton	Catawba State	Drake	Evergreen
Mandatory education	3 months study if no HSD; GED classes offered	3 months study if no HSD; GED classes offered	6th-grade level of literacy required	3 months study if no HSD; GED classes offered	3 months study if no HSD; GED classes offered
College degrees (courses at prison unless otherwise noted)	AA via local 2-year college; and see vocational education	AA and BA via state 4-year college; and see vocational education	BA via area 4-year college; AA via area 2-year college; and see vocational education	Correspondence courses without Pell Grant funding or other administrative support	AA and BA via out-of-state college
Vocational education	Optics, Building Trades, Heating/Air, taught by local community college (nondegreed)	AA in Restaurant Management; Medical Technology; Quality Assurance apprenticeship	AA in Business Skills, Auto Repair, Electronics, Horticulture, Building Trades	Auto Repair, Auto Body, Welding, Drafting; also 10 specific trades apprenticeships accredited thru nat'l organ.	Auto Body, Welding, Masonry, Machine Shop, Electronics; Printing and Cable apprenticeships
Prison industries (UNICOR)	Optics, Textiles	Cable Factory	Optics	Cable Factory	Cable Factory, Printing Plant
Drug treatment	1000-hr. in-resident program; 40-hr. drug education	1000-hr. in-resident program; 40-hr. drug education	Alcoholics/Narcotics Anonymous Groups	40-hr. drug education, support groups	100-hr. non-resident program; 40-hr. drug education

These circumlocutions are at the heart of the true place of programs in prisons. On one level, they certainly function, for both prisoners and staff, as rehabilitation—as a way to pick up or provide skills that might help prisoners to avoid crime. But programs are equally, or perhaps even more importantly, a way to keep prisoners constructively occupied. The fact that these programs in some sense dupe or bribe prisoners into cooperating with staff to keep the prison orderly is problematic for both groups, as I explain in the next section. But prisoners and staff are often willing to support a longer-term, more nebulous goal like rehabilitation primarily because they believe that programs also offer immediate, near-term institutional advantages.

The importance of keeping prisoners busy may not be obvious at first. But it stems in large part from a perennial problem of the prison: what do you do with people once they are behind a fence? The obvious answer is to make prisoners work. But like many popular proposals for prison reform, this is not easily done. Prisons are restricted by union and business pressure from producing goods that can be sold on the open market. While many prisons now have small-scale prison industry programs, the products they produce are restricted for sale to other government agencies only, and even this limited role for prison industries comes under sharp attack.[2] Politicians dislike the thought of inmates sitting idle, but they dislike more the specter of cheap prison-produced goods crowding out products made by their constituents. Another alternative, having prisoners serve as an auxiliary public workforce, is equally difficult to implement. As eager as leaders may be to take care of infrastructure and maintenance needs that public treasuries must delay for lack of funds, they do not want the scandal of criminals on the street, possibly escaping while in the process of fixing roads or cleaning up parks.

Under these restrictions, prisons turn to making work for inmates within the institution. Work assignments were mandatory for every prisoner in each of the prisons I studied. But there is a limited amount of cleaning, kitchen work, maintenance, and landscaping that inmates can do, particularly because staff need to supervise their work actively. Add overcrowding to the mix, and work assignments requiring a meaningful amount of effort and involvement become more and more scarce. In one prison, I watched as an inmate buffed the floor of the visiting room—about 400 square feet of space—slowly, over and over, for an entire afternoon. At other prisons, seven and eight prisoners are assigned to a job that one could do by himself; and at one prison, prisoners were on multiple waiting lists—first for their initial work assignment, and then for the more desirable jobs.

The resulting idleness can be extraordinarily painful for prisoners. Most enter prison with little mental and emotional preparation for what they will find. Prisoners freely admit that "jail is the last thing on your mind when you're out there in society doing wrong; you chose to do it because you're not looking at yourself being caught. Jail's not a reality until you go in" (4KH). Even those who think about the sentence may only consider it as a status symbol. Not until people are confined do they

[2] John DiIulio, *No Escape: The Future of American Corrections* (New York: Basic, 1991), 116–18. For a defense of the Federal Bureau of Prisons UNICOR program that obliquely addresses the many problems prison industries confront, see Richard P. Seiter, "Federal Prison Industries," in *Federal Prisons Journal* 1 (3) (spring 1990): 11–15.

realize what their sentence means. "I thought prison would be a walk in the park—it would be exciting to be with hard core criminals. Then after you're actually in, you realize you're bored, and you can't go home. The game's over" (1AZ). Lest boredom sound too mild a punishment, imagine emptiness, the consciousness that one has dropped out of the world, and the realization that one's time can never be returned. "There's so much I've missed, life's really passed me by. Here I'll sleep just to pass the time, but it's like wishing your life away" (3FV).

How do prisoners deal with their idleness? Some dream about freedom, remembering home and making plans for the future. They spend hours in front of the television trying to keep in touch with the world, and write letters to keep their loved ones in touch with them. But for most inmates, the first step in coping is to focus on what can be done within the institution. "Get into sports, stay busy. Don't think about the streets because if you do, your hair will fall out. I don't think about the streets, or my family, because I can't think" (3GC). Some lift weights, taking their pride from the shape of their bodies. Others participate in prison social groupings: sports teams, bands, or chapel-led prayer groups, all of which are organized by the prison; as well as hometown gangs, ethnic clubs, and religious brotherhoods, which exist semiclandestinely and are organized by the inmates themselves. And some participate in programs. "You add color to your time, instead of just doing it. Some people do it by weightlifting; school works for others, like me" (1AH).

School and weightlifting, however, are not quite equivalent. Part of the value of educational and other rehabilitative programs lies in the fact that they are activities with a purpose. If the intent were merely to keep inmates occupied or to extend a carrot for good behavior, television sets, gyms, and exercise yards would serve as well as schooling or treatment programs. In some prisons, in fact, recreation is all there is; it is cheaper to buy a weight set or put up a basketball net than to hire teachers. But education and training programs allow prisoners to create a facade of normalcy, or at least to prop up their dreams of a better life after prison. A teacher explains, "To make them sit around is demoralizing. Many of them are knowledgeable . . . maybe someone [had a trade] outside, and you can't put a person down for 10 years and not let him practice his trade" (4jm). A work foreman adds, "We have programs to make this setting as close to real life as possible, and to let them make something of themselves" (1o). Prisoners themselves often need the reassurance provided by comparisons with other prisoners, or with former comrades on the "street" who have not changed their ways.

> It [programs] keeps you busy doing positive things; the ones that don't participate have a weak mentality. I call outside, you know, and guys I know who

were 8 then, when I was 13, are telling me, man, we do this, we do that, we're gangbanging. I tell them, it ain't worth it, and they say, but man, it's a credit to you to be in jail, when you come out you got lots of credit. Shoot, that's stupid. Jail's no credit. (3GL)

The experience of inmates confined in minimum-security camps is instructive. These camps, for low-risk inmates serving sentences of under three years, are considered extremely desirable by inmates confined in medium-security institutions. Visiting hours are looser, more freedom of movement is allowed, and usually fences—a constant reminder of incarceration—are not built around camps. But once prisoners earn a transfer to a camp—ironically, often by participating in programs and acquiring a good work record—they find that the camps, being smaller, offer less work, fewer activities, and almost no programming options. The regret and frustration of these men was evident.

The plus here is that I'm closer to home, and the camp is laid-back and relaxed, but there's a psychological war because they are babysitting us. There's nothing constructive here because the staff don't get the inmates ready for society. At the [medium-security prison] you do your time better; it has more to offer in terms of education, rehabilitation, recreation. (4JM)

I wished they had more [programs]; I feel like I'm wasting my time here. If they had things, I'd go to them. [People go] when there is something to do, but there's not much. The rooms only seat 10-15, so you know they're not planning to bring much here. If there's nothing to do, there will be lots of confusion and anger. Like this morning: it was raining, we couldn't go out, and they were just fussing and fighting all morning. (4JQ)

Notice how careful this prisoner is to suggest that while he is "wasting his time," the other prisoners are the ones "fussing and fighting" in response to idleness. Although prisoners seldom admit that they themselves cause trouble when they are bored, frustration, monotony, and time to think about one's situation quite naturally lead to the escalation of small conflicts, to efforts by the strong to dominate the weak, and to attempts by prisoners to strike out at the people who enforce the grimness of the surroundings. As one staff member puts it, "You need to keep them busy . . . otherwise they have a lot of time to think about that fence" (2cx). Staff are blunt about their interest in programs: "If there were no programs, every inmate would be prone to violence" (5mm). "Idleness is horrible; it breeds trouble. . . . If the inmate doesn't have work habits in the prison, he sure won't have them on the outside, and if he doesn't have something productive to do on his off hours, he'll just get into trouble" (1h).

Prisoners echo these sentiments. The near-term activity a program provides is as much of a concern as the longer-term educational benefit it can offer.

> It's a tremendous waste of time to come here and not accomplish something. The best thing here is education. . . . Besides, the key is staying busy. If you're learning, you have to think about the subject. And that eliminates stress. (5MH)

> Well, I might get out one day, and hopefully it will help me. . . . [And it] give[s] the inmates something to do; you know, to keep peoples out of trouble, so they're not out on the yard doing something or getting assaulted. I know I'd be doing something if I didn't have something to do. (4KY)

> You could really see rehabilitation happening [at my last prison] if you let the programs work for you—they had all kinds of school and they worked you 8 hours a day—when you got off you were tired! (3FC)

The dual purposes of programs—as ways to keep prisoners busy, and as opportunities for self-improvement and a better life—are, in this telling, complementary. Programs keep prisoners busy because they provide rehabilitative opportunities that prisoners value: at the same time, the busy-ness prevents violence and alleviates boredom. But one can also glean from this a potential problem. What happens when programs do not alleviate boredom—or, conversely, when multiple options for relieving boredom exist? When programs serve only a rehabilitative purpose—when the skills they teach are useful, but not absorbing enough to distract prisoners or boost their self-esteem—neither staff nor prisoners are likely to consider programs a good deal. The reasoning can be carried even farther. Suppose that the prison was disorderly enough so that defenders of programs, regardless of the programs' actual merits, simply could not claim credibly that programs were helping to keep the peace. Programs, again, would be likely to lose support: staff, in particular, would dismiss their utility and look about for other ways of controlling prisoners instead.

The fact that support for programs is inextricably tied to the institutional needs of staff and prisoners has other implications as well. Although the overwhelming emphasis within a prison is on keeping order, prisons do have other needs: day-to-day maintenance, prestige or accreditation within a prison system, and the like. Prisoners also have needs other than those of keeping their minds off their imprisonment: spending money, contact with people outside prison, earlier release dates or furloughs, halfway-house placements, or transfers to a better prison. Given that staff and prisoners have multiple needs, a program whose implementation allows staff and clients to serve multiple purposes is a program that is more likely to be implemented. For instance, a vocational training program that saves the prison money by training prisoners to perform some essential repairs will be implemented before a program that takes up staff time but has no discernible return. Similarly, an industries program that allows prisoners to submerge their frustration in useful or challenging activity will get more prisoner participation in a prison where there are few other activities. Note that it matters little whether the multiple purposes served by a program's implementation actually complement it. In the case of Evergreen Correctional Center, one of the prisons in this study, a vocational training program that saved the prison money and brought accolades for the quality of the output actually encouraged the instructor to work with the most experienced students, many of whom had learned the trade before entering prison. He ignored the inexperienced students, who actually needed training; their training was less likely to add to his prestige.

Program-specific incentives and sanctions also play a role, but their impact is also mediated through the organization. Consider an example: a child condemned to stay after school for some infraction. The program-specific way to understand that sanction is by reasoning that most children want to get out of school as soon as possible, and thus will avoid behaviors that incur sanction. But now imagine that the school is situated in a neighborhood where staying after school is a status symbol, a sign of how "tough" a kid is. Within that context, the meaning, and thus the effect, of that sanction is different. A $25 stipend to a prisoner for attending class is meaningful as a bonus, but it is a disincentive if the prisoner's alternative is a prison job paying twice that amount in wages. Similarly, rotating from a job as a correctional officer into a job as a counselor or teacher can be a stepping-stone to future promotion in the prison system. But if promotions are also contingent on moving to a different prison in a different area of the country, and most staff prefer to stay in their hometowns, the value of this incentive to take a "program" job is much diminished.

The extent to which implementation is influenced by institutional purposes and frameworks, rather than by the program or policy-specific characteristics that program designers often worry about, shows the centrality of context to policy. An abstract discussion of the requirements for a good rehabilitation program is unlikely to include the need to keep prisoners occupied. By understanding how programs fit into the context of the prison, however, one may see why this tangential issue can be at the center of a program's fate. Prison staff and prisoners—for that matter, any group of program staff and participants—cannot be expected to administer, carry out, or participate in any set of activities unless those activities serve some purpose in their understanding of the work or life tasks they believe they must do, or unless those activities make their lives easier. On the other hand, this accommodation alone is not enough to ensure the successful implementation of programs. It is not only institutional purposes and needs, but institutional values as well, that programs embody and that can cut against rehabilitation.

The Values of Prison

> Once I got a call from a young officer to go over to one of the [housing] units. When I got there, there were hundreds of inmates—we were surrounded, and there were people screaming, things were flying. I was furious; and I just didn't think, I just stood in the middle of this hall and yelled, "All of you that don't want to be involved, go to your rooms; those of you that want to talk, go out to the rec [recreation] yard and wait for me; and any of you who aren't sure what to do, stay in the middle!" Well, they actually listened to me—there's no reason they should have done that, we were completely outnumbered.
>
> Later I turned to the young staff member and blew up. I said, if that ever happens again, you hit your body alarm! Don't ever get me into a situation like that again without reinforcements! You have to go by policy on something like that—but sometimes you get lucky. (Lieutenant, 1ad)

Do staff have the skill and the authority to maintain control over prisoners using rules and their own watchfulness alone? Or can prisoners be trusted, or bribed, to cooperate with staff in maintaining a state of order that both groups will benefit from? This dilemma is at the heart of a great deal of research on prisons and prison dynamics. Thus Sykes (1958) argues that prisoners and guards negotiate over the production of order, and argues for the incorporation of the inmate social system, with its maintenance of inmate solidarity and social structure, into prison governance (See also Wright 1993; Reisig 1998). By contrast, DiIulio (1987) argues that a "control" philosophy, in which prison wardens and lower-level staff make and enforce clear rules rather than negotiated agreements, is much more effective. The involvement of outside influences—in particular, of judges, elected officials, and reforming administrators—has been seen as both disruptive and salutary (Jacobs 1977; DiIulio 1990b; Marquart and Crouch 1998). The possibility of effective communication between prisoners and staff, and the use of incentives or behavioral "contracts," have also been frequent topics of investigation (Ellis 1993; Kauffman 1988; Fleisher 1989; Useem and Kimball 1989).

One way to sort through these differing evaluations is to realize that while debates over the best way to keep order are important, they are also unavoidable. Such debates exist precisely because no method of keeping order is sure. The predictable behavior instilled by routines can be taken advantage of as part of a planned disturbance. A display of power, by either staff or prisoners, can goad others into fury or retaliation; it can also itself become "preventive" violence. Communication always presents the possibility of mutual deceit. Incentives—or bribes—to maintain good behavior can cause violence if something expected is suddenly taken away, while sanctions, of course, can prompt rebellion or revenge. As Sparks, Bottoms, and Hay show in their study of two maximum-security prisons, one of which emphasized "control" and the other "liberality," the difference between strategies is not in absolute levels of disorder but rather in the types of disorder risked and tolerated. The riskiness inherent in the prison environment extends to the choice of strategy used to control that risk: prison officials, and by extension lower-level staff and prisoners as well, must choose to run some risks in order to minimize others (Sparks, Bottoms, and Hay 1996: 90–93).

Consider the lieutenant's story that opened this section. Outnumbered as they were, the young officer and the lieutenant could easily have been killed or taken hostage in the chaos. Either outcome would have made it impossible for the prisoners at fault to back down, and thus would have set the stage for an institution-wide riot. Thus, "policy" in this case would have been for the young officer to hit his body alarm—an institution-wide warning signal, at which all staff drop their jobs and run to the location of the alarm. The alarm itself, and the appearance of reinforcements, might have created just enough of a show of force to deter violence and allow the situation to de-escalate.

Instead, the lieutenant chose to do something else: he communicated with the prisoners, giving the prisoners themselves a chance to defuse the situation. Appealing to both their sense of self-preservation and to his authority, the lieutenant gave the prisoners a way to behave as individuals—some of whom might have had a grievance, some of whom just wanted to get out of there. In doing so, he prevented the prisoners from forming into a united front against the officers who might come to quell a disturbance.

Of course, this approach could easily have backfired, and the lieutenant's rueful statement, "They actually listened to me—there's no reason they should have done that," is evidence that he knows it. As a strategy for maintaining order in the prison, the choice between solidarity, force, and control, or instead communication, individual relationships, and flexibility, is one with no fixed rules and a high possibility of failure. Both cross-group communication and within-group solidarity are inherent and necessary characteristics of the prison environment. But the two also cut against each other, and programs, which favor communication over solidarity, cast the opposition between communication and solidarity into sharp relief.

Most prison administrators and trained prison staff recognize, in a hard-headed, unsentimental way, the importance of staff-prisoner communication. Mark Fleisher's *Warehousing Violence* (1989), a study of the maximum-security penitentiary, USP Lompoc, vividly explains.

> "Either we come to work willing to talk to them, or we better be willing to fight them," stressed [Warden] Christensen at a weekly warden's meeting of departmental managers and administrators. . . . Why place a strong value on talking to inmates? The answer is dangerously simple. A commonly used line-staff expression, "If the inmates want the place, they got it," reminds everyone that, anywhere, at any time, there are far more inmates than staff. On my first evening in the penitentiary, I helped supervise inmates in the mess hall during dinner. There were hundreds of convicts, and I wondered where the staff were, so I started counting: There were seven of "us." Those aren't great odds. Harmony, open communication, and rapport instantly took on new meaning. (Fleisher 1989: 49)

Nor is the dining hall the only place where staff find themselves outnumbered. Staff-inmate ratios of 1:3 or custody staff–inmate ratios of 1:6 may seem low, but staff are spread out over three shifts and large compounds. Thus it is not uncommon for a welding teacher to be alone in the shop with 30 inmates working with torches and heavy metal objects; for one recreation supervisor to be in a gym watching over 75 inmates lifting free weights or arguing over the outcome of a game; or for one correctional officer to be routinely locked into a housing unit to keep watch over 150 inmates at night.[3] Being outnumbered in these ways makes it impossible for staff to carry weapons. "They [the general public] think we carry guns in here. I tell them, puh-leeze! There are over 1000 inmates in here. You think, if I carried a gun, they wouldn't have them?" (Officer, 5md). A prison industries manager with time in both the state and federal prison systems is more contemptuous. "What makes me mad when I talk to people outside is hearing what 'they would do' if they were in charge. All these young state troopers—it's a macho thing with them. But (pointing to the cellblock) you can't carry your .45 in there with you" (4kf).

No wonder, then, that prison staff often see their task as one of psychology, not of brute force. The public, said one lieutenant, "all want to know what kind of weapon I carry. They don't want to hear that it's

---

[3] Officers are locked into units to prevent inmates from overpowering the officer and taking his keys. They maintain radio contact with staff at the prison and wear a body alarm, but otherwise they are alone during their shifts.

common sense and a quick tongue" (5ml). They maintain cynicism about inmate intentions without feeling that the response must be confrontational: "Everyone here has their scam they're trying to run . . . [but] to keep it down, you have to realize where you are and what they're interested in; you talk to each individually and you treat them with respect" (Officer, 4jk). Realizing that this approach might be seen as "coddling criminals," the staff I talked to are often somewhat apologetic.

> I was a drill sergeant in the military, so I was more hard-nosed when I came. I think the military generally is. But I found the best way to deal with inmates here is really just to talk to them; you get more accomplished that way. (Officer, 1b)

Prisoners understand and respond to this approach. They accept the presence and authority of staff with a surprising matter-of-factness, even when given the chance to denounce them. A prisoner's advice on how to deal with staff is most often like this inmate's: "Stay out of their way—they're human, and they have jobs to do" (3FK). Others admit that most problems between staff and inmates are two-sided. "They're fair if the inmates let them, but inmates can show ass just like the officers can. It's all with the individual. I always say if you want to be treated human, treat them as human" (3FD). Prisoners also know that their acquiescence can bring more favorable treatment.

> Every guard here is trying to win a popularity contest. Look, the young kids believe you shouldn't talk to staff, and they have a chip on their shoulder about staff. But here you don't have to be a stool pigeon to be friends with the staff. . . . Respect them, say hello to them; if you do that, they'll overlook the little rules you break. They won't come down on you as hard as the next guy because they know you're not into the serious stuff. (2CI)

Staff depend on the prisoners' good will—or at least the absence of open malice—to ensure their physical safety and their day-to-day peace. But prisoners need staff for exactly the same reason. They are much more likely than staff to be killed or hurt if a spontaneous disagreement erupts into violence; merely being a fellow prisoner is no guarantee of security. Prisoners are far from happy about their need for protection; the fact that staff can and do intervene to quell conflicts only emphasizes the power that staff have over them. But they grudgingly recognize that staff intervention is often the best way to ensure their own safety. And so they are often put into the odd position of complaining that staff are not doing enough to control prisoners, or are responding in kind to prisoner taunts and insults. A long-incarcerated, repeat prisoner expresses this idea succinctly, "Inmates are inmates—they're not going to change. Staff has to be the ones who are professional" (2CC). A more complicated reaction comes from this young prisoner, who himself has a record of violence. "The administration would rather see inmates kill each other than inmates hurting staff; it's them and us. They think they can treat us like dogs because we're inmates, so they're not going to get in the middle of a fight because they might get hurt" (3GL). The recognition of a need for law is interesting: while this prisoner attaches little condemnation to compatriots who break laws against fighting, he is quite clear that representatives of the law have an obligation to uphold it, even at the risk of their safety.

As one can imagine, this is not an easy position to be in. One of the reasons communication is so often emphasized is that, despite its utility, it is difficult to sustain.

> The staff here is under stress because people are hostile to the staff, even if it's subtle. You're in a dangerous environment; and it's not just physical stress, it's the mental stress of knowing you're locked up with 105 inmates and most of them don't like you. I try not to think about it too often, but you can tell from the divorces and the drinking problems that this is a stressful position. (Drug treatment specialist, 2dc)

The manipulation inherent in any relationship between staff and prisoners can easily backfire. Consider the following comments: the first made by a physician's aide, the second by a correctional officer.

> An inmate's job is to beat [manipulate, take advantage of] you. You just have to accept that sometimes you'll get beat. We're buffers; we're here to take abuse for the executive staff. Just accept that they're sociopaths. Prevent it— sometimes if you negotiate, make them think they're getting something from you, they'll stop. (Physician's aide, former officer, 1f)

> We can't solve much, but we can communicate with the inmates. I get along with them pretty well; they say I do pretty well, I can get the job done. . . . When you start out, they'll test you. I let them think they're fooling me; then I turn the tables on them to let them see where the line is. It's entertainment to them, and that's how I look at it too. (Officer, 3fc)

Note that both the physician's aide and the correctional officer may be deluded about how effective they are with the prisoners. By negotiating, the aide may in fact be giving the prisoners in question exactly what they wanted; meanwhile, what the correctional officer sanguinely calls "entertainment" may be much less entertaining to prisoners, who in his account are always outfoxed. But whether or not the staff are accurate judges of their effectiveness, notable in both accounts is the sense of being on the edge, of needing to out-manipulate the prisoners. One staff member may enjoy it; another may not; both reactions show the precariousness of the technique.

The sense that communication can be as difficult as it is necessary drives staff and prisoners to value its opposite: staff solidarity, and prisoner resistance. Outnumbered as they are, staff depend on the predictability of each others' actions. Solidarity ensures that if one person hits a body alarm, everyone else drops what they're doing and rushes to that person's assistance. More mundane expressions of solidarity, such as being able to count on staff to "back you"—to support your decisions without question so that prisoners are not able to play one staff member off against another—serve both as safeguards against manipulation and as tests of loyalty. In fact, for many staff, the two actions—"backing" each other and running to help when a colleague's life is threatened—are morally equivalent. Any relaxation of solidarity leads to a slippery slope: there must never be any doubt about where one's loyalties lie.

Solidarity is particularly threatened by staff-prisoner communication. Once staff begin to establish a rapport with prisoners by talking to them, acknowledging their side of the story, or resolving problems, accusations that they are not "backing" each other immediately arise. Think about the following prisoner's story.

> They gave me a shot [disciplinary report] and put me in the hole [segregation] for a week when I was grieving for my grandma's death. An officer talked to me like a kid and I just got mad because I was so upset. [But] then another officer talked to me after the incident and he understood what had happened; so some of them are good. (4KD)

From the prisoner's perspective, the officer who took the time to talk to him was simply showing some human sympathy, working on creating "harmony, open communication, and rapport." But from the staff's perspective, the officer who talked to the prisoner made himself look good at the expense of his colleagues. The fact that the "shot" was for insolence to an officer only makes the betrayal worse: in the eyes of the officer corps, an officer who excuses this kind of behavior is licensing prisoners' disrespect. Had the officer been able to revoke the "shot" out of sympathy with the prisoner's extenuating circumstances, his actions would have been the last straw: the officer who issued the original "shot" would have felt that his authority had been undercut.

A similar dynamic also exists for prisoners. The affinity and sense of interdependence that staff have for each other is less common among prisoners; prisoners commonly talk about "doing your own time"—staying away from other prisoners lest they get you into trouble. But while it may not power a unified front, prisoners do share a resentment of those who keep them where they are, and it is made worse by their vulnerability and their dependence. Remember the prisoner who said that "the young kids" had "a chip on their shoulder about staff" (2CI). Inmates brood about incidents where they feel that staff are deliberately going out of the way to emphasize their powerlessness.

> Yelling at you, like "You, get your butt in bed." They don't wait to discipline you until you've done something wrong; they push you too hard and say something smart to you because you can't react back. The way they talk to you is just unnecessary. (4KB)

And they respond with hostility and petty revenge, which serve both to make the atmosphere extremely unpleasant and to keep tensions high. "There's always a way you can make a guy's [staff's] 8 hours hard if he's a knucklehead. Some guys they'll cut his phone wires or jam the locks, or put defecation (sic) on the place where his ear goes, you know. And you know, 3 out of 5 of them will chill out after you do that" (5MA).

The push and pull between communication and solidarity is present at all prisons. When programs are taken seriously, however, the dilemma is exacerbated. Programs encourage casual interaction between staff and prisoners as a way of keeping the lines of communication open and keeping tensions down. They give staff an opportunity to talk to and understand the prisoners as individuals. Thus one vocational education supervisor muses, "In ed/voc . . . we don't remind them where they are—they don't have to be an inmate when they're working in the shop" (1p). Another teacher explains, "You have to be friendly to teach; you have to establish a rapport with them. There's a line, of course, but . . . they'll open up to us because we see them every day" (1x). And this is true not only for program staff, but for officers as well. As inmates are encouraged to look to structured institutional options to fill their time, the staff they look to for assistance are often correctional officers, whom they see every day, rather than teachers or program supervisors, with whom they are less likely to be familiar. Correctional officers, in turn, will informally incorporate this into their job description. Thus an officer is quite likely to explain that he deals with inmates by letting "them know I'm here to help them when I can, and I'll go higher [take the question to a supervisor] if I have to get a question answered" (3fb). Forty-two percent of all staff interviewed named "helping inmates" as part of their job description, or simply said that what they liked about the job was "working with the inmates."

Simultaneously, both staff and prisoners are wary of this contact. Officers and program staff constantly complain that the other group doesn't understand the "real" inmate. "The treatment staff come in and get to help these guys; they only see the inmates when they're a different person.

In front of the officers, they don't put on a show" (2cv). For prisoners, resistance to programs can be a way to maintain self-respect. At first, this may seem hard to understand, since prisoners so obviously benefit from the free education, the training and apprenticeships, or the drug treatment. But from the prisoner's point of view, the criminal justice system is primarily a system that deprives him of families and freedom, slapping him with a "Buck Rogers outdate" or "Santa Claus sentence."[4] Thus, for prisoners to concede that the system also gives them programs that might help them is, for many, too much of a concession. One does not take gifts from one's enemies. Explains one inmate, "When I started here, I didn't want to do programs because I didn't want to conform and stuff. I just came to do my time" (3GK). Similar comments are forthcoming from other inmates, who discuss how programs can harm one's reputation. "The ones that don't [participate] think it's a waste of time, and they don't want to be like 'them'—the staff" (2CG).

Nor are the problems of programs limited to the consequences of the closer interpersonal connections they foster. The demands of running programs can exacerbate conflict between staff by creating differences in priorities and information. Everyone agrees, for instance, that the overarching task of the prison is to keep inmates inside the fence. As a unit manager remarked, "The main job is security; you can't treat 'em unless you have 'em" (4jz). Yet what threatens security is often a matter of debate. At Drake, frequent bouts of bad weather required late work-call almost daily during some seasons of the year. For staff who supervised inmates working in prison industries, this meant unpredictable work schedules and delays in supplying their product to customers. They were understandably frustrated by this; their program was evaluated as a profit-making business. But the situation was made worse because they felt custody staff were unwilling to search for ways around this problem. Custody staff, for their part, felt the issue was trivial. One officer remarked, "They'll gripe because we won't let the inmates go out to work. They don't think that we're concerned that the inmates will disappear as they're going to work" (4jg).

Underlying such arguments is a deeper issue of power. To take the former example, if staff in prison industries are not evaluated by their output, and if the administration of the prison is not called to task for running an unprofitable business, then there are no great stakes at risk in squabbles over when the inmates get to work. But because staff must show results for their work, and because it matters to administrators that

---

[4] The first term describes sentences that are so long that the release date is in the twenty-fifth century (Buck Rogers outdate). The second is a sarcastic way of referring to the "generosity" of a system that gives out years like Santa Claus gives out presents.

there are results, a conflict over bad-weather procedures becomes a conflict over who has the power to see that their interests are respected. In other words, it is not the mere presence of programs in an institution that creates a problem; instead, it is taking programs seriously, and thus running the risk that different staff's needs will sometimes clash. Teachers who give individual help to students working at their own pace in an overcrowded classroom may not be able to monitor the passing of contraband between two inmates in a far corner of the room. A unit officer angered by an inmate's refusal to obey an order may write up a "shot," only to have it overturned by a counselor who knows the inmate has just been denied permission to attend his mother's funeral. Case managers struggling under the burden of a caseload of 150 inmates will resent their colleagues in a residential drug treatment unit where the population averages 80. And if such conflicts are accompanied by perceived or actual differences in salary, working conditions, or promotion potential between staff, the administration of programs can seem to be a zero-sum game among different groups of staff, where rewards or attention for some result in harder work for others.

Most of these differences—whether in the prison's basic strategic orientation towards communication or solidarity, or in the distribution of power and resources among staff—are conveyed through each prison's specific characteristics. Staff are not explicitly told that their prison emphasizes solidarity over communication, or the reverse. Instead, they learn which is more important from the prison's sense of history and mission. Just as teachers often find salient only the parts of a curriculum reform that harmonizes with techniques or teaching materials that they already have (Spillane 1998), what prison staff, and to a lesser extent prisoners, notice about programs are characteristics that are congruent with the values their colleagues profess and the styles of interaction that gain rewards. Sometimes these cues come from a rich body of oral history specific to programs: stories about how a particular requirement meant something else when it was attached to a different policy, or how policies are always changed two months later, or how no one takes a program seriously because it was only adopted to placate some congressman. Many of these cues, however, are not specific to programs: for instance, staff look to their warden's comments about staff and about prisoners, their prison's reputation within the prison system, and their own sense of staff hierarchies and centers of power within the prison.

Over time, this creates not only differences in opinion about programs at different prisons, but actual differences in programs. The BOP makes clear that part of its mission is to provide "safety, humanity, and opportunity" to prisoners, so that they can change their lives if they so desire (DiIulio 1990a:8). Staff at all of the federal prisons in the sample echoed this claim. But at Antelope Valley and Beaverton, prisons which made communication a priority, this injunction meant that prison staff bore responsibility for the quality of the opportunities provided. Because of the history of each prison, that responsibility was explained differently: staff at Antelope Valley talked about how the prison was set up as a place to pilot-test new programs, while staff at Beaverton emphasized their desire, and their history, of achieving excellence on multiple dimensions. By contrast, at Drake and Evergreen, the BOP's injunction was understood quite differently: it suggested that *prisoners* had an obligation to take advantage of the opportunities they were provided. There was no sense that the prison staff had any obligation to the programs: their obligation was discharged as long as programs existed.

The implementation of programs can and does happen under both understandings of "safety, humanity, and opportunity." But implementation that is also successful with respect to rehabilitation requires that institutional values consistent with the rehabilitative purposes of programs be present as well. Of course, prisons do not run on either communication or solidarity alone. But the extent to which one style dominates the other suggests something about how much the benefits of programs will be valued and the costs resented. In a prison where communication is valued, programs will attract more participation from prisoners and program staff will face less resentment from their colleagues. By contrast, in a prison where solidarity is central, the program characteristics that most arouse staff ire will be de-emphasized over time. Programs themselves will be abandoned or altered so that they enhance solidarity, and prisoners will be more likely to see programming as an attempt to manipulate them, leading to the rejection of programs, or at least to deep cynicism about their own participation.

From Implementation Success to Varieties of Implementation

In his classic, *Street-Level Bureaucracy*, Michael Lipsky argued that "street-level bureaucrats," rather than policymakers or agency directors, actually make policy. "They exercise wide discretion in decisions about citizens with whom they interact. Then, when taken in concert, their individual actions add up to agency behavior" (Lipsky 1980: 13). To take Lipsky's insight seriously is to realize that one cannot look at policy without looking at the people who implement it and at how they act while doing so. Richard Elmore sums up this "bottom-up" perspective nicely. "Unless the initiators of a policy can galvanize the energy, attention, and skills of those affected by it, thereby bringing these resources into a loosely structured bargaining arena, the effects of a policy are unlikely to be anything but weak or diffuse" (Elmore 1979–80: 611).

But galvanizing those affected by policy—either as staff or prisoner—is more complicated than it might first seem. In particular, it is not the program itself that wins support—thus, not support for education or job training or drug treatment in the abstract. Rather, it is what the program can do to help staff and prisoners meet their needs given where they are: what this particular program can do in the here-and-now. And it is how well the program fits with the strategies that staff and prisoners are already using to try to meet their needs: whether there is a fit, a clash, or simply a mismatch between the values that prisoners and staff use to guide their actions, and the activities that a program intentionally or unintentionally promotes.

When there is a match between programs and the prison's needs and values, implementation is *successful*. Programs provide a bonus to staff and prisoners, giving them new resources to meet demands they already face. And they do so in a way that is familiar to staff and prisoners, that they find or can make compatible with what they are already doing and what they believe. In this case, program activities will be logically consistent with rehabilitative goals. They might still not produce a decline in recidivism down the road, but they will be consistent with the learning or training that one hopes programs could provide.

Two of the prisons in this study, Antelope Valley and Beaverton Correctional Centers, show what this kind of implementation looks like. Antelope Valley and Beaverton are very different prisons: Antelope Valley has a history of being a "treatment" prison, in which new programs are often tested, while Beaverton is a rural prison where staff have a no-nonsense, "everyone-is-a-correctional-officer-first" philosophy. But in both prisons, program participation is widespread. Prisoners sign up for programs, both program and nonprogram staff feel that programs are integral to the institution, and nonprogram staff will even encourage prisoners to participate in programs. Students in the programs work actively during class time and can explain their work to a visitor. Teachers are engaged in the classes, and cooperate with schools in the community so as to maintain comparable standards. This latter aspect helps ensure that the program activities are consistent with rehabilitation: there is little busywork in the programs at either Antelope Valley or Beaverton, the necessary materials are available, skills and courses are taught in sequence, and each program has an overall plan that staff can explain.

But as Table 2.2 shows, there are several other logical possibilities as well. Programs provide resources to keep prisoners occupied: it is usually easier to supervise 25 prisoners in a classroom than on a work detail, and programs fund the class and the teacher to provide that supervision.

TABLE 2.2
Implementing Programs in Five Prisons

Prison-centered Needs	Institutional Values	
	Communication	Solidarity
Met by programs	**Successful Implementation** *Antelope Valley*: Variety and flexibility of programs encourage participation; emphasis on easy staff-prisoner communication; history of pilot programs informs staff that programs should be taken seriously. *Beaverton*: Seriousness and challenge of programs encourage participation, as do privileges for participation in programs; staff commitment to communication as a way of dealing with prisoners; reputation of excellence leads staff to support program quality.	**Subverted Implementation** *Evergreen*: Staff maximizes enrollment in programs so as to solve problem of prisoner supervision; prisoners resent staff and are not much interested in programming, but participate because of staff pressure; emphasis on solidarity encourages staff to modify programs to serve institutional needs.
Not met by programs	**Neglected Implementation** *Catawba State*: Programs enroll too few prisoners to make a contribution to prison order; programs seem like an extra burden and provide no visible benefits to staff. History of quality programs at prison and of easy relationships between staff and prisoners creates tolerance for program innovations, but rising frustration is evident.	**Abandoned Implementation** *Drake*: Staff emphasize solidarity among themselves and social distance from prisoners. Prisoners know little about the program offerings available and avoid participation out of resentment against staff. Reputation of excellent custody means program staff have no leverage to ask for changes that might benefit programs.

They might even provide opportunities for earning pocket money, or for prestige. But if the prison values solidarity over communication, or staff and prisoners interpret its history to mean that programs are unimportant, program implementation, with respect to the rehabilitative potential of programs, will be *subverted*. That is, the programs themselves will generate active participation, but in activities that are not plausibly related to learning, training, or other rehabilitative ends. Evergreen Correctional Center illustrates this type of implementation failure. The program staff, primarily teachers, at Evergreen, created an extensive set of literacy courses and vocational training programs. They also worked hard on outreach, meeting with prisoners to get progress reports on the courses they had taken and to suggest new ones. But once the prisoners were enrolled, the same teachers allowed them to sleep through class and hang out in the hallways of the education building. The curriculum included construction courses in which there were not enough hammers to go around, vocational math courses in which students were placed without the requisite preparation, high school equivalency courses that relied upon television movies to fill class hours, and a college program administered by an out-of-state campus that provided little, if any, supervision of the adjunct faculty who taught its prison classes. In short, while the enrollment and variety in the education program at Evergreen was high, the day-to-day activities that make up the content of their programs were not conducive to education.

By contrast, it is also possible to have programs with the opposite problem: where the day-to-day practices are consistent with rehabilitation, but attract little prisoner participation and disinterest, even hostility, from many staff. This happens when the values of a prison are supportive of communication and programs, but programs themselves offer few resources to truly keep prisoners busy. For instance, at Catawba State Correctional Center, classes were much more serious than they were at Evergreen: hands-on projects abounded in the vocational training courses, and teachers discussed curriculum seriously and were able to give pedagogical reasons for their choices. Teachers also worked intensively with students in individualized programs, rather than letting their students drift. But despite these promising signs, prisoners found other things to do with their time: playing sports, working in lucrative (comparatively) prison jobs, joining gangs. Correctional staff resented the additional security demands that programs seemed to require of them, and grumbled that the money spent on prisoners should have paid for more security staff or better raises. The upshot was a set of programs with very little institutional support, run by embattled staff, making the existence of even such good programs precarious. Implementation is *neglected*: programs exist but attract little participation, making their continued existence problematic; and the programs that do persist often do so because the program provides an outlet or name for something that people were already interested in doing.

One final option is possible. At prisons where programs are neither extensive nor challenging enough to keep prisoners busy, and where the value system emphasizes solidarity and provides no history supportive of programs, implementation of programs can simply be *abandoned*. Such is the case at Drake Correctional Center, the prison described at the beginning of the last chapter, in which students slept through class. Those students were mandatory enrollees: the prison system's policy is that those without a high school diploma must take at least three months of class. In other classes, which are voluntary, disengagement is shown in a different way: students simply do not sign up. On paper Drake has ten different vocational apprenticeship programs that can be combined with work assignments at the prison; rarely is more than one filled at a time. The program staff feel isolated among coworkers who suspect them of "hug-the-thug" behavior; the correctional officers and housing unit managers make no effort to encourage prisoners to enroll in programs. There is only minimal resemblance between activities that would provide education or counseling, and what actually happens in programs: one teacher is prohibited from introducing tools such as computers in her class, despite the proliferation of computers in the vocational field she teaches, because that skill is deemed too sophisticated for prisoners to be learning at taxpayers' expense. Essentially, Drake has abandoned implementation: while programming, classes, and enrollment all exist, the level of disengagement and the lack of meaningful programming are so severe that programs cannot be considered to have gotten off the ground.

The comparison between Table 2.2 and Table 2.1 is telling. From Table 2.1, it would be difficult to differentiate between the prisons; each seems to have a variety of program options for prisoners. But Table 2.2 makes the point that there is more to implementation than meets the eye: *what* exists must be understood in terms of *how* it exists. Programs exist in varieties: varieties of implementation, which result from variations in the prison context, and which in practice create programs that share little but the name. Achieving successful implementation is thus as much about creating the right context for programming as it is about getting the program's design, incentives, or structure right: it is about taking the needs of staff and prisoners seriously and on their terms, and about emphasizing—or promoting—values within the prison that can provide a "hook" for appropriate programming. Evaluating implementation that has already taken place can illuminate where staff and prisoners were ignored, or took their needs into their own hands. It can also explain why the virtues that advocates often attach to programs actually violate, or at the least miss entirely, what staff and prisoners most value.

3

Unsuccessful Implementation

THE USE AND ABUSE OF PROGRAMS

DRAKE, CATAWBA STATE, and Evergreen Correctional Centers are all, as prisons go, extremely well-run institutions. Although no prison is completely free from physical violence, incidents of inmate-inmate or inmate-staff violence are rare. The food is competently if not expertly cooked, the buildings are clean, and the noise only occasionally rises to deafening levels. None would be considered pleasant places to spend several years of one's life, and yet none resembles the kind of iron jungle that popular movies portray prisons to be.

Studies such as John DiIulio's *Governing Prisons* (1987) suggest that prisons with this level of order and amenities both make rehabilitative programming possible, and in turn depend upon programming to help maintain this level of order. On the surface, each of these prisons appears to support this claim. All offer institutional programming: high school equivalency classes, some job training and factory work, various opportunities for college education, and different kinds of drug-abuse treatment. The administration and many of the staff at each prison tell visitors that the programs keep prisoners busy and thus help maintain prison order, and there is no reason to doubt their sincerity.

But on closer examination, the programs' ability to offer rehabilitative benefits—to contribute to the education, training, or rehabilitation of prisoners—seems doubtful indeed. Basic resources, equipment, and coordination between classes are often missing. Program activities that exist on paper are underutilized or unused in practice. Teachers do little to teach or to encourage students to learn; when some teachers make efforts, they feel stymied by their colleagues and supervisors, and spend a good part of their energy on prison politics. Prisoners use class time for socializing or sleeping, with little interference from their instructors. Individual prisoners and instructors who are determined to learn and teach soldier on, of course; but the infrastructure that could improve the content of what they learn, that could motivate those who are more easily distracted, is absent.

Implementation with respect to rehabilitation fails at Drake, Catawba State, and Evergreen because programs do not satisfy the institutional needs of staff and prisoners, and/or violate institutional values. At Drake and Catawba, neither staff nor prisoners feel that they derive any institutional benefit from participating in programs. Meanwhile, prisoners feel that the programs are not challenging enough to keep them busy. They thus lose interest in participating. At Drake and Evergreen, the use of programs to create order also violates institutional norms about the importance of solidarity. At Drake, the conflict encourages correctional staff to refuse to assist, and sometimes actively stymie, program staff and activities. At Evergreen, programs are modified in ways that make them more useful to the prison, but less useful for rehabilitation.

The resulting lack of implementation takes on different forms. At Drake, where programs neither satisfy institutional needs nor mesh with institutional values, implementation is abandoned. Enrollment in programs is low and driven mostly by mandatory involvement; attempts to enrich programs are greeted with hostility. At Catawba, by contrast, many staff and prisoners are enthusiastic about programs; long waiting lists exist for all the prison's offerings, and the administration unabashedly supports programming. But because the programs are too limited in scope to address the demands of maintaining prison order, they do not provide an institutional incentive for their maintenance. Neglected implementation is the result; what little implementation occurs stems from individual staff activity and is constantly threatened with opposition. This lesson is underscored at Evergreen, where attention to the institutional benefits of programs leads staff and prisoners to support them. On the surface, then, the prospects for program implementation are more favorable than at either of the other two prisons. But because there is also a strong norm of staff solidarity, programs and program staff must justify their existence. Most programs collapse into a set of provisions designed to fulfill institutional needs, with little reference to how those provisions affect the quality of the education or training that prisoners receive. This subverted implementation is often hard to distinguish from successful implementation, because staff, and sometimes even prisoners, are supportive and often quite proud of the programs they run. Yet good as they are at maintaining institutional order, these programs do little to rehabilitate prisoners—and thus, in the long run, contribute to the perception that programs "don't work."

Drake, Catawba State, and Evergreen are well-run correctional institutions that struggle, usually successfully, with the demands of maintaining order in the prison. Each prison's staff and prisoners employ a mix of formal and informal strategies for doing so; some of these strategies make use of programs, while others depend on marginalizing them. In conjunction they show the range of ways in which the rehabilitative potential of programs often goes untapped in the overarching need to ensure the safety and smooth operation of the prison. But that same variety also implies that other ways of balancing the rehabilitative and the institutional benefits of programs exist as well. Though none of these prisons finds that balance, the ways in which they fail also point to the ways in which other prisons might succeed.

Drake—Abandoned Implementation

Drake Correctional Institution sits in a hollow at the intersection of two nondescript county highways, at the outskirts of a city whose manufacturing base is inexorably disappearing. As recently as fifteen years ago, union salaries from factories, power plants, and transportation financed the ranch houses, hunting vacations, pickups, and boats in the area; now, jobs take longer to find and are less rewarding when they arrive. Prison work is a good job here: it offers a reasonable salary and stable prospects. And, especially at the Federal Bureau of Prisons, it is professional work: officers are trained, expected to behave in accordance with a code of conduct that regulates behavior both on and off the job, and promised opportunities to advance.

Staff at Drake repay the professional benefits of the job with a deep sense of pride in their work and their colleagues. "[Drake] has a great work ethic that comes from this community. It's reflected in our regional standing too, and I can see it when I look at the files of inmates who have transferred here. I can almost tell where they're from just by seeing how the files are kept up" (Case manager, 4jo). They often display an almost macho sense of relish for the difficulties of their work. "I enjoy the excitement and the stress; there's never a dull moment here" (Lieutenant, 4js). "You get different inmates from different parts of the world, and 90 percent of them don't like you, so it's more interesting" (Officer, 4je). The companionship and support of their coworkers also adds to their satisfaction. "I guess I don't see any problems with the prison. Everyone backs you, and people who work here are just great" (Officer, 4jd). "We're easygoing, warm, we try to make people feel comfortable; we enjoy our work. The warden is a jovial guy, he tells stories and jokes, and we're homey and friendly people" (Unit manager, 4jc). "It's much better here than at other institutions. I don't know if it's the people, or the area, or if we're just basically friendly. People try to help each other out when you start here, and then it just keeps getting passed on" (Counselor, 4jl).

Not everyone, of course, shares the same level of camaraderie. Minority staff, for instance, can feel excluded from the easy friendship that other staff take for granted. "If you're not a homeboy, a local let's drink beer together type, you have it hard," one young black officer reports

(4jp); another, an older Native American, claims, "Until five years ago, it was a family-run institution. If you weren't born into it, or married into it, or a friend of it, you didn't work here . . . if you ain't from here, if you're different, you ain't gonna be here" (4jk). But while minority officers are the ones who are most visibly "different," many of the white officers also talk about the existence of an inner circle. "If your daddy didn't work here or your uncle's not a federal judge, you're not going to get far," says one white officer (4jg); a unit secretary complains, "They've moved people up too fast because they're good ole boys, they go to the right parties and dinners" (4ja). In general, however, even those who feel that they are on the outskirts of the institution's social life agree that a sense of mutual support undergirds staff interactions. "The correctional officers really do support each other when it's time to support each other," says the black officer quoted earlier; a black lieutenant adds, "They'll be friendly to you, but you won't be part of the circle. Things get done around here, though. . . . It's like a sister and brother might fight, but no one outside had better mess with us. The lieutenants stick together, and so does the correctional team. We feel like a family—we have the same goals and we have to support each other" (4js).

The lieutenant's phrasing—"we have to support each other"—is telling. The sense of mutual support that staff at Drake feel is more than a perk of the job, or a happy accident of shared backgrounds and cultures. Instead, it is a carefully cultivated and stringently maintained camaraderie. From the warden on down, supervisors make "backing" their staff a central part of their jobs: in other words, they make a point of supporting their staff's decisions, taking their concerns seriously, and preventing them from losing face even if they have made a mistake. A unit manager (the director of an inmate housing unit, who supervises counselors and case managers in the unit) says enthusiastically, "Ninety-nine percent of the time we make decisions, the warden backs us; he believes in unit management, and he backs us one hundred percent." In turn, he encourages his staff to back the officers, "Both my case managers used to be officers, so they work with the officers and don't feel that they're better than them. You can't have that attitude. I really think it's important to have the attitude that you are a correctional officer first" (4jz). A lieutenant echoed his sentiments, "I communicate with my staff, I let them know I've walked in their shoes and I remember my roots. I back them to the hilt and talk to them a lot. For their part, it helps them to know that there's someone on who will give them respect, and I give it to them" (4kd).

As both these comments suggest, "backing" your staff at Drake is also associated with a particular group of staff—the correctional officers. This is not surprising: within many prison systems, the statement that "everyone is an officer first" is an axiom. Security is everyone's job, the phrase reminds staff; no one should be too busy or too important to stop an inmate who breaks the rules, to keep an eye out for missing equipment or contraband supplies, or to break up a fight. At Drake, however, this often translates into a casual disrespect for those who are not currently officers: the medical staff, the prison industries foremen, and teachers. Take one conversation in the lieutenant's office: as I interviewed the lieutenant, we were interrupted by an officer who came in to say that the physician's assistant (often known as a "P.A.") was giving prisoners needles and allowing them to administer their own medical injections. One prisoner, he said, would have put the needle in his pocket and walked off with it had the officer not been watching; once the prisoner noticed the officer, he returned the needle to the P.A. At first, the lieutenant explained to the officer that official policy authorized the P.A. to allow self-administered injections as long as she did a needle count at the end of the shift. But when the officer persisted in his worries, the lieutenant agreed to talk to the P.A. about security, "if she's capable of understanding it." The officer laughed and agreed with the lieutenant; his tone and posture both expressed relief.

From the point of view of the correctional staff, this incident epitomizes good supervision. The officer felt free to report a concern; the lieutenant explained the policy, but did so in a way that took the officer seriously and preserved his self-respect; the conversation ended with a reinforcement of the bond between supervisor and staff. But notice, also, the loser in this situation—the absent physician's assistant, who had violated no policy but was nevertheless the target of good-natured contempt. Although it is usually unintentional on the part of correctional staff, the emphasis on security makes program staff easy whipping boys, foils for the self-respect and self-satisfaction of the officers or of those who can identify with them. And because the correctional officers are usually paid less, and work less desirable shifts than the mostly 9-to-5 program staff, castigating the program staff provides an outlet for dissatisfaction that might otherwise be turned against their own supervisors or the administration.

Another clear consequence of the "security first" strategy for maintaining camaraderie is the creation and maintenance of boundaries, of a sense of "them versus us" between prisoners and staff. At Drake, this is evident in the threat that staff feel prisoners pose to them. Asked, "Do you think the inmates here are hostile to staff?," 48 percent of the staff at Drake agreed. As Table 3.1 shows, this is a higher proportion than at any of the other prisons, and it is particularly striking because few prisoners have violent records or high security classifications at Drake—fewer than at any prison but Antelope Valley. Another comment that I heard more

TABLE 3.1
Staff Perceptions of Prisoner Hostility

	Antelope Valley	Beaverton	Catawba	Drake	Evergreen
"Some/most prisoners are hostile."	8%	32%	24%	48%	38%
"No, they're not hostile to us."	89%	65%	49%	38%	41%
"Inmates are hostile only when staff give them reason to be."	4%	3%	27%	12%	22%
(N=)	(28)	(34)	(33)	(33)	(32)

often at Drake than anywhere else is the desire for more leeway in the use of force, in particular to keep prisoners in their place. "When they [the prisoners] step too far across the line and we don't stop them, it makes their chest swell out. At the first sign of something, we need to send a crew in and remove him—nip the trouble in the bud. Bureau-wide, we don't have a lot of situations, but in some, force should be used to restrain people. Let them know we still run it, and not them" (4jb).

The creation of boundaries between staff and prisoners is obvious in less confrontational ways as well. One sign of this is a practice I saw at none of the other prisons in this study: the refusal to use prisoners' first names. Asked about mistakes that staff might make with inmates, a chaplain said, "Becoming too friendly—joking around, kidding, or calling the inmate 'Mr.' I'll call an inmate 'brother,' or outside of the chapel, use the last name or in a more formal situation, 'Inmate' and the last name" (4jq). A unit secretary agreed, "I never call them by their first names or let them call me by mine. It's a respect thing. I don't agree with first names— they're inmates, they're not here to be my buddies or have a good time" (4ja). A similar concern is most often cited by officers and attributed to nonsecurity staff: fraternizing with prisoners. "Mingling [with inmates] is bad because it breaks the bond that staff have with each other; they like the [work] foremen and they hate the po-lice [correctional officers]" (4je). Another officer muses, "We need to have more of an us-versus-them mentality, and not an us-versus-everybody mentality" (4kc).

The maintenance of staff camaraderie through all of these practices— the elevation of correctional staff, the concomitant if offhand scapegoating of program staff, and the distancing from prisoners—creates an atmosphere where the institutional benefits of programs are far outweighed by their costs. Staff are quick to say that programs can be useful—they "keep them [the prisoners] using their free time, instead of using it to tie us up in the courts. And because otherwise we couldn't control them. They can control the institution anytime, so we have to keep them happy for our safety. The institution isn't built for the security of this many" (Food service foreman, 4kb). Many also believe that prisoners should be given some opportunities to improve themselves, "hopefully, so they'll do something worthwhile in time. Hopefully, so they'll make good use of their time and have something to stand back on when they get out" (Secretary, 4jh). But even the supporters are equivocal. The secretary who supports programs is also quick to defend their limitations—"We deal with violent people . . . but we do try to help inmates. We can't let them have or do everything they want, but it's not a bad place for them" (4jh). And the foreman clearly believes that while programs can keep prisoners from causing trouble, part of the reason prisoners can cause trouble is a lack of control. "The inmates are getting more rights and getting more and more vocal . . . we get tied up with answering grievances, and it's important to have that, but it gets old quickly because the inmates use it to tie up the system for the purpose of tying it up" (4kb).

This ambivalence about programs would not be very significant if it were confined to staffs' personal musings and private beliefs. But it overflows into prison practices: into peer relationships with program staff, into decisions that affect the day-to-day operations of programs, and into staff interactions with prisoners who might be interested in programs. Teachers cannot easily dismiss the type of casual disrespect that they receive as mere good-natured, offhand ribbing. Instead they see an institutionalized disrespect for programs that leaves them out of staff camaraderie, that precludes their accomplishments from being recognized and rewarded, and that puts them continually on the defensive.

[Q: I wonder if you feel that other staff understand what your job is and support what you do?]

In education, yes. With other departments, sometimes they say we're babysitting, that we just sit down and get money for doing nothing. Most of the people who say that are officers who didn't like school, and barely made it through when they were there. (Teacher, 4ka)

No—when you're in recreation, everyone else thinks all you do is throw out the balls and nothing else. Custody doesn't understand why I shoot pool with the inmate; but my job involves games, and I can get information from them that way. (Recreation supervisor, 4jw)

No—they don't understand and there's not much support. They don't like us helping the inmates. They think they should make an inmate's life as miserable as they can. Custody's attitude is, get out of my way because you got nothin' comin'. Education and psychology, on the other hand, try to help the inmate. When I was in custody [working as a correctional officer], I guess I had the same feeling, but I had to change when I got to education because you can't degrade people if you're going to do this job. (Vo-tech instructor, 4jm)

One of the ways that the lack of institutional support is most apparent to teachers is the pressure for "numbers," or for higher participation rates in the GED and vocational training courses. Of the five prisons I visited, Drake was the only place in which the staff talked about feeling pressure to increase enrollment. On the surface, this might indicate that Drake placed a high priority on education. But as the education staff see it, this concern is dictated by their supervisor's fear of looking bad in regional comparisons; in other words, Drake was under pressure because their participation rates were lower than everyone else's. Education staff resent this pressure because they feel that they are already working hard, with little support.

[Q: *What do your supervisors do well? What should they pay more attention to? What are the biggest problems they face?*]

They have to pay more attention to whether their instructors are accountable—they have to focus more on the quality of education. They should stop emphasizing numbers, or favoring the amount of time you spend at work over how you do your duties . . . they should stop worrying about how much time you spend out of the classroom—at the ladies room, or making copies—and just about whether the students are learning. [Their biggest problem is] the pressure for numbers, I guess from the region; they don't consider whether we have the staff to produce those numbers. And also, not being able to find qualified staff. (Vo-tech instructor, 4jn)

[Our supervisor] wants us to do his job so that he'll look good, but he already said there'll be no rewards for us if we do a good job, because he doesn't get any. (Teacher, 4ka)

We have excellent people in some areas, like education—but at Drake, education is considered the lowest form of everything. People have the attitude—why would you teach these guys? So we'd like to hear, once in a while, that we're doing a good job, and not just—"why don't we have more students?" They should try to help us, not threaten us when we don't have the numbers without telling us how to get the numbers up. (Vo-tech instructor, 4jm)

What explains the low numbers at Drake? Clearly the lack of classroom challenge and motivation is part of the problem. Teachers devote their class time to helping the students who approach them with questions about their individually paced assignments. Most of their students, who are enrolled because class is mandatory for those without a high school degree, simply sleep through class without fear of reproach. Students in the vo-tech classes are more alert, but the shops themselves have an air of quiet disuse and abandonment. This latter fact is particularly odd in light of the fact that on paper, Drake appears to have an excellent apprenticeship program: ten different trades, in areas such as auto body and mechanics, cabinetmaking, dental technology, welding, drafting, maintenance, electrical work, plumbing, and quality control. Such trades courses usually have long waiting lists at other prisons; at Drake, few prisoners even know that they exist.

The lack of challenge, and the perception of a lack of programs, means that prisoners gain few institutional benefits from participating in programs. Participation does not make the day go by faster, because it is not interesting and absorbing. Prisoners are unlikely to feel that they are "doing" their time, or deriving some positive improvement from their incarceration; instead, they are aware that they are being babysat. "They put books in front of you and they don't care—I sleep so much in there I quit" (4JH). "In the GED class, the teachers don't really help you. There's just a couple of good [inmate] tutors; but if they weren't there, it wouldn't be productive" (4KD). "With the drug programs and stuff, it's self-taught—so we just bullshit together. The staff don't really do much" (4KR). "They [the education department] get $2500 for my taking the class; that's my understanding. I'm sure that they don't care if we learn, or what we do when we're out. But that's the same with me; I don't care about what will happen to them when I leave" (4JC).

As the last quotation suggests, since the programs do not offer the advantage of challenge or interest, prisoners are apt to look for concrete benefits to participation—financial incentives, offers of "good time" or early release, favorable consideration for halfway house placement. The lack of such incentives serves as a further reason to reject participation. "There are more people beginning to turn the programs down. . . . They need to teach values you need at home—how to get a job, how to get back your wife. But they're [the prisoners] not getting that, so they're bitter. They [the prison] get money for them [the programs]. They could care less about us. They just want you to be in bed when they tell you to be. If they cared about education, they would give you rewards too" (4KB). "They [the prisoners] go just because they [the staff] make them go; or they'll put you in the hole. It's all forced. . . . I would like to see them give good time for education. Since they get money for the program, why not give me something too?" (4KJ).

But the disaffection with programs is not only due to the lack of material or experiential incentives for participation; it is also a reaction against a staff whom prisoners consider overzealous and disrespectful. Interactions with Drake staff leave most prisoners with no sense that the relationship is anything but adversarial. Staff thus provide no cues to suggest that mainstream society might accept prisoners back upon release; and they help to strengthen the image that prisoners already have of themselves, as outcasts and outlaws. "There's nothing here, and I didn't want nothing to do with Drake. When I first came, it was all right, but then they didn't care when I got sick. Plates aren't clean; you can't like people if they treat you that way. Before, at every institution I've been in, I programmed" (4JA). "I've been all over the federal system. This is no good at all. There's nothing in the canteen, the staff treats you like dirt, like little kids; the food is bad; this is the worst place I've seen . . . the warden here is nothing; we don't see him . . . they have to train people in more advanced stuff, like radio technician. In the state prison, we worked on computers, TV, radios; here, they won't let us bring any people from the street to teach us" (4KF).

Of course, there are exceptions to this pattern: some prisoners find individual staff members who reach out to them, or are so motivated that they ignore their bad encounters with some staff and attract others who take them seriously. Their stories clearly show the influence that good relationships with staff can have on program participation. One young prisoner currently works in prison industries but is enrolled in no other program. "There's nothing else here to do; you have to look to rehabilitate yourself" (4KM). Unlike most of his colleagues, however, he has not come to this conclusion through hearsay.

> I took all the classes in the psychology department, because people have to put in the initial effort. Change your mentality, or you will be back. . . . I want an education, so I can say I did the time, but I didn't waste the time. I want to say, look what I did with it! I don't want a factory job when I go out; I want a job where I can provide for them [my family] correct, or I'll hustle to do it.

This prisoner's unwillingness to take a factory job, and his awareness that crime is a continuing alternative, can be taken as a lack of commitment to abide by the law, no matter the cost. And yet, both he and the welding teacher can be given credit for ensuring that his rejection of factory work is at least an informed rejection.

> I wanted to take college courses, but I can't take them here, it's almost impossible to get them. . . . I took the welding class because the teacher kept insisting, and no one had ever done that for me before. But I just couldn't get interested in it. Many people here are willing to take college, but there's nothing here.

Another prisoner, whom staff enthusiastically spoke of as a model prisoner, had overcome the lack of college courses at the prison by finding out, on his own, about correspondence courses that he could take instead. He is understandably enthusiastic about the unit team and the education staff who went out of their way to help him take courses that are generally unavailable to prisoners at Drake. "The team recommended me for a UNICOR (federal prison industries) scholarship so I could take this course [in business management] . . . the team's really helped me all the way." But his experience also shows why he is the exception and not the rule. "It's really hard to communicate with the college and get this started. There's lots of paperwork to do with the staff at the college; it was really difficult. . . . Education was afraid even to give the application to me here"(4KS).

The difficulty that these prisoners faced in taking college courses was a function of both staff disdain and administrative policy. At the time of this study, Drake was one of the rare federal medium-security prisons that did not have a college program.[1] This idiosyncratic decision, the result of the warden's philosophical opposition to allowing prisoners to use federal financial aid money, had wide-ranging effects on the quality of Drake's programs. The involvement of local colleges with prison programs serves two purposes: it enriches the prison's offerings by supplementing them with college-level academic subjects, but it also allows apprenticeship programs to be held to outside standards. Such colleges provide a curriculum identical to their courses outside the prison, and sometimes even hire the same instructors to teach "inside" and "outside." They administer the same exams and other evaluations that they do for their on-campus students; and give degrees and/or certification to the prisoners who pass the courses. In turn, the colleges are paid with Pell Grant money that prisoners who enroll in the courses can apply for. The prison gains a college program without additional expense; the students have access to an education certified by an accredited institution; and the local colleges receive additional funding.

The absence of a college program at Drake does not only mean that it is forced to offer fewer (and lower-level) program options than other prisons. It also keeps the prison from patterning its programs on good information about the trades or skills being taught. Without outside accreditation, prison administrators need not adhere to any outside institution's prescribed course of study. Thus they can veto any proposals to teach skills that may be too dangerous or too "good" for prisoners. Implementation with respect to rehabilitation is clearly threatened as a result. Teachers, of course, may know which skills are necessary because of their professional training. But the lack of administrative support, and their peers' disdain and distrust, means that they do not have the autonomy to make use of their knowledge. For instance, one vocational skills

---

[1] With current restrictions on prisoner eligibility for Pell Grants, such programs are now less common.

teacher complained that she was "not allowed to teach inmates who know anything about computers computer-aided design. That basically means that they aren't going to be able to get a job, because everyone uses computer design now" (4jn). But correctional staff regarded her frustration with complacency: "I think when you go to having college courses, or design class with those special machines, that's too much" (Officer, 4jd).

The implementation of programs at Drake is thus threatened, not only by institutional values and norms about staff solidarity, but by institutional values and practices that reject some types of programming in particular. Drake does not intentionally provide inferior programs. Instead, its administrators are worried, justifiably so, that prisoners might use computers to break into confidential records, the welding workshop to make weapons, their electricians' skills to sabotage the prison's security system, and the like. They can even make a case for refusing to allow college programs that the Bureau itself approves, perhaps because they fear public relations or political fallout in an area where few can afford college. But such arguments are successful because staff share these values: seeing primarily the problematic aspects of programs, nonprogram staff felt justified in disdaining programs, and program staff were cowed.

What if the prison administration, by contrast, were committed to programs? Perhaps with a different warden and education administrator, implementation could be more successful. This, of course, is the implementation strategy most often tried: bring in a reforming administrator, and he or she will make programs work. (Nathan 1993) But while administrative commitment to programs and their rehabilitative potential is important, it is not sufficient, and can sometimes be counterproductive. Unless attention to programs is coupled with an understanding of institutional values, like solidarity, that might be threatened by more attention to programs, and unless staff and prisoners receive the institutional benefits that make them willing to participate in programs, implementation will still fail. While it may go farther than at Drake, where programs were barely implemented, implementation is still likely to be neglected or subverted. The case of Catawba illustrates why even good leadership is not enough.

Catawba—Neglected Implementation

In many ways, Catawba State Correctional Center is the most interesting of all the prisons. At 1,800 prisoners, it is one and a half times larger than Evergreen, the next largest prison in this study. As a state facility, it holds the greatest number of prisoners with violent backgrounds. Walk through the grounds of this prison and instead of the small groups of two or three prisoners in the other institutions, one sees packs—large groups of prisoners milling about together, communicating in shouts and taunts. The arrival of a staff member only slightly subdues the noise, and the presence of a staff member with authority actually increases it: prisoners stop supervisors to complain loudly about an injustice, to present a request, or simply to get attention. A quick walk through a courtyard with an assistant warden takes half an hour because of our constant stops to address prisoner concerns. Most of the staff we pass, by contrast, do not stop to hail the assistant warden; nor does he always remember to greet them.

The chaos contrasts oddly with the physical setting of Catawba. For as a collection of buildings and grounds, Catawba is peaceful and attractive. The old brick building one sees from the parking lot is a dignified three stories; while most of the other buildings are prefabricated, they are spread out on a compound that includes grassy knolls and stately old trees. When prisoners come to Catawba from one of the state's famed maximum-security prisons, expecting the bars and tiers they left behind, the wide-open spaces and rural location come as a shock. The surroundings are not only markedly different from those at other prisons; they are a stark contrast to the city ghettos where many of the prisoners grew up. As this prisoner comments: "There are trees and stuff here—you can see the outside, and there are animals—there's just more life" (3GK). Prisoners are encouraged to take advantage of the grounds through a liberal movement policy: at specified times, they can go to the recreation yards freely, or even to other housing units. While passes are used, they are pro forma. The recreation yard is large and includes a basketball court, a horseshoe pit, a running track, and a refreshment stand, where prisoners can purchase snacks with their pocket money.

But the most powerful symbol of Catawba's relative freedom is the fact that prisoners receive keys to their rooms—and thus can come and go as they please. This prisoner, barely out of his teens but already a veteran of the maximum-security prison, recounts his astonishment when he was transferred to the medium-security Catawba:

> I was in the max joint [the maximum-security prison], and you spent most of the time in your cell. If there was movement, it was only for 1–2 hours a day to the yard, and then to meals and back to your cell. [But at Catawba] you have a key to your room—when I got here and they gave me a key, I tripped out. One of my [gang] associates told me, "Hey, man, take that, it's your key" and I thought they was trying to set me up [thought they were trying to get me in trouble for having a prohibited item or planning an escape]. Lots of guys cry

about this place but I tell them, you ain't never been in no max joint, you ain't never been in prison. You had swords, shanks there—and the po-lice they don't even mess wit it because they scared. This here is paradise, for real. (3GL)

It is hard to miss the irony in these privileges: prisoners come and go as they please, but only within the boundaries of their confinement to the prison, and staff can and do enter the rooms at any time, to count, inspect, and search. A cynic might say that the only freedom prisoners have at Catawba is to lock themselves up. And prisoners, of course, realize this; as one remarked, "Catawba doesn't have walls it has fences, and it doesn't have cells it has rooms, and you have a key—but that's the only difference I can see—it's still a penitentiary" (3FD). Another way of putting this is that the chaos in the prison is, for the most part, permitted chaos. The prisoners' freedom is real, but it is also circumscribed.

Perhaps more ironic is that prisoners play as much of a role in keeping themselves circumscribed as the staff do. As the young prisoner describes, the chaos in the prison is disorderly but it is not really dangerous, or at least, not dangerous relative to more controlled institutions. The freedom of movement does not breed more "swords and shanks" (varieties of handmade prison knives); nor do the prisoners perceive the "po-lice," or correctional officers, to be scared of them. Instead, even gang members like the young prisoner quoted above know that abusing the freedom Catawba offers is the surest way to get sent to a much less pleasant prison. "You know they make you do what they want, and we do it, not because we're afraid of them, but shit—you don't want to go to seg[regation], or get shipped out of here, because this joint is sweet" (3GL).

The contrast with the maximum-security prisons where most of the prisoners started their incarcerations also helps to account for their generally good relationships with staff. As opposed to prisoners at Drake, where the distrust and distaste for staff is widespread, prisoners at Catawba give staff their due. "Most are fair—they'll give you a break, because they know you're stressed" (3GI). "Most of them are ok; I hardly be around them, but I like them" (3HB). "Some of the officers have an inferiority complex; since they have the rank, they have the ability to give [disciplinary] reports to you, and they will. But that's not here, you get what's coming to you here" (3HD). Organizing responses like this into general categories, one finds three: staff treat prisoners badly; staff reciprocate, treating prisoners well if they are treated well; and staff are generally good, treating prisoners with some humanity and respect. Table 3.2 shows that compared with other prisons, Catawba's prisoners are much less likely to complain that staff treat them with disrespect, and more likely to give staff credit.

TABLE 3.2
Prisoners' Evaluation of Prison Staff

	Antelope Valley	Beaverton	Catawba	Drake	Evergreen
"Staff treat prisoners badly, without respect."	24%	21%	14%	34%	47%
"Staff are ok; they leave you alone if you leave them alone."	57%	61%	57%	46%	42%
"Staff here are pretty good; they treat you human."	19%	18%	29%	20%	11%
(N=)	(37)	(44)	(35)	(35)	(38)

Note: Prisoners were asked an open-ended question, "The next set of questions is about staff here. I wonder if you can tell me about them. What are they like?" Answers fell generally into the three categories displayed above.

Staff sense and return this matter-of-fact acceptance. As Table 3.1 showed, only 24 percent of the staff at Catawba, as compared to 48 percent of the staff at Drake, find the prisoners to be hostile. The contrast is particularly striking because, as Table 3.3 shows, the backgrounds of the prisoners at the two prisons would lead one to expect that the practices of the two prisons should be reversed: only 17 percent of the prisoners at Drake are incarcerated for robbery or the use of violence, compared to 82 percent of the prisoners at Catawba. Table 3.1 also shows that twice as many staff at Catawba—27 percent compared to 12 percent—consider staff, not prisoners, to be at fault when prisoners are hostile. "To certain staff, they [the prisoners] are hostile—and sometimes there are reasons for it. There are some people here I can't stand either. But I never felt any danger, and there's no reason for me to—I'm always honest and fair" (Grounds foreman, 3gg). Staff at Catawba make distinctions between the prisoners' previous behavior and their behavior once in prison. As this officer says, "The major problem here is anger, which is why they're a problem to society. But I don't feel unsafe, like I'm looking over my shoulder all the time" (3fd). They credit the prison's environment with the prisoners' behavior; as another officer says, "Once they see the freedom and space here, though, they calm down. I'll talk to them and wait for them to come around" (3fc).

But at the same time, the freedom and space that calms the prisoners down puts the staff on edge. Staff shortages and overcrowding combine to make the staff feel as if their work is continually spinning out of control. One lieutenant, who says that he likes "everything" about his work, nevertheless sums up his frustrations succinctly: "There aren't enough

TABLE 3.3
Instant Offense Profiles

	Antelope Valley	Beaverton	Catawba[a]	Drake	Evergreen
Drug/Liquor	41.4%	48.3%	18%	51.7%	53.7%
Robbery	14.8%	16.6%	29%	13.6%	17.9%
Violence	7.0%	9.6%	53%	3.0%	4.2%
Extortion/Fraud/White Collar Crime	7.3%	3.3%	NA	3.4%	2.4%
Total Population	789	933	1777	1061	1115

[a] Because Catawba uses a different classification system, these are not exact comparisons. The instant offense percentages were calculated from the respondents at Catawba who agreed to release their offense data. A look at Catawba's own classification system suggests that these numbers may slightly underestimate the violence profiles of inmates in Catawba.

people, and we can't do things the way they should be done" (3fp). Another officer elaborates:

> We're shortstaffed, so no one gets a vacation, and there are not enough command staff to go around. . . . We always thought our job was pressing buttons and closing cages; now we find our job is solving problems and answering questions . . . [but] with people coming up to me and three or four other things happening, I can't always deal with the problems. . . . I don't know if security is lax here, but there needs to be more control. People don't call to follow up on passes, and they should. They should also be stricter in taking good time [docking the prisoners' time off for good behavior], not downgrading tickets [not finding the prisoner guilty of a lesser offense when he's written up for a violation of prison rules]; if they enforced the rules more, it could affect their [the prisoners'] behavior. (3fg)

Two things are evident from this officer's musings. First, his belief in communication—"our job is solving problems and answering questions"— coexists with a fear of disorder and a desire for more control over the prisoners' activities. He is committed to communicating with the prisoners: "The 'don't bother me' attitude—when you come in with a chip on your shoulder—is really bad, because the problems could be important. You have to respect them [the prisoners] because they're people too" (3fg). But it does not make the job easier; and when he is pressed for time or has too many tasks to perform, the need to communicate makes his job harder.

Second, the target for much of this officer's frustration with prisoners is the command staff. They are the ones who are not around, who are not requiring compliance with procedure from their officers, and who are downgrading tickets and allowing prisoners to keep their good time. The line staff's contemptuous assessment of superiors from the lieutenants on up to the warden stands in sharp contrast to Drake, where the staff were almost uniformly enthusiastic about their supervisors. "The lieutenants; they're pencil pushers. And the captains too—you never see them" (Officer, 3ff). The warden and assistant wardens come in for charges of micromanagement: "I fired an inmate and wrote a ticket on him. The warden sent him back to me even though he fronted me [challenged my authority openly]. The warden doesn't back you at all. You're damned if you do and damned if you don't" (Grounds foreman, 3gf).

The unhappiness with supervisors is notable because issues of solidarity and staff conflict are usually thought to arise between program staff and correctional officers (Josi and Sechrest 1996; but see Steadman, Morrissey, and Robbins 1985). But at Catawba the staff's antagonism is directed mostly toward the prison administration because, almost uniformly, Catawba's education staff are appreciative of the correctional officer corps. They hold the officers blameless even in disputes about the relative claims of programs and security. "We [program and security staff] have two different agendas, but it's not a problem. . . . I have no problems with officers telling me what to do, and while sometimes I drift, I never do so to the extent that someone might be injured" (voc-ed instructor, 3gb). "Security is #1; it has to be, even for us. All the teachers know that security is first, so there aren't any differences because of that" (voc-ed instructor, 3ga). One GED teacher explains disagreements between program and security staff as a byproduct of the difficulties that the officers face. "I think the administration does things that security questions and that make their job more difficult. . . . The bottom line is staff need more backing from the administration. This is especially true with officers—they don't have any support, so they don't carry out policies like removing gang paraphernalia. The command staff needs to intervene in situations like that, not just let officers take the heat" (3fz).

The staff's unhappiness is particularly acute because, in sharp contrast to its perceived neglect of the security staff, the prison administration is openly and actively committed to providing opportunities to prisoners. While Drake's warden prevented staff from creating joint vocational education programs with the local community college, the warden at Catawba went looking for a college partner in a different city after the community college in his area bowed to public pressure and decided to stop teaching courses to prisoners. While Drake's administration prides itself on its strictness with prisoners and makes staff satisfaction a priority, Catawba's warden and several of his deputies consider themselves reformers, doing their best for prisoners and encouraging an often-reluctant staff to follow their lead.

Part of doing the best they can for prisoners is providing a range of programs. From sports teams to speakers, ethnic clubs to drama clubs, a prison newspaper to a range of trades and college courses, Catawba provides numerous opportunities for both recreation and education. There are some conspicuous exceptions: the drug treatment program is minuscule, consisting primarily of a few Alcoholics and Narcotics Anonymous (AA/NA) groups, and the prison industries program, an optics factory, has a waiting list of several years. (Prison industries, though technically a work assignment like the kitchen or grounds crew, is considered a "program" in most prison systems. Because it offers pay for performance rather than a fixed stipend, often teaches prisoners a marketable skill, and enforces work habits in a way that normal work assignments do not, most prison administrators consider 'industries' to be as much 'training' as 'work.') Expanding either program would require more money from the state, unlikely when every expansion of programs is overtaken by the overcrowding that is currently Catawba's most pressing problem. But where the education and recreation departments have been able to expand their offerings, either by enlisting the assistance of cooperating colleges or of volunteers, they have done so. As a result, the atmosphere in the education buildings is as different from Drake as can be: every class is packed full and every student has a project at his workstation. Despite the fact that Catawba's individually paced approach, like Drake's, leaves students on their own, prisoners at Catawba do not complain that their teachers "don't teach." Instead they credit the teachers for their learning. "You go at your own pace and no one rushes you. That's what's good; so you have lots of time to think. . . . The GED teacher here is a genius. He breaks everything down so small that you have to get it; I got my GED in three months!" (3GC).

Teachers display a sense of purpose and of control over their work that is missing from their counterparts at Drake. While at Drake teachers speak primarily about what they wish but are unable to do, teachers at Catawba describe the choices they make in their programs and their attempts to cope with the day-to-day problems that arise. The business technologies teacher, for instance, explains why she chose to teach an easier but less-widely used word processing program over a popular but more complicated one, and explains the placement test she initiated to screen her students (3ga). The basic education teacher talks about how her supervisor has encouraged her to learn ESL (English as a Second Language) skills so as to better assist the Hispanic students (3gc). The vocational education instructor in the laundry recounts how he designed the curriculum from scratch and the compromises he makes when the steam for his presses is shut off (3fx). The choices themselves are not particularly notable; certainly the judgments behind any of them could be questioned. What is notable, though, is their belief that they have the space and the authority to innovate and to make decisions, and thus that they will be allowed to use the information they have to make the programs as useful in rehabilitating prisoners as possible.

The ways in which teachers can use this autonomy to protect the rehabilitative aspects of programs, insofar as they understand them, are evident in their response to mandates from the state's correctional education division. In order to increase the numbers of students in the college program, the state put pressure on teachers to eliminate placement tests for vocational training courses. It also ordered each vocational education class to adopt a state-standardized textbook and statewide lesson plan (thus making it possible for transferred prisoners to continue their studies). The instructors objected to these changes: they felt that placement tests were necessary to make sure that students had command of some basic skills, and they objected to the lack of continuity for students in courses that had been using a curriculum other than the one the state chose. They used their control over their classrooms to fight back. Some simply continued to require a placement test. Others banded together to create a "vocational math" course, in which students were required to enroll if they wanted to sign up for a particular trade. They also coordinated a joint response to the curriculum change, as this instructor gleefully explains: "We were told to do nine weeks' curriculum in six weeks. [This was so that all courses in all prisons could start fresh with the new curriculum on the same day.] What happened is that I, and other instructors, gave everyone incompletes. The administration was furious" (3gb).

It is important not to take this as a claim that the teachers made the right choices, or that standardizing curricula and abolishing placement tests are self-evidently contrary to good education. Just because the institution gives program staff the autonomy to protect the rehabilitative aspects of programs does not mean that staff will use their autonomy wisely. But when program staff are not given that autonomy, they cannot protect their programs even if they know what to do. Compare the responses of Catawba staff—covert and open resistance to mandates they consider unreasonable—to Drake staff, who do not organize to protect their programs but instead get bitter, blame their supervisor, and feel impotent.

As this story suggests, the institutional values that support programs can come from many places. The fact that Catawba's staff emphasized communication with prisoners and (for better or worse) felt little solidarity between ranks meant that interaction, which programs foster, did not threaten them. On top of this, the warden and other top administrators emphasized the importance of programs, in word and deed. This support made it legitimate for teachers to advance their professional understanding of how to teach an effective program, even when the specifics of their understanding challenged the administration's. Even the environment of Catawba helped: programs seemed to be an appropriate accompaniment to the landscape that calmed prisoners down and gave them a second chance.

But in the long run, it is hard to sustain programs if they are *only* consistent with institutional values. Unless staff and prisoners find that their prison-centered needs are met by the programs, their opposition or simple disinterest will lead to program neglect. And at Catawba, this is the case. The staff's sense of overwork and of resentment toward their supervisors pits them in an odd competition—not against the prisoners, per se, but with the prisoners in a struggle for attention from the prison's administrative staff. They do not see the prisoners as antagonists, but they do see their interests as antagonistic to the prisoners'. When the prisoners get programs, the officers wonder if the money is coming out of their staffing budget; when the prisoners argue their way out of a disciplinary sanction, the officers lose face. Thus comments like these are common:

> You write tickets and it goes nowhere; it seems like they [the prisoners] have more coming than you do, because they can badmouth you and you can't say anything back. (3fe)

> [The prisoners get] recreation—time's a lot harder if you're laying around. But sometimes I wonder why we take people out to other institutions [for sports competitions within the prison system], for example, when we don't have money for supplies we need. (3fx)

> The inmates are given things that are pure benefits, too, when the officers are put at risk: we have no floor officers [roving officers who keep an eye on the prisoners and can be called for assistance], but we put someone in the mailroom so that it's open on Saturdays! (3fq)

> The command staff don't do anything about the short staff—they keep having programs to pacify the inmates but they don't do anything for us when we don't have the staff. (3fk)

As the last quote suggests, programs get caught up in this competition. The officers recognize the role that programs play in calming the prisoners and maintaining order; many of them even enthusiastically support programs. But their own sense of deprivation and their feeling that they are being overwhelmed by sheer numbers leads them to see programs as a burden as well as a benefit. This officer's complaint is one of the mild ones:

> The programs for inmates are great, but if there's no staff, we can't sustain them. For example, if they open up a program in 118 [one of the activity rooms], we might have 300–500 inmates there. If there's no staff, we won't see

them moving shanks or trafficking in drugs, but that's what they do if they're all together. . . . We can't open the library until we can detach an officer at 7, or let people use the gym, because we just don't have the officers. (3fl)

Other officers see programs as not only an imposition on their already overwhelming jobs, but as the wrong method of keeping order when the ratio of staff to prisoners is so small.

They [the prisoners] need some activities to control the inmates, but this is going overboard . . . if it got harsher, at first it would be harder to control, but after awhile they wouldn't miss the freedom—just do it [remove the programs and privileges] slowly. (3fu)

I would focus on knowing where the inmates are at all times—exactly. We could write it down if we wanted to, but why bother, even though we're supposed to? We've got 400 acres here; of course we don't know. The Department of Corrections should focus on running more like a military outfit, but the only thing military about this is how they treat us [the staff]. . . When we don't have the manpower, we have to have uniformity—put them in lines and only let them move under order. (3fs)

Over time, this kind of frustration has a serious practical effect on program operations. At a big prison like Catawba, where the smallest counseling case load is 150 and the largest 450, prisoners depend upon the correctional staff and their work supervisors to tell them about programs they could apply for, to give them permission to take time off and go to the education building to research options or sign up for programs, and to supervise the library, activity rooms, and education building. By pleading lack of bodies or an excess of duties, nonprogram staff can turn program activities into activities that exist only on paper. Their unwillingness to help with supervisory duties can also force teachers to spend more time on monitoring students rather than teaching, thus affecting the quality of programs as well.

Paradoxically, Catawba has more officers per prisoner than the other prisons in this study (see Table I.1). More programs might even be more useful than more staff at creating order over the long-term. Currently, only twenty-seven percent of the prisoners at Catawba are enrolled in education/vocational programs. Staff cuts and funding shortages mean that 200 mandatory students alone are on the waiting list for basic literacy instruction—more students than are currently enrolled in the literacy and GED programs combined.[2] Programs relieve disorder not only by

[2] State law requires prisoners to be in school if they test below a sixth-grade level of reading and math skills, and to stay in school for ninety days, or until they have mastered that level of literacy, whichever comes first. After that participation is voluntary, though encouraged. Thus, the school is under pressure to cycle mandatory students through quickly

occupying those who participate in programs, but also by creating a critical mass of inmates who are not willing to tolerate peers behaving in ways that could jeopardize the programs. Without sufficient funding for programs, however, prisoners who want to participate are not occupied, and thus fewer prisoners overall contribute to the critical mass necessary to preserve order. Thus, staff must cope with the extra burdens that programs entail while receiving few of the benefits; it is no wonder that they see program-related duties as an additional irritant.

Unfortunately, the lack of preexisting staff support for programs means that additional funding to expand them would probably not create the necessary support. Increases in funding for programs would do little to address the cost of programming at Catawba: the staff's sense that their concerns always come second to the prisoners' needs and desires. Instead, increases in funding would likely produce the opposite effect, making staff feel even more neglected. Although the budgets for programming and for hiring officers are separate, staff assume that money for programs is diverted from money for staffing in the correctional ranks. If their numbers do not increase as funding for programs increases, their resentment would hurt not only their morale but also the operation of programs.

Nor is it clear that prisoners would greatly increase their participation in programs were spaces to increase. Given the long waiting lists for programs, this claim is counterintuitive. But because prisoners know that waiting lists for programs are long, they tend to get on lists simply to keep open the opportunity of enrolling in the future. When space finally opens up for them, they are often involved in other activities and thus decide not to enroll. Thus, while the waiting list is a good indicator of interest in programs, it is a less reliable indicator of actual future participation.

This disjunction between interest and participation exists because for prisoners, as for staff, participation in programs is a function of how well programs satisfy their prison-centered needs. One big cost to enrolling in programs is absent at Catawba; unlike prisoners at Drake, prisoners at Catawba are not deterred from enrolling in programs because of their resentment toward staff. But in the absence of reasons to reject programs, the relative availability of benefits from programs and from other sources is still important. Here, Catawba suffers. Prisoners often look to programs for material benefits: pay increases, institutional privileges, or

---

once they have completed the mandatory ninety days of enrollment, regardless of whether their skills have improved. Though many students stay on through the GED classes, encouraging them to do so is counterproductive for the program. Waiting lists for the college and trades programs are equally long. The long waiting lists discourage enrollment even after openings become available; prisoners who start with some interest in a course lose it by the time their name comes to the top of the waiting list.

preferences for halfway house and early release that can come from participation. But at Catawba, although most jobs start at $20/month, and can pay as much as $45, the pay for being in class is only $15/month. Attending classes, therefore, requires a real financial sacrifice, especially from prisoners who depend on the monthly stipend for their only source of spending money. "I work in [prison] industries, and I watch TV. I tried to study English and math, but I left it so I could work in industries" (3FW). In addition, overcrowding has eliminated the single cells that used to serve as rewards for program participation and other indices of good behavior; all prisoners now are housed at least two to a cell. And the determinate sentencing under which most new prisoners enter makes no allowance for programming. While prisoners earn "good time" (time off their sentence), that time off comes automatically as a consequence of avoiding misconduct "tickets," rather than as a reward for proactive behavior such as program participation.

Despite the absence of material rewards, education, vocational training, and drug treatment are still worth participating in if the classes themselves are interesting. Here Catawba does much better; the reputation of the teachers is generally good, the classes are fast-paced and full of hands-on projects, and the trades offered are attractive to prisoners. Prisoners are satisfied enough so that they participate in spite of complaints that the courses could be more challenging; note the contrast to Drake, where prisoners refused to participate in classes where they would do little more than sleep. Participating in classes also brings a peculiar inducement: as the result of a court decision requiring equal educational opportunities to be provided for male and female prisoners, female prisoners are brought in from a neighboring prison to attend classes. The chance for routine contact with the opposite sex, not to mention the sexual teasing and horseplay that staff cannot always prevent, is particularly attractive in the otherwise sexually segregated world of the prison.

Prisoners' explanations of their and others' participation reflect this mixture of incentives. Although male prisoners almost never say that the presence of women brings them to programs, for instance, they are quick to link other prisoners' attendance to the women. "I went to school for self-improvement—so it wasn't wasted time, but filled time. . . . they [other inmates] do it for good time, to see girls—but also to better themselves" (3FV). "I've always wanted to improve myself and I have time on my hands that I might as well utilize. I used to take an art class too . . . slowly but surely you realize that education is where it's at. Also, it gives the males and females a chance to mingle; in one way, that's negative, but they're still learning" (3GM). "I'm in auto mechanics because I love cars. I never took the time to go to school on the street, so since I have to be here, I might as well better myself" (3FF). "I'm in GED and sports, because I never did anything productive before, I never had the opportunity. The atmosphere here is a lot better, so I want to do programs; and sports gives me the opportunity to be with the other guys" (3FM).

But as the last quotation suggests, participation in programs is not the only way to occupy one's time in an interesting and constructive way. The wide variety of leisure time activities at Catawba can do more than complement rehabilitative programming; it can provide an alternative to programs. This prisoner's discussion of running is reminiscent of others' discussions of class: "I love running, and I help coach basketball. I used to be in ABE (adult basic education) classes, not anymore. I'm an athlete and running is my first sport. It relieves a lot of tension and it gives me a sense of direction. I took ABE courses because they were mandatory, but I stayed in them until I got a job that paid money—then, you know, I just went with the flow" (3FR). Another prisoner was active on the Latin Committee, a social group for Latino prisoners, and in sports, "because it makes doing time easier, and gets camaraderie" (3GK). Now close to his release date, he wonders if he was right to let his other activities substitute for school.

> When I started here, I didn't want to do programs because I didn't want to conform and stuff, you know, I just came to do my time. But maybe that was the wrong attitude, I should have used the time to get my education, but I didn't want to before. I always loved to read, though—anything real, like World War II history or the Civil War; I'm reading about the Vatican and Latin America now. . . . I tried school once, but something on the outside made me mentally worried, which is stupid because you can't do nothing about it in here anyway, but I was too occupied and I dropped it. (3GK)

Some might argue that prisons should not spend scarce resources to encourage people to participate in programs, when prisoners are not self-motivated enough to prefer an education to an extra few dollars a month and the opportunity to play basketball, or when students are not committed enough to stay in class when the pressures of their lives distract them. I return to this question in Chapter 5. But if nothing else, these prisoners' stories show the fragility of participation in programs. Prisoner involvement with programs is the result of many homely motivations: companionship and self-improvement, stress and boredom, interests and availability, self-respect. Just as with staff, therefore, the organizational context of programs is crucial. In Catawba, where the prison administration cares about and supports the rehabilitative potential of programs, and where staff-staff and prisoner relationships are not overtly antagonistic, the context for programs is much more favorable than at Drake. And yet issues that seem to have little to do with programs—understaffing in the correctional ranks, dissatisfaction with correctional supervisors, overcrowding, and a large variety of recreational activities—can all affect the institutional support that programs receive, and thus their prospects for expansion and improvement.

The example of Catawba suggests that programs can remain side-lined—tolerated, but essentially irrelevant—without the institutional support to make them an integral part of the way the prison functions. But getting that support is not easy. Institutional support often depends upon factors that are not obviously linked to programs, as at Catawba. As the example of Evergreen will show, it can also be purchased at too high a price, with the cost exacted in program quality.

Evergreen—Subverted Implementation

A tower stands watch over the winding drive down to Evergreen, and visitors state their business through an intercom before being allowed into the parking lot. This is a layer of security dispensed with at the other prisons, where drive-up-and-park entrances are standard. Inside the reception building, the anteroom where visitors wait for their staff escorts is placed squarely in front of the barred guardroom that monitors all access to the prison. The corridor to the warden's office boasts a display case filled with weapons made clandestinely by prisoners in their cells and seized during searches or after disturbances. On the walls hang black-and-white photographs of the prison's first buildings, group pictures of the early staff, and pictures of the various directors of the Federal Bureau of Prisons.

All of these details would seem to indicate a prison much like Drake, where the preoccupation with security colors everything from staff relationships to program implementation. But Evergreen's memorabilia and security arrangements are instead reflections of its sense of history. One of the oldest prisons in the federal system, Evergreen has had its share of famous criminals and legendary wardens. Its high profile in the Bureau makes Evergreen a good place for ambitious staff, who use the connections they make at Evergreen to transfer out to other prisons with a promotion. But befitting Evergreen's sense of history, the young up-and-coming staff do not determine the character of the prison. Instead, the staff who have the most influence on the culture of Evergreen are the "homesteaders"—staff who have been working at the prison for several years and who consider themselves the prison's institutional memory.

Every prison, of course, has homesteaders. But in the Bureau, which encourages staff transfers as a way of standardizing practices and providing experienced staff for its new prisons, promotions are often contingent upon one's willingness to accept a transfer. Homesteaders are often considered unpromotable because of personal eccentricities, or less committed to their jobs than they are to the families, side business ventures, or hobbies that keep them in the area. Homesteaders, of course, resist this characterization. But their claim to experience seldom gains them a hearing from supervisors and colleagues who are themselves "movers," or who aspire to be.

At Evergreen, by contrast, homesteaders are prominent members of the supervisory staff. The captain, the highest-level correctional supervisor, has been at Evergreen for almost ten years; the education supervisor for more than twenty. All the counselors and teachers I interviewed, positions in which there is normally a great deal of turnover, have at least ten years at Evergreen; for many of them, it is the only federal prison at which they have worked. Almost all of these staff spent some time as correctional officers before transferring to their present jobs; all work additional overtime doing officer duties in staff shortages or prison emergencies. Unlike their counterparts at other institutions, therefore, they do not consider themselves outsiders because of their program positions, and they brush off anyone who might try to exclude them. "Put it this way," one teacher, with nearly twenty years at Evergreen, explains, "mechanical services and caseworkers too, we went through wars together here. One of my best friends was killed here. The only staff I don't respect is a dirty staff [a staff member who takes bribes or smuggles contraband], or one that won't respond to a body alarm." Asked about teamwork, he is tolerantly condescending to the officers who at other prisons would condescend to him. "Yes [I'm satisfied], but there's a lot of green staff here. You can't blame custody, because half of their staff is kids. With experience, you'll have more teamwork" (5mo).

The numbers of homesteaders and their prominence creates an alternative source of legitimacy within the prison, one that cross-cuts the normal program-custody division. Remember that at both Catawba and Drake, the correctional officers and their supervisors—the lieutenants and captain—are the emotional linchpin of the institution. Their ranks are the most numerous, their jobs require the most irregular hours and physical danger, and their function is as the guardians of the prison's purpose—keeping prisoners safely inside the walls. Thus, at Drake, comments such as this one from a unit manager are typical, "The main job is security; you can't treat them unless you have them" (4jz). Program staff often counter with the claim that they are doing "security," but it is a claim that needs to be made and defended—not one that, like the correctional staff's, is accepted without question. But at Evergreen, while custody and program staff still complain about each other, a second rhetoric is available—the rhetoric of experience and dedication to the institution, demonstrated by the length of one's tenure. Rather than falling on the custody-program division, the line between experienced homesteader and "green" mover brings in many of the program staff, while isolating most of the young correctional officers. Since the officers are in an entry-level position at an institution that promotes and sends away many of its officers, by definition most officers will not have been at the prison for a long period of time. Thus, in my random sample of staff, 44 percent had been at the prison for more than seven years. This group included both of the correctional supervisors in the sample, but only one officer. By contrast, eleven of the twelve officers in the sample had been at Evergreen less than seven years; their average time at Evergreen was two and a half years.

But it is not just the homesteaders' length of tenure and positions of responsibility that give them their self-respect and their sense of importance to the institution. Rather, they claim that they are better: more likely to have the experience necessary to govern effectively, and more likely to put the interests of the prison above personal ambition.

> The homesteaders here have been really good because they maintain stability, even though that's contrary to the policies of the BOP. When people move a lot, decisions aren't made to benefit the institution, they're made to look good in the short term. They feel like they won't have to deal with the consequences, that's someone else's problem. Look at this metal building out here; some administrator put that in as a cost savings on a concrete building, but now it's a problem because it requires so much maintenance. (Teacher, 5mv)

> It runs pretty good; the people who want things to change are people who never worked here. I worked the cellhouse last night [substituted for an officer], and nothing's changed there in 4–5 years. . . . We've got a real good staff. We're fortunate in this department because all the people are from here; the caliber of the person who will move around is different. It's people who are here for a long time who carry the load. (Teacher, 5nd)

> You've got an older worker here; he's been around through disturbances and strikes—they've seen so many mission changes that they know to be security-conscious. (Lieutenant, 5nf)

> [It's] the nature of the beast; people go into supervisory positions when they're not seasoned enough, just because they need to staff new institutions. They give them training, but you can't beat experience. (Counselor, 5mj)

The younger officers pick up on this set of attitudes. Although they are not directly its targets (or at least, not until they get a promotion and become movers), they complain that Evergreen is old-fashioned, that it has developed a distinctive set of practices not common at other institutions. Since most of them have not worked at other prisons, they cannot identify exactly which practices these might be. But they sense that they would have more control, and perhaps by implication more prestige, elsewhere.

> This has been a good education, but the place is in a groove and I want to be where I can have some input. At a new place, it would go by the letter with just a few curves; at Evergreen, there are too many curves. That's why they say if you can work Evergreen, you can work anywhere. (Officer, 5mf)

> We need administrators with degrees here, with more education. But no—this is all a good old boy system. A lot of people aren't really educated, and there's not a lot of communication here. People are frightened of repercussions if they say anything; sometimes I feel that the judge sentenced me to twenty years here. . . . It's not run like anywhere else—this is a unique place to be. I can't explain it; you just have to be here. (Officer, 5md)

The young officers direct most of their discontent not at programs, but at their supervisors in custody—who are likely to be experienced home-steaders, and who stand between them and a promotion to a prison where they might have more input and status. "Your evaluations are done by people who don't know you. . . . They never try to make you look good—I think some just remember you when you do something bad" (Officer, 5mp). "They [the lieutenants] sit in their office and drink coffee, smoke cigarettes, and watch the compound from there; they harass the officers and not the inmates. They should be mentoring. . . . The new people come in and they're hot charging. They see that their senior peers are very unprofessional—it's eight hours, they say, don't kill yourself. That kind of attitude is trouble" (Officer, 5mq). They also complain about a lack of recognition; it is particularly telling that while most staff mention morale as a problem, the experienced staff tend to say that morale is currently good but needs to be maintained, while the younger officers complain that their morale is bad because they are not appreciated. "The ones who get employee of the month never have any contact with inmates, while we're here 24/7 [24 hours a day, 7 days a week], with nothin' comin' [no consideration] and always catchin' the shit" (Officer, 5nc).

The cleavage between the homesteaders and the movers has two implications for programs. For one, the reflexive scapegoating of program staff, so common at Drake, does not get off the ground at Evergreen. The status of the experienced program staff is too assured, and the fellow-feeling between homesteading officers and their young, up-and-coming colleagues too shallow, to allow program and custody staff to separate into two opposing camps. Instead, conditions are ideal for programs to be accepted as tools for keeping order: they are the way in which the program staff does its part for the security of the institution, just as the custody staff does its part by monitoring prisoner behavior. But this rationale also puts pressure on the program staff to organize programs so that they do serve the institution's needs. As we will see, this has serious consequences for their rehabilitative potential.

The belief that programs are useful to the institution is widely shared across the prison, perhaps even more than the staff themselves realize. On the part of program staff, this is not surprising. One recreation assistant, for instance, explains, "Everyone understands that our number one priority is security, but there are things that branch from that." In his opinion, however, the officers could stand a little reminder. "Like when I bring the supplies in for Bingo prizes, the correctional officers at the back gate can't understand it. The officers like it that the inmates are tired, but they don't understand the process of making them tired." In his opinion, for the sake of security, the officers should lighten up. "The correctional officers come in on them too hard, and antagonize them" (Recreation assistant, 5ma). Another teacher explains the difference between correctional officers and education staff but insists that there is no real contradiction.

> We're trying to help inmates; we have to come onto them as people. Other staff can be more authoritarian; officers, especially, can't be too friendly. They're trying to keep them in a dorm, so it's a different relationship: everything is by the numbers, it's more adversarial. We're doing what they're doing, we're just working on it in a different way. (5mb)

But the officers I spoke to did not disagree. Not one officer complained about program staff who coddled prisoners, or programs which were too extravagant. They agree that programs are "a pacifier . . . education makes some people feel good about themselves, and it's the best use of time for the inmates" (Officer, 5mh). Other officers tend to put it more colorfully. "The official party line, and I concur, is that it [programs] keeps inmates busy. We understand that rehabilitation is dead and stinking—that never worked. But as for keeping inmates busy, yes, it has definite positive effects" (Lieutenant, 5ml). Another lieutenant explains,

> Society now thinks we should lock them up and throw away the key. That don't work. You can't build enough prisons if you're going to do that. We can't keep up with either the staff or the space this way; Congress has to realize that we need an alternate way of dealing with crime. We need programs. (Lieutenant, 5nf)

The marked acceptance of programs has something to do with the feeling of solidarity between the homesteading program staff and their homesteading counterparts in custody. The psychology department, which in many prisons is considered a refuge for people who want to "hug the thugs," goes out of its way to make friends in the institution, expanding its mandate to work with staff stress as well as prisoner issues. As one psychologist reflects, "[Normally] the psychologists won't have the same level of credibility as custody, but over the years, I think we've earned it" (5mk). The staff in education routinely puts in overtime to substitute for officers on training or out sick, or to help process new prisoners when a transport comes in—a sharing of duties that happened at none of the other prisons in my sample. Even in the performance of their own duties, the program staff go out of their way to coordinate with the rest of the institution. For instance, in each of the federal prisons, education staff are assigned to particular housing units to serve as liaisons between the department, the unit staff, and the prisoners. In theory, they should attend the unit team meetings, held weekly, where unit staff meet for rotating reviews of each prisoner's prison activities and release planning. In practice, however, this is difficult; teachers are almost always teaching classes in the hours when unit meetings are held. Teachers thus routinely excuse themselves from meetings. But at Evergreen, the staff almost never miss a unit team meeting; teachers routinely cover each other's classes so that each unit's liaison has time to go to the prisoner reviews. Thus, when the counselor or case manager suggests that a prisoner enroll in a class, the education liaison is there to tell the prisoner what he needs to do and to follow up on the suggestion later on. The teacher is also able to suggest alternatives for prisoners who are not participating in programs; to call prisoners to account, in front of their counselor and case manager, for not attending classes they have signed up for; and thus to prevent miscommunication between the unit and the education department.

But the acceptance of programs also has something to do with the programs that the homesteading program staff create. One consequence of overcrowding in the prison is the lack of work assignments for prisoners, and of the staff to monitor prisoners at work. Education staff, convinced that the purpose of programs is first to keep prisoners busy, stepped in to alleviate this problem by assigning as many prisoners as possible to a half-day of class. Class sizes were increased, and vocational education programs were opened to students who had not yet received their GED—a practice unique to Evergreen. The resulting influx of students helps to alleviate the work shortage, as two prisoners scheduled for half-days of class can also share a full-day work assignment. It is also an efficient way of monitoring prisoners, as a teacher can watch twenty-five students in a classroom while a foreman can only keep track of ten on a work detail.

These policies, however, seriously affect the quality of education. The large class sizes result in a variety of skill levels in a class. At a minimum, this makes classes much harder to teach. As one teacher explains, "There are too many students in one class with too many levels; I know I don't get to all of them. Mandatory education is good, but there are always three or four who don't want to be there. They ruin it for the rest because you spend all your time on them. . . . I spend lots of time revising my curriculum, because the level of students is always changing" (5mb). Other problems are more basic. One vocational education instructor comments, "I get more and more students all the time. I have twenty-one now, when there's only room for fifteen in my shop, and tools for fifteen." A lack of tools naturally makes it difficult for students to learn and practice their skills. The need to use education assignments for monitoring also makes it difficult to dismiss students who are disrupting class or not taking it seriously; any student who is dismissed needs to be found a work slot that will occupy his time. Thus, supervisors emphasize holding students accountable for being at class (rather than being out where they aren't supposed to be, in the recreation yard or in their housing units). Once there, however, students study or not as they please, with teachers assisting the ones who wish to learn. Others simply doze in a corner or take long breaks in the hallway.

The quality of the vocational education programs is also threatened by the eagerness of staff to be useful to the prison in other ways. Teachers proudly boast of how much money they save for the prison factory by making or repairing necessary tools or contracting out their services. In theory, of course, it is good to give inmates experience with hands-on projects for real customers, in order to teach them useful skills. But the potential also exists for programs, when they are primarily justified by the benefits they can produce, to focus on getting good workers to produce those benefits. And that production often comes at the expense of giving them a thorough education, or of helping slower students to learn the necessary skills.

The reallocation of priorities results in numerous practices that make sense from a production standpoint but not a training one. In one class, the instructor proudly led me around a group of display cases showing prizes his students had won for particular projects. One or two of those students were in the workshop, bent over machines; another five or six played the radio and chatted idly; the rest were in a classroom attached to the workshop. Talking to the students working on the machines, I discovered that they were part of the team who had won the prize for the last year; everyone on the team had been skilled in the trade, union-certified with more than ten years' experience, long before entering prison. They didn't "study"; instead, they had been assigned to projects upon entering the class and spent their days practicing their trade. Those playing the radio, by contrast, hadn't had any training before coming in; the teacher didn't spend much time with them, as they did not learn quickly enough to produce the prize-winning projects or the orders that came in for the shop's work. The other eight students were in the classroom studying textbooks: textbooks, the instructor told me dismissively, that it was a waste of time to give them, because they didn't know the math necessary to do the problems. He said that he skipped chapters when math came up: a teaching technique that most probably results in a somewhat piecemeal understanding of the topics.

Such problems did not afflict all the vocational education courses; not all made money for the prison or saved it money by producing services in-house. But the importance that the staff placed upon making sure that the programs brought institutional benefits to the prison meant that supervisors cared little about distinguishing between programs that were also providing a good education to prisoners, and programs that were not. As long as the programs existed, enrolled students, and helped out the institution in other concrete ways when asked, they earned their keep.

Perhaps the best example of this approach is the college program at Evergreen. Unlike the college partners at other prisons, the college that sponsors Evergreen's program is located hundreds of miles away in another state. "Colleges" such as this one were the unintended beneficiaries of the Pell Grant program. To establish eligibility for the grants, they maintain a small campus; however, their real financial support comes from the off-campus extension courses they run at prisons and some military bases. The school employs an administrator at the prison to hire local teachers who moonlight from their regular jobs. The only courses that are offered to the students are courses in which there is enough enrollment to provide a profit after paying for the program's overhead; the rate at which courses are provided (and at which degrees can be earned) is thus very slow. The teachers themselves are a mixed group: some high school teachers, some teachers from the local community college, a real-estate agent. As there is no mechanism for evaluating their work, nor even of coordinating their classes with concurrent classes on campus, the courses are of uneven quality.

By contrast, when a school whose program is primarily on-campus runs a college course for a prison, both its resources and its monitoring and evaluation stand behind those courses. The courses are pegged to concurrent offerings on campus and similar tests are given; students can take the courses that are not offered in the prison by correspondence. The courses offered in the prison are considered part of the school's offerings when the college is up for accreditation or review. Under such conditions, inmates take courses and earn a degree equal to one on the street. Evergreen had in fact had this kind of program in the past, when it contracted with a local, two-year community college to run its program. But it switched to the current partner because it was technically a "four-year" college, thus allowing the education administrator to say that he had upgraded his department's offerings. How likely it was that anyone would graduate with a BA, or how much respect the diploma might command, was not considered.

The program activities I have described are not the outcome of some malicious intent toward programming. But they show what happens when the dominant institutional value governing prisons is one of solidarity. Staff at Evergreen do not intend to teach badly; they simply do not much consider the rehabilitative potential of programs a yardstick for their work, and no one asks them to do so. Of course, any education prisoners receive is more than they would receive in the absence of programs. But it is also easy for program staff and administrators to settle for this explanation, or not to find it troubling at all. Their long terms of service to the prison, their personal loyalty to their coworkers, and their belief that their programs are first and foremost ways for the prison to occupy the prisoners and maintain order all lead them to modify programs so as to increase the numbers of prisoners monitored. Were the education staff to identify with a professional community of educators and less with their prison colleagues, or if programs were valued for reasons other than their obvious contribution in helping to maintain order, staff might have reason to try to balance the monitoring of prisoners with the educating of students. But as it is, there is no check on the ways in which programs can be subverted during their implementation.

The fact that programs often do very little to educate prisoners raises the question of whether such programs satisfy prisoners' needs for something to keep them occupied, to keep their minds off prison, and to make their lives in prison a little easier. The relationship is not direct: without a familiarity with the subject matter or at least some previous training, for instance, prisoners cannot tell if they are getting a comprehensive education in a particular trade, or a truncated one. But the signs that the rehabilitative qualites of programs are neglected are evident to them.

> They don't really help you, they just give you the work and go over it. It's not like a regular class—people are all working on different things. . . . Some guys play, and you can't study because the teachers don't control the class. They need to be at the board more, and have the class all be on the same thing. . . . I don't think the prison wants you to be educated. They just need a place to put you so not everyone's at UNICOR (prison industries)—they're not really teaching us here. (5MK)

> Here, I took ESL; I finished in one day. The teaching they show you nothing here; the administration is no good. In New York State [prisons], the English class was very good, GED was good; not here. (5NU)

> I know a guy who spent 240 days in them [the GED classes] and he can't read or write. In the next [class]room, they're just watching TV; they're not learning. (5MZ)

As criticisms of programs, comments such as these may or may not be fair. "Have the class all be on the same thing" is operationally difficult when skill levels are too widely mixed; the second prisoner may have made it through ESL quickly because his English had progressed beyond the class curriculum; a prisoner's inability to read even after eight months in class could have as much to do with his ability and diligence as with the teaching. But as commentary on the day-to-day nature of class activities, these descriptions confirm my own observations. In terms of involving the prisoners in absorbing and challenging day-to-day work, work that allows them to forget that they are in prison and instead take pride in their achievements, the programs at Evergreen fall short.

This is not to say that learning, in and of itself, cannot serve as an incentive for participating in programs. This prisoner's desire to get an education carries him through a set of courses that he is completely unprepared for and did not choose himself.

[Q: *What programs have you been involved with here? Why?*]

I'm in GED and welding—I don't know how I got into the class, they put me in, I don't know how. I asked to go to school full-time, but they wouldn't let me; that's what I really need. My reading and math are both bad.

[Q: *Are you satisfied with the programs here, what they offer and how they're run?*]

You've got to teach yourself, because the teacher's in the room but he's got no time really to help you when you don't know anything. Welding is hard for me because I don't know the math you need to do it. I am satisfied with it though.

[Q: *Are many people here involved with programs? Why do they do them?*]

Lots of people are. I don't know why—I never questioned them; but I want to learn and I got nothing but time to do it in. I don't want to just be cutting grass; everyone can do that. But I never had a chance to go to school, so I just want to get my education and affirm Christ.

[Q: *How far did you get in school before you came here?*]

Fifth grade, but I didn't learn anything in fifth grade.

The danger is, of course, that at some point this prisoner will become frustrated with the disjunction between his elementary-level math and reading skills and classes that do not really address his educational needs. But ironically enough, his experience also proves the rule: for him, in contrast to many of his counterparts, classes *are* challenging and absorbing. His near-total lack of background makes everything a struggle, while awareness of his limited knowledge makes every new bit of information, every new skill, a victory. Other prisoners also manage to make programs interesting for themselves by piling them up: by taking several courses so that they are consistently challenged, or by becoming an expert in some skill so that they can practice it. One of the prisoners, who had become well-trained in a vocational education class, stayed with it after he graduated, following an individualized apprenticeship program. He describes his reasons.

> I run a computerized milling machine in the shop here, and I spend a lot of time writing programs and making molds. I'm in the apprenticeship program . . . because it's a tremendous waste of time to come here and not accomplish something. The best thing here is education. I was also in the drug program—I did it because I had to, but once I was in it, I realized I had a problem. I did all the therapy here. Besides, the key is staying busy. If you're learning, you have to think about the subject. And that eliminates stress. (5MH)

Prisoners with less determination, however, participate because of other inducements. Few material benefits are provided for programs at Evergreen: there is no special housing or early release time. Unlike Catawba, though, prisoners do not take a pay cut for participating in programs, and even receive a $25 bonus for finishing the GED sequence. Thus, there is no particular reason to avoid a program assignment and, as one prisoner says, "most people are trying to duck the kitchen, for at least half a day" (3NV). There are also some costs to not participating. Evergreen is strict about pegging its pay scale to the completion of mandatory education, and the presence of the education staff at their reviews reminds prisoners that staff pay attention to education when considering a prisoner's preparation for halfway house placement. Some prisoners are even threatened with segregation for refusing to go to mandatory classes.

The fact that most programs are not challenging enough to provide experiential benefits to prisoners, coupled with the fact that participation is often motivated by avoiding the costs of nonparticipation, make involvement with programs a matter of some resentment and not a little happenstance.

> [I did] ABE, pre-GED, welding VT, drug education, drug therapy, print and cable shops, and I learned to be a baker in food service too. Why? I thought I was going to get parole! That's what they told us when we got here—program, stay out of trouble, and the parole board will give you some consideration. But now I went before the board and they told me to max out my time [to serve all of my sentence], so I decided I don't need this. (5MA)

> I don't like the teachers. They won't let you do what they can. They eat, drink, read the papers, but I can't do any of that in class. I participate real good if I

have my cup of coffee, but they won't let me have that now. . . . School has to be only if you want to go—you can't force someone to learn. When they tell you you have to go, too, you hate it more. That's the way it is with me now. (5MD)

I'm in the AIDS class, by accident. This friend of mine and I got caught in chapel when they called movement [when the period for prisoners to go from place to place on the prison grounds without a pass ended], and found out they had the AIDS class there. So we listened, and I got interested, and we decided to go. There's nothing else to do, and it's educational; some day when we get out we're going to need to look at that stuff. When I came in before there wasn't that much about it; now it's all over so it's good to know. (5ME)

I have participation because they force me to be—they don't help you nothing outside [when you are released]. . . . It's a cover for the business that the government has here. Putting people in prisons is big business—it looks good outside, but they don't give us nothing here. It's better to give the programs to the babies on the street so they won't come here. (5NP)

The ill-will that many of these prisoners display is compounded by the fact that prisoners at Evergreen find staff uncongenial. As Table 3.2 showed, nearly half say that staff treat prisoners without respect. Despite the efforts of the education department, only about 47 percent of the prisoners in my sample voluntarily participated in programs; this is similar to the 44 percent at Drake, where prisoners felt similarly angry with staff. But this fact also shows how limited prisoners are when faced with programs of poor quality. At most, they can refuse participation, and even that must be weighed against the costs of not participating. They have little leverage to make the programs better.

And yet there are important differences between the way implementation is subverted at Evergreen and abandoned at Drake. Subverted implementation is harder to recognize as an implementation failure: the number of available program options would satisfy most outside observers, and the widespread support for programs among staff would seem to suggest that programs are firmly established. For proponents of rehabilitation, this is in some ways a particularly dangerous situation. The deceptive appearance of support means that problems with the programs are harder to spot, and negative or disappointing outcome results are likely to be blamed upon prisoners or program design, not on implementation. The willingness to conclude that programs are primarily good for improving the prison environment, and not for their rehabilitative potential, might in fact testify to the many programs that are subverted rather than implemented successfully.[3]

[3] For the argument that programs are primarily good for keeping peace in prison, see

But the fact that staff, and even prisoners, do "get something" from program activities at Evergreen, like the fact that the staff does emphasize communication with prisoners at Catawba, means that program implementation rests upon a firmer foundation at these prisons than it does at Drake. If staff and prisoners at Evergreen are predisposed to think of programs as useful, or at least usable, they might more readily accept an additional set of reasons to value programs. If staff and prisoners at Catawba are already predisposed to communicate and maintain cordial relations with each other, they might be more receptive to an argument that additional programs would only help them in that effort.

Attempts to improve implementation with respect to rehabilitation along these lines would first, however, have to be sensitive to the context that already exists at Evergreen and Catawba. Often it is impossible to improve program implementation by focusing on the easy solutions: better leadership, more funding, more training of staff. Increased funding would be the obvious way to address the long waiting lists for programs at Catawba. But staff, already frustrated by the lack of money for staffing and by an administration they feel is unresponsive, would likely greet an expansion of programs with resentment. Similarly, an attempt to decrease class sizes or to change admission and teaching practices in the programs would likely lead "homesteaders" at Evergreen to roll their eyes and complain that prison administrators were micro-managing them.

Instead, any attempt to improve program implementation at these three prisons would have to address the organizational factors that operate behind the daily interactions among staff and between staff and prisoners. At Catawba, this might mean thinking through the elements of prisoner monitoring that staff find most burdensome, and redesigning program activities so that the expanded programs visibly alleviate staff burdens. It might mean making programs more attractive to prisoners by reducing the disparity between the educational stipend and prison wages. These options would help programs seem more useful to staff and prisoners, thus earning their support. At Evergreen, by contrast, programs are already useful: the problem is what they are used for. But changing values at Evergreen would have to be done within the context of the homesteading system. For instance, veteran staff might be asked to develop techniques for teaching the least-prepared students, who, not coincidentally, are often the "young punks" that cause the most trouble in prisons. They could be sent to courses that might train them in new ways of teaching,

---

DiIulio (1991) and Wright (1993). For another example of subverted implementation, one in which the prisoners seem to be getting more of their institutional needs met through the program, see Craig and Rogers (1993).

but also be told explicitly that they were to bring their long experience to bear on the problem. They could then justify their changes in class organization, and (hopefully) the increase in meaningful program activities, by explaining that working with the "young punks" would help the prison solve one of its most pressing problems.

Other possibilities for improving program implementation, with respect to its rehabilitative potential, no doubt exist. But what those possibilities must take note of is that program implementation is often not about programs themselves. Instead, it reflects a set of organizational beliefs and practices that are not centered around programs, but which have implications for programs nonetheless. Drake's culture of staff solidarity and distance from prisoners, Evergreen's culture of "homesteaders" and "movers," are not built around support or opposition to programs; they would persist even if programs were to disappear entirely. But their effect upon programs is great. The task, then, must be to harness existing elements in the organizational context to the implementation of programs: to remake programs so that their implementation satisifes the needs of staff and prisoners, and to identify ways in which prison values and rehabilitative values can be made consistent.

This does not mean that practices and beliefs need not change; it suggests, however, that change must start from the practices and beliefs that are already accepted within the organization. At Drake, Catawba State, and Evergreen, programs fall victim to prison contexts that they could not accommodate. At Antelope Valley and Beaverton, successful implementation starts with that accommodation.

4

Successful Implementation

THOSE WHOSE vision of a prison is Alcatraz jutting above the waters of the San Francisco Bay might be surprised at how unobtrusive Antelope Valley and Beaverton Correctional Centers are against their landscapes. The winding, two-lane highway that leads to Antelope Valley Correctional Center first snakes past a series of industrial parks and company campuses, each set off in its own buffer of landscaped acreage. Like them, Antelope Valley's buildings are low-lying and new-looking; its large parking lot is full of neatly planted saplings and the entrance sign is sleek, almost corporate. The area outside Beaverton is also traversed by a winding country highway, but this one cuts through fields of corn and soybeans, standing thick as the eye can see. Occasional woods and farmhouses break the monotony, but one has to look pretty hard to find the wood-cut sign that indicates the prison turnoff. Once you are there, the long gray buildings seem to blend into the long gray sky.

"Corporate" for Antelope Valley and "rural" for Beaverton describe more than their surroundings. At Antelope Valley, the staff think of themselves as educated professionals, moving up the career ladder in the Federal Bureau of Prisons (BOP), applying modern methods of prison management to the prisoners in their custody. Fifty-eight percent of the staff have some college or a BA, and another 16 percent have graduate education. By contrast, the staff at Beaverton are from the surrounding area: as one lieutenant said affectionately, "people here grew up in a small town and they're slow, there's no hurry" (2dh). Nearly half—48 percent—of all staff have only a high school degree and/or technical training. Forty-three percent have some college or a BA, and only 9 percent have done graduate work.

The difference in staff backgrounds is accompanied by a difference in prisoner backgrounds. About two-thirds of the prisoners at Antelope Valley have no history of violence; whereas about two-thirds of the prisoners at Beaverton *do*. For about half of the prisoners at Beaverton, that violence was considered "serious"; only a quarter of the prisoners at Antelope Valley had "serious" violence in their background files. Eighty-seven percent of the prisoners at Beaverton had been sentenced to five or more years; only 67 percent carried that much time at Antelope Valley. And a final factor, usually considered relevant to prisoner unrest: while Antelope Valley and Beaverton hold similar proportions of black prisoners (41 and 36 percent, respectively), Antelope Valley also has a substantial number, 31 percent, of black staff. Less than 3 percent of Beaverton's staff, by contrast, are African-American.

As one might expect from these differences, the two prisons carry out the rehabilitative project in very different ways. Antelope Valley, as prisoners and staff will tell the visitor, is "unique" (1f), "laid-back" (1BD), a "showplace" (1i). The prison has a history of being a site for experimental pilot programs and initiatives, all carried out against a backdrop of deliberate informality and ease between staff and prisoners. The informality has become a taken-for-granted part of the prison culture, even though it causes numerous interpersonal and interdepartmental problems within the prison. Programs thrive here; the most serious threat to implementation is complacency. Beaverton, by contrast, is almost defined by its ordinariness. Its staff emphasize how it is a "place that sticks with policy" (2ch), and the prisoners describe their relationship to staff as one where you "don't be disrespectful and don't be familiar" (2cc). Each group is uncomfortable with some of the associations of programs: staff fret about the benefits that prisoners receive from programs, while prisoners are suspicious of the types of programs and the reasons they are offered. But in general programs do well at Beaverton out of a shared if wary pragmatism: both staff and prisoners believe that they are better off when prisoners are busy with something worthwhile.

The particular institutional values and the details of staff and prisoner interaction will naturally differ from place to place, from warden to warden, and from time to time. But that Antelope Valley and Beaverton can be so different shows that these variations do not make successful implementation impossible. Instead, the conditions for successful implementation can be met in a variety of ways. As long as programs meet the institutional needs that staff and prisoners experience, and as long as institutional values can be made consistent with programs, successful implementation can occur.

This chapter shows how Antelope Valley and Beaverton have, in different ways, carved out a role for programs that complements staff strategies for managing prisoners and ensuring their own safety, as well as prisoner strategies for maintaining their dignity, safety, or comfort. I describe each prison's set of standard operating routines and assumptions, from both the prisoners' and the staff's perspectives. I explain how programs fit into these practices, and how they are buffeted by the tensions inherent in each prison. And finally, I explain how the conditions that create successful implementation could break down in each prison, returning us to the examples of unsuccessful implementation in Chapter 3.

Antelope Valley

Go to Antelope Valley on a sunny day, and you will see its compact courtyards, neat lawns, and spotless walkways dotted with numerous clusters of two and three men, casually attired in T-shirts and jeans, talking as they move from building to building. A few officers distinguishable by their neat gray and white uniforms, and men and women dressed in business suits or office attire, walk past the clusters at a brisker rate; they nod or hail each group they walk past. Sometimes they'll stop and engage in conversation, at times about nothing more serious than the basketball game on TV the night before. Other times the conversation is more involved; the officer, or the suited staff, will often close it with, "All right, come see me later and we'll work it out."

In the words of one veteran officer, Antelope Valley is "relaxed" (1b). From the fact that prisoners wear their own clothes to the easy rapport that staff have with prisoners; from the accessibility of prison administrators to the disdain that one correctional officer, a former police officer himself, expresses for colleagues who "think they're the PO-lice" (1r); Antelope Valley is not only like no prison movie on television, but like no prison that most of the inmates, or staff, have ever been or worked in. Both groups, in fact, tend to describe it by what it's not.

> [At the other two prisons] you always had to have a mask on—you show no emotions, you be a hard convict. Antelope Valley is a joke—it's the first place I've laughed or smiled since I've been in. (Prisoner, 1J)

> There's an us-against-them syndrome in prisons, often, which is not good—but that doesn't happen at Antelope Valley. (Counselor, 1ac)

> Here, it's just really different. At a penitentiary, there wouldn't be any problems [with inmate informants] because you would be standoffish—you would never be alone with a staff. (Prisoner, 1AO)

> I was a drill sergeant in the military, so I was more hard-nosed when I came. I think the military generally is. But I found the best way to deal witn inmates here is really just to talk to them; you get more accomplished that way. . . . Some people think inmates are thugs, and how you treat them doesn't matter. But I see them just as other humans now; they have their own personalities. (Officer, 1b)

Here at Antelope Valley it's good for me. The good staff here, they don't fuck with inmates. You can talk to staff here and they will listen, that's not true everywhere. (Prisoner, 1A)

People are very protective of the atmosphere at Antelope Valley. We have a lot more tolerance for the inmates' individuality, though there is a clear line, and everyone knows where that is. You can see it in transfers especially, as they get acculturated to the place. (Doctor, 1g)

Equally as striking as these comments is the frequency with which people make them. In response to two questions, "Sometimes people say that inmates try to 'get over' on or manipulate staff. Does this happen? How do you prevent it?" and "What's the most common mistake that a staff member might make when dealing with the inmates?," 71 percent of the staff at Antelope Valley invoked some variant of "be responsive to inmates" or "treat prisoners with respect," and condemned their colleagues who failed to do so. By contrast, about 50 percent of the staff at Beaverton, Catawba, and Evergreen gave a similar answer; and only 30 percent of the staff at Drake shared this view. Staff at Antelope Valley are certainly not alone when it comes to believing in responsiveness as a way of dealing with prisoners, but it is a central value, in a way not seen at other prisons.

This responsiveness, of course, needs to be understood against a backdrop of expectations about prison behavior. Neither staff nor prisoners at Antelope Valley have any illusion about the fact that one group is the keeper and one group is the kept. The comparisons which prisoners make—the "hard convict" who shows no emotion, the penitentiary [maximum-security prison] rule that prisoners never mix with staff, lest they be seen as "snitches" or informants—show that even a little interaction, small talk about basketball or about an inmate's children, is considered a lot. Such pleasantries go a long way towards making the prison a more "natural," more comfortable place to be. But this responsiveness is also a form of mutual manipulation: of inmates, who will be less likely to bear grudges against staff that could lead to riots; and also of staff, who if given the sense that they are "special" to a prisoner, might be moved to allow him extra privileges or extra consideration. Their communication is not false or feigned, but it is stylized: it is the interaction of people who manufacture an ease they do not wholly feel.

The adoption of a stylized communication with prisoners is nicely encapsulated in the comments of another correctional officer, a former Marine who described his job as being "responsible for the safety of the inmates, to look after their welfare, and to make sure none of them leave until they are supposed to" (1e). Asked whether inmates tried to "get over" on staff, he vigorously agreed. "I strongly believe that a majority try to. They receive a lot, they have more rights here, but they also want more. It's like they have to be incarcerated, but they want everything that they can get." This officer's lack of trust is real. But so is his conviction that the way to handle that lack of trust is through responsiveness.

> You've got to treat inmates as you would like to be treated. Handle their problems just like your own; or think about how you would like to be handled if you did something wrong. Most people [referring to the general public] think the institution is crazy. But it's nothing like TV; there's not so much contraband, for instance. Others think inmates have it too good. But if inmates had no rights, no programs, I couldn't go to work. If they had nothing to look forward to, what would stop the violence?

The role of programs as an integral part of responsiveness is also clear from this quote. Tellingly, the officer links "rights" with "programs," and both with his own safety. Other staff share this formulation: with few exceptions, they go out of their way to express their conviction that the programs are "for me—it makes my job a lot easier" (Officer, 1i). "Prisons are places for punishment, but to keep them safe, clean, and functioning, you have to have programs and funding," explains a program supervisor (1m). A case manager at Antelope Valley, who in other prisons would spend most of his time working with the paperwork of prisoners about to be released, transferred, or wanted by the courts for appeals or new charges, instead describes his work as primarily focused within the prison. He also links responsiveness with programs:

> The first thing, and the most important, is to get along with the inmates—the warden puts a lot of pressure on you to get along. The second is to determine the needs of the inmates and marry them with programs. Part of it is setting them up for release, but most casework is focused on institutional programming here; halfway house is just part of it. (1k)

The emphasis that Antelope Valley puts upon "marrying" prisoners with programs is evident in its high rate of prisoner participation. Eighty-one percent of the inmates I interviewed at Antelope Valley participated in programs. While I was unable to get figures from the prisons that would verify differences in the number of participants in programs at each prison, the wide variety of programs at Antelope Valley adds credence to this figure. The prison boasts literacy and high school equivalency (GED) programs; a two-year AA in business administration; three vocational education courses, in optics, building trades, and heating/air conditioning repair; an intensive, 1000-hour in-resident drug treatment program, another program for sex offenders, and prison industries employment in optics and textiles. Forty percent of the prisoners I interviewed at Antelope Valley actually participate in two or more of these programs.

But as the comparison with Drake and its ten vocational training courses shows, the variety of programs is not enough to explain high participation. Looking elsewhere for causes, it would not be unreasonable to suggest that, as with the staff, the looser and more relaxed environment of Antelope Valley is at the heart of these high participation rates. But while the cordial relationship with staff has at least an indirect relationship to prisoner participation, there is little evidence that the relaxed environment itself makes a crucial difference. Prisoners certainly approve of the fact that they have fewer restrictions at Antelope Valley than they did at other prisons, although as I will describe later, this lack of restriction has a downside as well. But in discussing why they participate in programs, prisoners do not mention the freedom as an incentive. Instead, they emphasize being active and staving off boredom, in a way that could mean something in the future.

> The education staff is down to earth; they treat you like you're a person, with respect. The normal staff, some of them are okay, and the work supervisors are all right. [*What programs have you been involved with here?*] I'm in GED class—I was put in, but I would be there anyway. I want to study computers after I get my GED. And I'm in UNICOR—I have to, because I have to pay a fine and I need money; I try to save but they pay us nothing. It's almost like slavery. (1AL)

> I'm in this apprenticeship program with UNICOR. In the winter I'll start college. It won't help me in my job, but it will help me to pass the time; right now there's sunshine, so you should be outdoors, but in the winter you go to school. I want to study literature, writing, speech—that will help me later on. The training with UNICOR is excellent; the boss is good, and he really teaches us how to do everything. [*Do most guys here get involved with programs for the same reasons you do?*] Well, when it gets dark early, the nights are very long; and they want to better themselves. (1BC)

> [I'm in] UNICOR optics, and optics classes in the afternoon. I try to block out lots of stuff to get through the day. [*Do most guys here get involved with programs for the same reasons you do?*] Well, some guys do it to pass the time, others to prepare for the future—they could offer more [programs here]. The optics class is pretty good, the teachers are pretty knowledgeable, but the equipment is bad. On the other hand they do want us to learn the craft, so the old machines are okay. The UNICOR supervisors are pretty prejudiced, I think. (1T)

Several things are evident from these quotes. First, notice that staving off boredom and increasing one's skills are inseparable as motives for participating in programs. "The nights are very long; and they want to better themselves" is the classic formulation of this; one gets the sense that without the push of boredom, the pull of "bettering yourself" would not be quite enough to get prisoners to participate. Second, notice that while these prisoners have good things to say about particular staff, they are not particularly grateful, and in fact quite openly critical about many aspects of the prison. Their participation in programs comes not because they have been encouraged by the staff or seen the error of their ways, but because they have decided that they will benefit, in both short- and long-term ways, from being in a program. As a corollary to this, the prisoners are careful to emphasize their own agency, their own decision-making ability. "I was put in, but I would be there anyway." In an environment where much of what a prisoner does is involuntary, maintaining the appearance of choice is important even when the reality of that choice is suspect.

The emphasis on deriving benefits from programming can be seen in an interesting phenomenon at Antelope Valley: it offers so many programs that prisoners will request transfers there to participate in one program, when actually it is another program that interests them. "I'm in vocational training; I wanted heating and air, and I transferred to Antelope Valley to get it. I'm in the drug program [too] because it was the only way to get to Antelope Valley" (1G). For some, there is also the more conventional set of benefits for participating in programs: "I'm in the drug program because it got me closer to home, and they promised me halfway house afterwards—it didn't come through, though. Besides, I was ready to change my life. . . . I have a grandson now, and I wanted a family with my girl. I built up my body and I took more pride in myself" (1K).

Mere variety of programs, however, is not enough to provide activity and self-satisfaction. For programs to interest prisoners, they must actually keep prisoners busy, and busy in ways that prisoners believe they benefit from. My visits to different classes and to the worksites, always unannounced, showed that Antelope Valley strives to reach these goals, although it does not always succeed. In education classes, for instance, a strong commitment to individualized education by most of the teachers resulted in classes where a small group of students each worked in his own workbook while the teacher circulated, helping and checking up on the students. One or two students could always be spotted daydreaming or sleeping, but while the teachers did not do much to dissuade these students from sleeping, they also did not hold the class back for them. In vocational education classes, similar patterns obtain: while there is a good deal of chatting across workbenches, most of the students work on their projects during the class period, and are engaged enough to explain to a visitor what they are doing and why.

Clearly, however, more could have been done to make the programs busy and challenging. The image of Antelope Valley as an institution that pioneers programs can be detrimental, leading to complacency, in particular among the more settled staff. Education staff, for instance, stress in their interviews that their literacy and GED programs gave them "lots of freedom to help inmates the way I want to; my supervisors aren't always on my back" (1q). Yet this freedom is not always well-used. Antelope Valley's techniques and range of course offerings, while not inferior, are certainly not out of the ordinary when compared to the other prisons I visited. For instance, in the variety of courses offered, contact with schools in the community, and enthusiasm from participating inmates, Beaverton far outstrips Antelope Valley. Yet expanding the range of opportunities is not actively on Antelope Valley's agenda, a fact made more surprising because of its reputation.

Nor does Antelope Valley always make the best use of the programs it has. Consider the textile factory at the prison, in which a dearth of orders leaves the workfloor quiet. Prisoners assigned to work there simply lounge through the day; although numerous little tasks could have been performed to clean up the remnants of past orders, improve the infrastructure, or increase their skill levels, staff do not demand and prisoners do not volunteer to do any of these things. The education classes I saw were also of varying quality: while the individualized classes of six to seven are small enough so that the students could command a significant amount of teacher time, the workbook and self-test format allows students to move slowly without being challenged to push themselves harder. Comments by both participants and nonparticipants in programs have the level of activity as a theme.

> In UNICOR, there's no work and people sit all day. It's stressful because there's so much dead time. (1AO)

> UNICOR (textiles) was a sorry business; nothing is planned or organized, and the guys' time is wasted when there's no work . . . the work they have now—you tell me why a man would want to learn how to sew! If you're going to better yourself, you need a job to better yourself with. There's not enough here to keep you busy. (1BB)

> The education staff is pretty good but they're interested in their quotas and not the learning of the inmates. (1O)

> If it were outside, the students would be more dedicated and learn more. Here the atmosphere's too relaxed; people don't want to be there. (1BA)

One should not overlook the hypocrisy in prisoner complaints that the programs do not keep them busy enough. In both the textile factory and the education programs, prisoners could have found activities to keep them busier. Take this prisoner, who complains that "I was in air conditioning for two to three months, but the person teaching it wasn't helping me. It was all self-taught, so I quit" (1AR). One could easily suggest that he made the wrong decision in response to an unsatisfactory program; he could have shown the kind of motivation that would have made it easier for a teacher to help him. But it is also important to point out that most of the prisoners who complain about the level of activity in programs either stay in the programs despite their dissatisfaction, or find other ways to keep themselves busy. All of the prisoners quoted above, for instance, are enrolled in programs in addition to, or in place of, the ones they complain about. Taking prisoners at their word by keeping the level of challenge and activity in programs high is part of the key to ensuring that prisoners have an incentive to participate in programs, instead of finding, as at Catawba, other ways to keep themselves busy.

The widespread participation in programs at Antelope Valley creates a self-sustaining cycle. Prisoners find something to keep themselves occupied; staff see that prisoners are participating and attribute the order and lack of hostility, at least in part, to the programs; they in turn support the program staff and encourage prisoners to participate. But while this cycle can have great impact on participation, it cannot, by itself, create program activities that are conducive to rehabilitation. Evergreen, after all, sustains staff and even some prisoner participation with programs that do little to foster rehabilitation. What makes programs different at Antelope Valley?

The answer lies in its set of institutional values. At Evergreen, the sense of solidarity among staff leads them to use programs as ways of helping each other out. Encouraging prisoner participation in programs fits into that interpretation. Monitoring the rehabilitative potential of programs does not. Neither would any program innovation that would cause problems for other staff in the institution, or for that matter, any expectation that programs would create closer relationships between staff and prisoners. At Antelope Valley, by contrast, a carefully cultivated sense of the need for communication, and a particular interpretation of professionalism, cushion the tensions that programs can cause in a prison environment.

All prison staff will acknowledge some need to be responsive to prisoners. But the extent of that interaction at Antelope Valley has a particular historical origin. Antelope Valley was built as a prison in which pilot programs could be developed; though it is no longer put to that use, the history forms part of the prison staff's knowledge about the prison, and thus their interpretations of events. For instance, staff link the looseness of Antelope Valley—the fact that prisoners move freely, wear their own clothing, and interact in a friendly way with staff—with a rehabilitative project. As this correctional officer says, "Antelope Valley is an experiment; inmates are given more freedom, more respect here; the inmate always has a voice. Senior officers tell me it's different at other institutions" (1a).

This history justifies the hiring of professional, often highly qualified staff to run the programs at Antelope Valley. There was some movement between the correctional ranks and the counselors, drug treatment specialists, and teachers who staffed or supervised the programs, but almost all of those who moved to programs had at least an MA, experience in the specialty from previous work outside the prison, or both. This was a major reason why Antelope Valley's programs could maintain high standards. A foreman in the optics factory who is an optician is able to judge, for instance, that although the optics factory lacks a licensing program for the inmates it trains, "they'll learn all they need to know here to get that [the license] when they leave" (1p). In addition, the drug treatment and sex offender programs were performed as part of carefully designed, national studies with their own protocols to follow; this led to frequent evaluations and inspections, reports on outcomes, and constant tinkering to improve procedures. The college and vocational education courses followed a curriculum that was simultaneously offered at an accredited sponsoring college for its regular students; some of the vocational education teachers ran their own businesses as well. Such links give the staff the sense that they are part of a larger professional community with common standards that should be met, or exceeded; they also give them accurate knowledge of what those standards are.

Moreover, Antelope Valley's history of innovative programming not only justifies the hiring of highly qualified staff, but also supports any explicit interest they have in rehabilitation. One unit manager I spoke to, for instance, transferred to Antelope Valley in large part to work with its programs. "I get to use my communication skills, interpersonal skills, to create options for people, to bring about changes in their lives. It's a great challenge—we have an entire world in 47 acres forced to interact and get along" (1ae). He continues,

> I believe in reprogramming. I think we should force people to reevaluate their lives—none of this [leading a] horse to water stuff, that's rehabilitation—by creating an environment where you work and go to school, where there are role models and a drug program you can use. We need to encourage them to participate, and punish them for not participating; give them benefits for participating, by pulling out our whole bag of sanctions and then afterwards communicating with them. We should tell them that this place stinks; that if you don't change, you'll be back. Look for nerves to push, like their family. Especially for the people here under the new law—we are their lives, this is their community: we can work out here how to create societies that work, and then take that model back outside.

He pointedly calls his vision "reprogramming" rather than "rehabilitation"; as all the staff knew, the Bureau of Prisons publicly emphasized, over and over, that it does not "rehabilitate": it only offers "opportunities." But whatever he terms it, clearly he sees his job as supporting and working with programs.

Few staff who are enthusiastic about programs at Antelope Valley have as fully developed notions about the role of programs as this unit manager. But they share his sense that they are the corrections professionals of the future. "We're a step above [the state prisons] in dealing with inmates, because of our programming," said one program supervisor (1m); a work foreman suggested, "I think it would really be an enlightenment to [the public] to see the professionalism and humanity of [Antelope Valley]" (1p). An officer explained, when asked why the Bureau spent money on education, vocational, or training programs, "It's really a new look—it's to prepare inmates for returning to society. In the past, they just thought, lock them up and throw away the key" (1r).

But while professionally trained or experienced staff are more likely to have the knowledge and desire to run quality programs, their presence alone cannot ensure quality programs either. The comparison to Catawba is apt here; although the teachers in their programs had well-designed curricula and took pride in their work, the innovations and the procedures they want can be undercut by other prison staff. As I argued in Chapter 2, treating programs as an important part of the prison's mission can cause tension and disagreement among staff with different jobs, because their needs clash and there is no accepted rule of thumb—such as "custody staff are always right"—to resolve disagreements. See the way in which these two comments, both in answer to a series of questions about support from other staff and teamwork between different departments, parallel each other:

(*From a teacher*) There's sort of a mind-set which is a negative attitude towards rehabilitation and programming. . . . The correctional officers, especially, need to be more sensitive. For instance, they need to respect program time; they'll often walk into the classrooms when [lessons are] being conducted because they're looking for someone. (1y)

(*From a correctional officer*) Other staff, though, don't understand my job as a correctional officer, they don't understand that custody has to overrule their activities sometimes. For example, when we have to clear the compound, the inmates have to be out of there; and other staff don't understand that they can't move inmates around just because they want to at those times. I think we know the inmates better; sometimes the secretaries, or education people, see only the good side of inmates. (1c)

Unlike Drake, where the teacher might complain but the correctional officer would blissfully override her concerns, or Catawba and Evergreen, where the teacher would probably go out of her way to accommodate the officer in his search, at Antelope Valley the teacher and the officer complain about each other. Neither gains an advantage. Both feel misunderstood and underappreciated.

The tension that such day-to-day conflicts cause is a destabilizing force within the prison. But it should also be noted that there is more than one way to combat these tensions. At other prisons, of course, the philosophy that "everyone is a correctional officer first" is supposed to solve problems that arise between staff with different jobs. But at Antelope Valley, this philosophy takes a back seat to a belief in the problem-solving properties of communication—to the belief that tensions work themselves out with more understanding of the demands of different posts. Thus, neither the teacher nor the correctional officer quoted above feels that the solution to their aggravations lies in giving her or his own job precedence. Instead, their answers to the question of creating teamwork are nearly identical.

(*Question: What would encourage teamwork among staff in different departments?*)

(*Teacher*) More awareness of each unit's needs, and a better sense of the big picture.

(*Correctional officer*) For staff and staff problems, more communication.

Of course, each person believes that more communication would lead to more respect for his or her own job. But thinking of the solution as "communication" at least admits the possibility that one could better understand everyone else's needs as well. For instance, the correctional officer quoted earlier as being frustrated by the rights that prisoners receive nevertheless points out, "Different views will always cause tension, but I think if people realized each other's goals, it would be ok. When you have a different job, you have different goals. For instance, a work foreman really needs to be a friend of the inmate. On the other hand, I don't need the inmate—as an officer, my needs are completely different" (1e). And several staff mention "cross-development training," a Bureau-wide initiative to prepare staff for promotions by learning about other positions in the prison, as a way of promoting teamwork. "We're caught up in what we do, and think that's the most important; we don't see others' point of view. Now there's cross-training, which is great, but it's only for department heads. It should be for regular staff members too—the empathy and knowledge that would come from it would be good for regular staff members" (Counselor, 1ac). Whereas custody, unit, and program staff in

other prisons often disagree about how to resolve misunderstand-
ings among themselves, at Antelope Valley majorities of each group
agreed that communication, with each other as well as with prisoners,
was essential.

The willingness to use communication as a way of resolving conflicts
makes it possible for both programs and custody to be part of the legitimate work of the prison. As we have seen, this means that staff are more
likely to be aware of the needs of departments other than their own, and
more respectful toward their coworkers. Equally important, it also means
that the stakes are low in any particular conflict between programs and
custody. A defeat for program staff does not mean that programs will be
abolished; a defeat for custody does not mean that their next set of suggestions will go unheard. Because partisans on both sides know that they
will not lose all the time, they need not make every battle a battle to the
death. And because each group is secure in its own niche within the
prison, there is no need to anticipate or look for weaknesses in the other's
position. In this prison, for instance, a prisoner had recently escaped with
the help of a gullible staff member in a program position. Not one member of the custody staff sought to blame the escape on the laxness of
program staff in general; only one even remembered to mention it. Instead, it was several staff in education and drug treatment who recounted
the story to me, always as an instance of how they needed to be more
careful.

Another potential problem at Antelope Valley is that one of the chief
incentives that programs provide staff, the ability to change career paths,
is missing when prisons hire program staff "from the outside." One of the
advantages that programs can provide staff is the chance to move from an
entry-level officer's position into a multiplicity of jobs. Some of these positions require specialized training, but the Bureau has tried to lower the
barriers to obtaining such training by creating "cross-training" self-study
modules, which staff can use at their leisure. Some institutions also provide on-the-job training for staff interested in changing jobs, and many
have an informal policy of giving preference to staff who have experience
as correctional officers. The variety of opportunities helps prevent burn-
out: staff who are tired of one job can apply for something different.[1] This
avenue of identification between program and custody staff is closed off

---

[1] Many state prison systems, often under union pressure, have adopted similar measures.
Under the Illinois "upward mobility" system, for example, seniority, when accompanied by
specified types of training, can be counted in lieu of a college degree. The federal system has
an important edge in providing such opportunities, however, because entry-level staff are
more likely to have college degrees and/or experience with various jobs in the military. See
Table 1.81, "Characteristics of Federal Bureau of Prisons correctional officers," in Maguire
and Pastore (1998).

at Antelope Valley. Thus, one might expect correctional staff to resent the outsiders hired to administer and teach programs; not only are these outsiders less likely to defer to correctional officers, they also limit the promotions and job opportunities available to staff.

But this problem is less difficult than it might be, again because of Antelope Valley's uniqueness. Antelope Valley is a "training institution" for the Bureau: staff who have shown potential as leaders are often transferred to Antelope Valley for a few years of exposure to its "unique" characteristics before being promoted and sent on to other prisons. Thus, while staff do not believe that the programs at Antelope Valley will eventually yield them a promotion in-house, they do believe that learning to cope with and accommodate program demands will earn them a promotion elsewhere. Their belief that they have been selected as the cream of the crop helps to mitigate the need to compete against program professionals for status; after all, as is evident from their comments, the young officers consider themselves professionals too. "I always conduct myself as a role model officer [an honor graduate from the BOP training program at Glynco.] . . . [This] is a training facility, so there's always something you can learn here" (1z). Another young officer talks about the Bureau in comparison to the states, "We're the white-collar institution— we set the states an example, and have expectations that others don't have" (1i). Moreover, the fact that staff can link the tensions between program and custody staff to the Bureau's conception of Antelope Valley, rather than to program staff who don't understand the job of a prison, makes the demands placed upon them by programs easier to accept. Sabotaging the programs or openly opposing them would mean sabotaging the Bureau's purposes as well as the program staff's, and Antelope Valley's ambitious staff would consider that both disloyal and unwise.

As this implies, however, the willingness of staff to cooperate with attempts to maintain program quality at Antelope Valley is very much a function of its uniqueness. It would be a contradiction in terms for every prison to be "unique" in the same way; and in part, the availability of other prisons in the federal system allows for some self-selection among staff. Those who really cannot stomach the stylized cordiality and informal interaction at Antelope Valley never apply for transfers there; there are other prisons at which they can work and from which they can advance. This suggests that Antelope Valley's model of prison management and program implementation may have limited utility. To staff at other prisons, Antelope Valley's stylized informality is enough to make it seem like a different world—a world in which the boundaries between staff and inmate are relaxed enough to seem threatening. Shorn of the rigid rules of behavior that can provide protection within an environment structured by the fear of violence, Antelope Valley seems, to staff at more traditional prisons, like a disaster waiting to happen. If this environment is necessary for programs to be implemented, it is unlikely that they will be.

What is important about Antelope Valley with respect to the implementation of programs, however, is not its style of interaction. Instead, it is the way in which that style allows prisoners and staff to see programs as a way for them to achieve their goals, while mitigating the tensions that programs can cause and the challenges to institutional values that programs can pose. Other styles of interaction can function just as well in this task. At Beaverton, staff and prisoners are more overtly wary of each other; the easy conversation of Antelope Valley and the sense that rules are merely guidelines do not exist. Yet programs also flourish at Beaverton: on the staff's part, because of a belief in communication and a dedication to "policy," and on the prisoners' part, because of the ways in which programs are—and are not—structured.

Beaverton

After a visit to Antelope Valley, a walk around Beaverton is like a walk around a deserted factory. Prisoners have ten minutes on the hour to move from place to place; they move with a bell system to the mess hall, to the gym after meals, and to the housing units at the end of the day. For the most part, even in the summer, prisoners are inside. When they speak to staff, it is usually brief, formal, without cordiality but with politeness. Staff, too, move through the institution in a businesslike manner. They don't stop to chat with each other, much less with the prisoners. By contrast, scheduled break times—shift change in the officers' locker room, noon meals in the staff mess—are warm, good-humored, even rowdy. But once on duty, the no-nonsense approach is cultivated; staff say what they have to, little more.

This leads to some interesting contradictions. Beaverton staff consider themselves good at "interacting" with inmates. As one correctional officer says, "Basically, the BOP's philosophy is to treat inmates as humans—and they are." Another, asked if he feels the prisoners at Beaverton are hostile, replies, "No—we have some real good interaction here" (2cx). A teacher and former correctional officer elaborates, "Most [of the inmates] are cooperative and interact well with staff, but staff interacts well with them. We do an excellent job of talking to inmates here" (2ci). Yet notice the way in which these comments are phrased: interaction is a BOP philosophy, something that starts with staff, a job. Though no less sincere, these staff are not starting from a set of beliefs like those at Antelope Valley, where staff talked about the individuality of inmates. The businesslike contacts, the absence of cordiality, tip the observer off that if there is "good interaction" here, it is interaction on a different level than the stylized informality of Antelope Valley.

A story from a prisoner helps to illustrate the difference. This prisoner begins by explaining that he has had more problems with the staff than other prisoners at Beaverton. "Here, people will sit with the officers and talk. I'm more extreme." He got more extreme, he says, because of an encounter with the lieutenants after he arrived.

> When the Rodney King incident went down, they called me in to the lieutenant's office and told me a reliable source told them I was planning something. I told them the source was crazy and after they got in my face for awhile, the lieutenant said I seemed like a good guy, but if they really thought something was happening, they'd throw me in the hole [segregation]. I don't care about that, I'm new law [I can't get time off my sentence for good behavior], but you see psychologically, they're trying to handicap us. If this was an orderly institution, they should accept us, not try to break us down. (2cw)

Most staff at Beaverton would consider this "straight up" behavior—telling the prisoner their concerns and giving him a chance to discuss them, rather than putting him into segregation on suspicion. But it is a far cry from the "friendly" interaction that one might see at Antelope Valley, and it is "good" interaction primarily in the sense that, as this prisoner says, it is an effective use of psychology and power. Contrast this, however, with an experience at a maximum-security penitentiary during the Los Angeles riots: when staff heard rumors that the prisoners were going to riot, they did not bother to waste time talking. Instead, they locked the prison down, to forestall even the possibility of a disturbance. The prisoner quoted above would probably prefer this treatment; in an odd sort of way, locking everyone up to prevent a crisis acknowledges the power that prisoners wield. But the cost in terms of personal freedom, mobility in the institution, and staff-prisoner tension would be great.

Some prisoners—in particular, prisoners with strong antigovernment attitudes—found Beaverton's "interaction" disrespectful. But most accepted the tradeoff and understood its advantages; they were willing to accept the staff's "interaction" as the price of a greater degree of freedom. They were willing to do this because most saw Beaverton as "pretty mellow; they [the staff] don't mess with you intentionally" (2CS). As one prisoner said, "The officers are laid back unless they're rookies. They go by the book and just go on until they get laughed at by the other cops" (2CW). In return, the prisoners followed the same rule: prisoners didn't mess with staff.

> Don't be disrespectful and don't be familiar; it'll get you into trouble sooner or later. (2CC)

Overall, they're decent. [*What's the best way to deal with staff?*] Avoid them; it's easier to do time if you stay away from them. Resolve what you can on your own. (2CG)

They're not too bad; I can't criticize. There's so little employment around here that I think you get a higher-quality officer than at other places [*What's the best way to deal with staff?*] Ignore them; just act as if they're not there. (2CQ)

Since I've been here, they don't dog me, and I ain't got arrested [given a disciplinary sanction]. The Man treat you as you want to be treated. (2DV)

Avoiding staff—staying away from contact and its attendant problems—is a tried-and-true tactic for staying out of trouble at any prison. But at other prisons it is often accompanied by disgust and anger; the implication is that only snitches fraternize with staff. At Beaverton it is simply prudence, the prudence of the inmate who says, "I stay away from them, that's more respectful" (2CN). Each group has its own world, and while the gap can be bridged by interaction, it is better if the need to communicate does not arise too often.

This set of beliefs about the usefulness of interaction—staff who believed that interaction helped control prisoners' behavior, and prisoners who felt they could interact with staff, but not too much—suggests that willingness to support or participate in programs will be understood in the same way. Staff are mostly cynics about rehabilitation, but they admit that the programs might make a difference, for some. And in the meantime, they improve the atmosphere in the prison.

[We have programs] to keep them busy, and to give them a reason to get up in the morning. It's a lot safer for us if they are content with where they are—that's what recreation is for, for instance. But it's also to let them be productive if they choose. . . . [discussing the culinary arts program, in particular] When they get in the program they're given the sense that they can do something. They can take pride in what they're doing because they can see it, taste it when it's good. That's why I think vocational training opportunities are really good; we should have more of them. (2ca)

Well, education gives you a better self-image; if you have a skill, you can get a job—plus we know that guys in programs are not management problems. . . . Overcrowding leads to inmate idleness; there are fewer ways for them to do their time, fewer niches to fit into. That's why I think we really need more programs here. (2cf)

The more that's given, the more the possibility that they may be better off when they get out. We teach some responsibility, education, a trade. But it's also more to take away, more tools to enforce cooperation from them. (2cn)

Their pragmatic approach to programs—an "it-might-be-good-but-at-least-it's-useful" approach—is reminiscent of Evergreen's. Indeed, one might expect Beaverton to be a repeat of Evergreen, where staff support programs for their utility to the prison but in doing so, they subvert the programs' rehabilitative potential. Instead, what one finds at Beaverton is extraordinary. Evergreen's education department ran an extremely limited selection of college classes through a distant college, and showed little interest in monitoring the course offerings. Beaverton, by contrast, not only contracted with several neighboring two- and four-year colleges to teach introductory courses on site, but also provided prisoners the opportunity to register for almost any other campus course at the local state university, through a correspondence arrangement. A professor teaching a campus course in which a prisoner enrolls simply sends the lectures, assignments, and texts to the prison; the prisoner does the work and sends it back. When special materials are necessary, instructors send those too: thus, a student interested in geology was mailed rock samples on which to do his analyses.[2] Students go on to earn degrees that are fully accredited by the college; in fact, the year before I visited Beaverton, one prisoner had graduated as the valedictorian of his class. In addition, Beaverton runs an apprenticeship program in the prison's factory, and two vocational programs: a course in culinary arts that results in an associate's degree, and a program in medical technology. A residential drug treatment program completes the prison's offerings.

These programs are accompanied by some incentives. Enrolling in the drug program, and to some extent in other programs, gave prisoners priority for the more desirable housing units "on the hill" in the compound. Interestingly, prisoners were quick to attach this motive to others while disowning it for themselves, as does this prisoner. "[I'm] in Alcoholics Anonymous, group counseling, and the drug program—I want to better myself. Many [guys] do, but there's no incentive to [participate in programs] under the new law—others get involved just to get to the top of the hill" (2CE). But as at Antelope Valley, the major reasons for participating were to fill time and to fill it with something useful, as in this prisoner's explanation: "It helps me stay busy, and keeps me in a positive situation" (2DC). More than at any other prison, the sheer quality of Beaverton's programs, the level of intellectual challenge and the value of the training, seemed to motivate prisoner participation.

> I was in the food service training program. I've been cooking for years, so I wanted the certification. Especially at my age, certification means something, and I learned a lot. (2CC)

---

[2] This arrangement did have its limitations. The prison authorities refused to let prisoners study chemistry, because the possibilities for misuse of chemicals were too great.

They have the best education in the federal system here. Blacks really need education; they didn't get it on the streets. So the older guys will tell the younger ones that they need school, they should take advantage of the opportunities here, just like the older guys will push religion, let the kids know there's something more to life. (2CA)

They need to expand education. Cutting it out is stupid, because education is the most effective way of lowering recidivism. Are they deliberately trying to keep convicts convicts? But the teachers are great. (2DP)

I made progress in the drug treatment program—it helps me to think rationally. Otherwise I wouldn't do it; I probably wouldn't even be doing this interview. . . . It's good for the young ones, they have good chances here. A program like the drug program can change your lifestyle. (2CK)

As at Antelope Valley, part of what makes programs good at Beaverton is the intensity of the experience they provide. Programs are not just for skills. They also, and perhaps more importantly, give those who participate a purpose in their prison lives, and a social group of teachers and fellow prisoners who reinforce that purpose.

I look forward to getting up in the morning now. When you're working, there's a sense of not being here—and the instructors are great. . . . You don't become mentally lazy, and get worse off than when you came in. You have to do something constructive for yourself or else it's pure hell. (2EA)

The care that goes into programs can be seen in many ways. Unlike at Evergreen, where program staff deliberately expanded enrollment in programs so that prisoners would have somewhere to go, Beaverton limits access to its programs. In the culinary arts program, for instance, ten new students are accepted per year, with an overall enrollment of twenty. The payoff is evident to even the most casual observer of program activities. Teachers could describe their lesson plans and their overall curriculum; students could describe what they were doing and how it fit into what they had already learned; classrooms were filled with active students and engaged teachers. Programs are not constrained by security needs in ways that inhibit their ability to function: despite the fact that knives, drills, and other potential weapons are used in both the culinary arts and medical technology programs, they go on, with the only caveat being that prisoners with serious histories of violence were ineligible to participate. Contrast this with Drake, where the possibility that computer skills could be misused was enough for the administration to prevent instructors from teaching any computer skills.

The culinary arts program is a good example of Beaverton's programs at their best. It not only trains students in a range of skills: it gives them a daily chance to practice those skills in the employee cafeteria. The students create elaborate lunches every day, with salad, appetizer, two main courses, and dessert; each is lovingly garnished with little decorative touches. More importantly, they do everything from ordering ingredients to composing the menus, from serving the food in regulation white toques and aprons to cleaning the kitchen afterwards. As part of their training, they also keep up with, and receive a degree from, the restaurant management sequence at the local state college. Graduates of the program have, upon release, taken jobs with Club Med, the Marriott Corporation, and landmark hotels and restaurants.

Just as important as what this program does, however, is what it does not do. In a prison without concern for maintaining the training capacity of the culinary arts program, instructors could be directed to primarily train students to provide meals in large institutional settings, so that they could be assigned to prison food service positions upon graduation. Under the right conditions, of course, allowing graduates to keep up their skills in the kitchen would be a benefit; the tradeoff, however, is that prisoners would not acquire the skills to cook in settings other than cafeterias serving 900 at a seating. This would make it hard to fulfill the requirements for the associate's degree or to find restaurant work in the future. As far as I could tell, this possibility was never under discussion at Beaverton. The culinary arts program had full autonomy to design its curriculum without reference to the prison's needs. In fact, the food service program at Beaverton required the outfitting of a separate kitchen, because the instructor was adamant that students learn to use kitchen equipment that would be available in any restaurant kitchen.

What leads Beaverton to look beyond the institutional needs that programs can satisfy, allowing them to preserve their rehabilitative potential as well? The key is in the way that excellent programming fits into the prison's institutional values: in particular, with a philosophy they call "sticking with policy." Some staff joke about it a little, but most are deadly serious; Beaverton dots every "i" and crosses every "t," from the important to the trivial.

> Well, at Beaverton we're known for our cleanliness and our meetings; people who come here from other places say it's just unreal here. We're also known for going above and beyond, following policies to the letter. (2cd)

> What's special is our way of doing custody. We go one step farther with security, we take the BOP policy and then go extra. We measure the trucks that come in and out, we do our counts perfect; everything is safety and security first. (2db)

> I don't think we're special, but troublemakers at other institutions aren't troublemakers here. We joke around a little, but we're pretty professional, and we stick with policy. (2cm)

Beaverton is a place that sticks with policy—it gets awards for excellence in that. And it emphasizes security. (2ch)

Numerous staff told me that Beaverton was "probably the best-run institution in the US; it got the highest ACA [American Correctional Association] score and unit management here was rated at the highest level" (2cj). Staff feel that they are "number one—it's always been outstanding here. There's lots of pride—other people come, or we go for audits, and you can tell we're outstanding in sanitation, etc. for the Bureau" (2cc). No fact is too small to brag about: staff can list officers who graduated, with honors, from the Bureau's mandatory training program in Glynco, Georgia; they remember different indexes, from the Bureau or from the American Correctional Association (ACA), which rank them highly; and, of course, they are even proud of their sanitation.

These values give programs a hook. Beaverton has no history of being a prison with innovative pilot programs or sophisticated treatment facilities: unlike Antelope Valley, there is no reason for staff to take for granted the presence of programs or the tensions they can cause. But because programs can be interpreted as simply one of the many things that a prison should do well, they fit in. Thus, pride in programs derives not so much from a devotion to programming as from a concern for the markers of excellence. Beaverton staff care about being seen as the best.

It is important to emphasize that this belief in Beaverton's excellence is a local value, not one shared by the BOP as a whole. Tucked away in a rural area, Beaverton does not have the reputation that older institutions, or showier ones, have. Certainly no one outside of Beaverton, either at the other institutions or at the BOP's Central Office, ever suggested to me that Beaverton was the "best-run institution in the United States." Evergreen's history and location, and Antelope Valley's reputation, make them "training" institutions; Beaverton is not. When supervisors with experience in other prisons explain why Beaverton "works," they do not cite, as Beaverton natives do, the dedication to policy. Instead, they point to local foibles, charming as they might be.

It [Beaverton] works. People here grew up in a small town and they're slow, there's no hurry, so they tend to think before they react. They'd rather talk than fight. Also they take care of each other—the staff will ensure that worthless staff don't get into trouble; it amazes me, but it does work. (2dh)

Thus, despite its rankings, working at Beaverton does not put one on the fast track: it is not a prison from which the Bureau promotes quickly, or a prison to which it sends new supervisors for training and seasoning. While Beaverton, like other federal prisons, gets its supervisory staff from transfers, they regard their posting there as a duty rather than a career move. One newly arrived lieutenant explains:

Beaverton historically has taken the very difficult cases and they have done well—inmates who should have been in a penitentiary but get lost there have come here and don't get lost. It's also known for doing the basics very well. But—most of the people here haven't been at other institutions. They're simple people, especially because of the area, and they don't always value outside experience when someone brings it. And, because of the remoteness, very few people want to come here. (2cy)

But while this lieutenant's assessment is in fact quite positive, those who are part of the institution want something more than a reputation for "doing the basics very well." And if programs are part of that higher profile, then programs deserve support.

Of course, programs create the same kinds of tensions at Beaverton as they do at other prisons. Inevitably, correctional officers look upon programs with some suspicion. Fifty percent of the custody staff I interviewed reminded me that teamwork happens when, as this lieutenant says, "[you] just make sure everyone knows they're equal; don't let education think they're better than corrections" (2cp). Officers complained that treatment staff might have started out as officers, but "they've forgotten what the trenches are like. They've forgotten security, they're very comfortable, and they don't do shakedowns anymore" (2ct). This correctional officer also clearly thinks that program staff's reaction to "the deuces," the prison-wide warning that a staff member's body alarm has gone off, is wanting. "When the deuces go off here, everybody runs—but I notice that the noncustody people come but don't jump in" (2df).

Yet notice what is not a feature in these quotes: the complaint, as at Catawba or at Drake, that programs are an extra burden upon staff. For all their complaints, these officers accept their program colleagues and, implicitly, programming, as important to the prison. Thus the officer who complains that his colleagues have forgotten the trenches offers a solution which implicitly recognizes the importance of all positions—not just custody—to the institution. "Get people to work security once in a while, to refresh their understanding of the job, and custody should go out to other departments too—cross-development is a good idea" (2ct). Though cross-development training was heavily encouraged by the Bureau during this time, staff at Antelope Valley and Beaverton were the only ones to mention it as a tool for creating teamwork. Even the officer who condemned his colleagues for not jumping to action at a body alarm is remarkably forgiving, though somewhat imperious. "Everyone's custody first; what we need to do is work together consistently. I shouldn't think that all I do is custody, or teaching, or drug counseling" (2df).

Table 4.1 illustrates this. Twenty-seven percent, nearly double the proportion at the other prisons, say that there are few divisions between program and custody staff at Beaverton. Another 29 percent believe that

TABLE 4.1
Staff Evaluations of Divisions Between Different Posts

	Antelope Valley	Beaverton	Catawba	Drake	Evergreen
More attention to custody needed	21%	38%	27%	39%	41%
More attention to programs needed	11%	6%	18%	24%	13%
More communication between different posts needed	61%	29%	44%	21%	34%
Few divisions	7%	27%	12%	15%	13%
(N=)	(28)[a]	(34)	(34)	(33)	(32)

Note: Responses compiled from answers to two open-ended questions: "What would encourage teamwork among staff in your department? Among staff in different departments?" and "People often talk about a difference in outlook or behavior between 'treatment' staff and 'custody' staff. Do you see that here?"

[a] Not all staff at Antelope Valley were asked this question. The total N for Antelope Valley is 31.

communication and cross-training would solve any remaining problems. Beaverton is trying a difficult balancing act: it attempts to resolve staff tensions by creating a common "correctional worker" identity. Yet unlike Drake, where this effort leads to the marginalization of all noncustody staff, Beaverton turns the adage that "everyone is a correctional officer first" on its head: because everyone is a correctional officer, everyone deserves respect. One program supervisor, a professional who did not have previous correctional experience, explains. "Beaverton has a correctional-worker personality, and there's a heckuva lot of camaraderie and support. The central theme is that everyone is a correctional officer first and there's respect for everybody because of that" (2di).

The difference from a prison like Drake or Evergreen may be subtle, but it is important. Remember, for instance, Evergreen's habit of encouraging program staff to pull overtime, substituting for officers in the housing units or with new prisoners who need processing. At Beaverton, this does not happen. Each area is responsible for its own unit: as we have already seen, program practices do not change to become "more useful" to the prison. But this goes the other way as well: even when coordination would improve the programming, it does not happen. To give just one example, the college program's practice of scheduling classes in the afternoons made it difficult for people to work in UNICOR and still take courses. Because the jobs in UNICOR pay so much better than other types of prison work, forgoing them in order to attend college is a significant financial sacrifice. In contrast to Antelope Valley, however, supervisors seldom give prisoners time off from work to attend classes during the day. Ironically, the other option, scheduling all the courses at night, is impossible because so many courses are offered at the prison. As a result, the combination of industries and education is much less common than at other prisons. Unlike Antelope Valley, where program staff went out of their way to coordinate different work and study options, at Beaverton each program was responsible for its own turf.

Relationships between the correctional officers and the program staff followed the same pattern of respect and distance. In contrast to Antelope Valley, the teachers and counselors in the drug program are often former correctional officers, and officers and unit staff praised that fact. When there were problems, they were willing to attribute most of them to the fact that prisoners behaved differently with different staff. Thus this officer's statement is typical: "Yes, [there is a difference in outlook between treatment and custody staff], but it's only because we see different inmates. They change. Many of the treatment staff came up through custody, so it's not bad, but they have to work harder at seeing our side" (2cr). The program staff—teachers, counselors, program supervisors— did not socialize much with the rest of the staff, or with each other; even the staff who had worked as correctional officers for many years described themselves as the type who stayed to themselves. But they did not feel isolated from their coworkers in the prison. "We're moving towards more acceptance and support. Some of the staff are less supportive because they've seen treatment programs come and go, but there's lots of cooperation" (2cz).

Beaverton's approach to programming is one that most correctional officers, and probably most correctional administrators, would find more congenial than Antelope Valley's. The focus on custody first, but programs in their place, allays the fear that the prison might be held accountable for the outcome of programs: for the prisoners' actual reformation after release. It is also more consistent with the law-enforcement conception of correctional work; most staff do not go into prisons expecting to rehabilitate prisoners. Ironically, Beaverton's approach to programming may even protect programs, because it prevents routine annoyances between prisoners and staff from being blamed on programs. For instance, at Antelope Valley, correctional officers were fond of complaining that the prison's "unique" treatment philosophy meant that officers' disciplinary reports were often ignored. At Beaverton, officers complained as well. But because programs were not such a focal point, they attributed the times when a prisoner was given no more than a mild reproof for an incident to idiosyncratic reasons—correctional supervisors or unit staff who were too lenient, too afraid of lawsuits, or too enamored of their own rank to remember that their first loyalty should be to the officers on the front lines.

However, just as Antelope Valley's approach to program implementation has some distinctive weaknesses, so too does Beaverton's. Both approaches falter when the particulars of the prison culture itself are considered, wrongly, as the key to implementation. Antelope Valley's stylized interaction and reputation for treatment, and Beaverton's respectful distance from both prisoners and programs, work because they fit within the existing context of the prisons. In other words, they address institutional needs that staff and prisoners have, given their environment, and they make use of values that are specific to the prison itself: not some abstract set of needs or values in general. Successful implementation is successful in the making: it lies in the fit between policy and the local values and needs that policy can address. Antelope Valley and Beaverton are thus not models to be followed slavishly; instead, they are examples of the kind of adaptation that makes policy implementation successful.

Creating the Conditions for Successful Implementation

The promise and the challenge of basing successful implementation on local values and needs, rather than on blueprints developed from a distant analyst's bright ideas or even from other successful programs, is that the resources in local organizational environments are both infinite and infinitely malleable. The values that sustain rehabilitation programs at Antelope Valley are not to be found at Beaverton, but an alternate set of beliefs—in "policy" rather than "experimentation," in "excellence" rather than "professionalism"—essentially fulfill the same function. Meanwhile, Catawba draws its justification for programs from yet a different source: the prison's open, relaxed environment, especially in comparison to the harsher prisons in its state system. Even at Drake and Evergreen, where prison values are used to justify the abandonment or subversion of programs, an alternate rendering is available. At Drake, the beliefs that "everyone is a correctional officer first" and that staff back each other up could have been interpreted to validate the program staff's contribution to custody, just as the correctional officers were validated. At Evergreen, the respect for history and experience could have been used to undergird the development of master teachers, who could give the other prisons in the BOP the benefit of their hard-earned wisdom while continually perfecting their craft. The differences between Antelope Valley and Beaverton show that each prison can develop programs with rehabilitative potential that are also imbued with each prison's distinctive sense of self.

The fact that Drake and Evergreen's values had the potential for re-interpretation suggests, however, that programs at Antelope Valley and Beaverton could be unsuccessfully implemented as well. The tensions in each regime are obvious. At Beaverton, the belief in respect for all staff positions could disintegrate into the assertion of correctional officer supe-riority so evident at Drake. At Antelope Valley, the burdens its regime of openness places on staff and prisoners could lead, as it did at Catawba, to rejection and resistance.

At Beaverton, "everyone is a correctional officer first" is an assertion of priority: it is a claim that differences in job, authority, and educational background must give way to central tasks that everyone shares. Ideally, it suggests that although "correctional officer" is the entry-level position in the prison, it is also the most important position, the source of one's pride in one's work. But that ideal coexists with the fact that the jobs of program staff seem easier, and are usually better paid, than the jobs of the officers. Officers, especially those who look for promotions and don't get them, are quick to see the contradiction. This officer's complaint was influenced by his own disappointment with the promotion process, but others were sympathetic with his frustration. "Put officers first—make sure we're better paid than UNICOR—they only work Monday through Friday. We're locked down here with the inmates" (2cq). He continues,

> The Monday-Friday people take lunch hours, we live with their disrespect and their disrespect to the inmates. They don't understand our concerns, they don't interact with the inmates, and the unit teams aren't here either [aren't around in the evenings, when crises always seem to happen]. . . . There would be more teamwork if others looked upon custody not as the bottom but as correctional officers. They don't show us respect at all, don't help us with our duties. But they're custody too. We need to have concern for all our staff—instead the evening shift didn't even get the leftovers when they had the national correc-tions officers party on our shift, so we couldn't go. (2cq)

As the section on Drake shows, were the views of this officer to become more widespread, the influence on programs could be substantial. Cer-tainly giving officers concrete markers of respect, such as higher salaries or options for managing the difficulties of shift work, would not detract from programs. But respect can also become a zero-sum resource, when the desire to "put officers first" leads not to rewards for them but to disrespect for the staff who are not officers. The teachers at Drake, for instance, felt so cowed by not being officers that they limited their inter-actions with students, stopped offering ideas for program innovations, and avoided making requests that might cause inconvenience for the officer staff. In some cases, the desire to underscore the officers' high status could even lead to the prison administration's refusal to allow prisoners any kind of specialized training or credentialling, out of a sense that it would be undeserved.

This is particularly true when staff have concerns about programs' fairness or cost. "Sometimes you wonder, though, if they have the money to spend millions on these programs, they should have the money to do a decent medical plan for the staff" (2da). And another related concern, one that surfaced much less often at Antelope Valley, is fairness. Since almost half the staff at Beaverton lacked a college degree, the range of college programs available to prisoners is an irritant. "[There should be more vocational programs . . . to replace the college courses. I agree with the GED. But I don't have college, and I'll never have the money to afford it—why should they be able to go to college free and let the taxpayers foot the bill?" (2cw)

There is a distinct race and class dimension to such concerns. Of the eight staff who feel that prisoners received too much—too many programs, too much free food, medical attention, or the like—seven also feel that, as lower-middle-class whites, their chances for promotion and mobility were unfairly limited. (The eighth, a Hispanic man, insists that neither race nor class limited his, or anyone's, mobility.) These comments, for instance, are typical.

> [Do you think race has a lot to do with whether or not someone gets ahead in America? Does it affect you?]

> Blacks can get ahead by working, but they complain that "you have to give it to me." I've been denied a job because of my race.

> [Would you consider yourself a member of the working class, lower-middle, middle, or upper-middle class? Do you think class differences have anything to do with whether or not someone gets ahead in America?]

> I'm lower-class; because by the time I pay my medical and retirement, I have no money left. Class differences do matter, because if you have money, you have different values, your money will help you, and your name will take you places. The middle class can't move up, and the lower classes do all the work. (2cq)

Seventy-three percent of all staff who feel the same type of frustration also feel that prisoners receive too many benefits. Although these staff represent only one-third of the staff at Beaverton, the combination of concerns is striking.

It is not clear, of course, whether a lack of personal mobility brings with it a resentment of programs that help other people, or whether frustration with one's own situation and anger towards others are just two different ways of expressing one's fundamental hostility toward other races. But it suggests that hiring and promotion freezes, a downturn in the economy, or an increase in racial tension in the larger society, might all overflow into staff hostility toward programming.

The possibility that Beaverton's climate of support for programming and its rehabilitative potential could disappear underscores the significance of communication as a strategy for keeping order. Programming inevitably raises issues of fairness, in relation both to prisoners and to other staff. When those issues are exacerbated by the difficulties staff face, either on the job or in their personal lives, staff naturally try to close ranks, to ostracize or convert the staff who benefit from programs, and to emphasize their difference from and disdain for prisoners. But if communication is the preferred strategy, one which staff accept as the best way to help them stay safe and get satisfaction from their work, the impulse to seek comfort and support from exclusion will diminish. Communication does not give staff an interest in programs themselves: that comes after elements in the prison's history and practice are mined to provide support for the rehabilitative potential of programs. Communication does, however, give staff an interest in the kinds of interactions crucial to program survival: the willingness to work with prisoners who are one's adversaries, and the willingness to work through the inevitable staff conflicts that programs create.

An established regime of communication does not, of course, mean that every staff member will buy into it. At Antelope Valley, communication is more than a strategy—it is practically a religion. The stylized responsiveness of Antelope Valley could possibly be imitated at Catawba, but would be unlikely to take hold at any other prison in this sample, or at most prisons nationwide. Even here, though, there are dissenters. Consider the way in which this Antelope Valley officer equates programs, program staff, and the difficulties of his job.

> If I were warden, I would enforce strict adherence to policy, give officers better custody training, and put in benefits like childcare for employees; I'd also scale down the vocational programs. [*Do you think your supervisors would agree with these ideas?*] Some of the custody staff would agree, but the warden and executive staff—of course not, because it would threaten their livelihoods. The teachers would protest and they'd [the executive staff] lose their jobs, that kind of thing. [*What would encourage teamwork among staff in your department? Among staff in different departments?*] In our department, more camaraderie; . . . teamwork among different departments is less important; basically, if each group did its job well, we'd be fine. It's not as important as getting our team together. (1w)

This correctional officer was in a minority of three among the staff I interviewed; significantly, all three were also frustrated about their chances for promotion, feeling that their point of view was unwelcomed and unappreciated by their supervisors. But it is difficult to say how many other staff might have shared this sense that programs were to blame for their difficulties, but chose to take a more pro-program approach in their interviews. More importantly, if circumstances changed—if more aggressive prisoners, miscommunication, lack of funds, or other problems were to make the stress upon staff more severe—more staff would probably find programs a convenient target for their frustration.

Antelope Valley's staff perform a careful balancing act in believing that "society probably thinks prisons are lawless—but they don't have to be if we treat people right" (1d). As we saw at Catawba, however, once staff are no longer satisfied with the level of security they get from "treating people right," both support for programs and the prison's "unique" atmosphere could disappear. One of the biggest problems at Catawba, the lack of trust between line staff and the administration, is already evident at Antelope Valley. Comments such as these, from Antelope Valley staff, are reminiscent of the contempt in which Catawba staff held their warden and the lieutenants.

> The upper management really manages, with the inmates appealing everything to them and their coming back saying "don't be too hard on the inmates." . . . there's lots of bending of policy. The administration is very inconsistent in its treatment of inmates. (1ab)

> I think people get lax; they take a good place for granted, and they don't have solidarity. (1o)

More communication between staff could resolve these problems without harm to programs. But if that is not forthcoming, the resultant stress could eliminate all the advantages in reduced tension that programs originally offered to staff.

Staff are not the only ones who can turn against a strategy of using communication to produce order. Prisoners can as well. At first, this might be hard to see. But prisoners experience staff disagreements as "lying"—staff saying one thing and doing another, either because staff are unwilling to violate the appearance of cooperation by directly refusing a request, or because one staff member's decision can be so easily overruled by another's. They also equate the laid-back atmosphere with "pettiness"—an insistence upon enforcing rules about personal property, food, or contraband. Paradoxically, such rules often go unenforced in a more dangerous prison, where staff control movement around the prison more strictly, but also try to avoid enforcing rules that could cause a prisoner to lose his temper and start a disturbance.

> Antelope Valley's so laid back that every little thing, they lock you up for. (1BD)

Yesterday we were horsing around, one guard was watching us, no problem, he was laughing. Another comes by and tells us to "stop playing." I'm a grown man and I don't need him to tell me to stop playing. In state prisons, they're not so picky or particular about cleanliness. Antelope Valley is the pickiest but the federal system's all generally the same. These guards couldn't live at other institutions. . . . [But at the] state prison we were fighting roaches and other inmates. Here it's different. (1F)

Antelope Valley and the state are very different. At a state prison, it's down to earth, there're more risks so guards know how far they can push, and snitches are in danger of their lives. Here . . . staff have their own rules. You can never tell what's forbidden or not; they don't like you to do the little things that make your life easier. (1M)

As these quotes suggest, the prisoners are not about to riot over the staff's "pettiness"—they recognize, and generally prefer, the lack of danger and the less tense atmosphere, even if it has its costs. But were prisoners to begin to consider the emphasis upon program and program participation as "picky," they could react by rejecting programs. This teacher suggests a possible dynamic:

The students who don't want to be in class, but have to because it's mandatory—they direct their hostility towards you. This is especially true for the recommits; they have to do a new 120 days of education every time they come. They don't know that's a BOP policy, so they blame it on Antelope Valley's being "heavy." (1x)

A student who ran afoul of the mandatory education policy for prisoners illustrates this teacher's observation.

[*Generally, what are they (the staff) like?*] Antelope Valley is a federal reeducation camp—they try to downgrade you and they build you back up again according to their ideas of improvement. Most programming is just to break you down and I resist it. They make a concerted, covert effort to break you down. (1V)

This prisoner is out of the ordinary; prisoners who are compelled to take GED courses at Antelope Valley are more likely to emphasize that they would be there anyway. Part of his anger is owing to the fact that he considered himself a "political prisoner," imprisoned for violating gun possession laws that he felt were illegal. As Drake shows, prisoners transform their anger at staff into a wholesale rejection of programs. While the same behavior is unlikely as long as Antelope Valley continues to mix strict enforcement of some policies with a general policy of tolerance and free movement, an influx of embittered, angry prisoners, or a change in the atmosphere for which Antelope Valley is known, could inspire a backlash against programs even at this "program institution."

No magic bullet exists for implementation. No particular set of values or incentives is best suited to the successful implementation of programs, either in prisons or in general. Instead, the ability of any particular set of organizational practices and beliefs to foster the successful implementation of a program can only be measured in terms of the incentives it provides, at any particular time, for staff and clients to participate in the program, and in terms of the match between existing institutional values and the program activities they will justify. Thus, while Antelope Valley and Beaverton are both successful at implementing rehabilitative programs, neither provides a foolproof model. Instead, tensions that already exist in each prison show how easily the implementation of programs could be subverted, or could disappear.

Nor are the threats to program implementation only internal to the prison. The reigning philosophy of rehabilitation—one that emphasizes that prisoners need to "want to be rehabilitated," rather than the prison's obligation to provide programs that are at least plausibly rehabilitative—sets up important barriers to the successful implementation of programs. These barriers are not primarily those of values—as I have shown, values that are not directly about programs can still support efforts to maintain the rehabilitative qualitites of programs. Rather, they are barriers to the incentives that successfully implemented programs provide for participation. Incentives, this philosophy holds, fly directly against the common wisdom that participation in rehabilitation programs is insincere when it is undertaken for reasons other than the desire to change one's life. In other words, if prisoners really "want to change" their behavior, they should be willing to participate in programs without reference to any immediate incentives. By contrast, if prisoners are not interested in reform, their participation has no real significance: it will not further the aims of the policy, at least insofar as the policy is intended to help ex-prisoners avoid crime. I examine this question in the next chapter.

5

The Importance of Successful Implementation

RECASTING THE DEBATE OVER MANDATORY
AND VOLUNTARY PROGRAMS

CHARLES ANTHONY is a "three-time loser": a prisoner on his third incarceration. In a previous stint, he learned to do upholstery work at a prison factory; after release, he held an upholstery job for a year. But the lure of drug money pulled him back. Now he says, "This is my third time doing time, and the one thing I found out is you can't know what you're going to do. You can't go out thinking I got this skill and I'm going to find me a job in it; sometimes you can't. Even people leaving school with a degree can't always know what they're going to do" (5MB). He hasn't given up on work as a way of avoiding crime: "I think I want to do something new when I get out; obviously, my vocational training before didn't do me no good, so maybe I should try something new." But his tone and his words all indicate that a job is only peripheral to his sense of what it will take for him to stay out of prison again.

> For some people, if they don't feel any hope or think they've got a chance in life, they'll go back to the same thing. If he does stay out, he'll get involved with something to keep him away from what he was involved with before. Or sometimes he's just tired of going to jail. But he might decide not to take chances and go to a shelter, which is like prison except you can leave. Or he'll take the chance and do something wrong, and once you do, that money is like an addiction.
>
> I don't know what gives you hope; you just gotta know yourself, and realize that lots of people are struggling to make it out there, it's not just you. And don't abuse it when you do get money, because then the government comes after you.

Charles Anthony is a hard case for proponents of rehabilitation. Unlike many of his counterparts, he does not talk eagerly about being determined to avoid prison again; in his musings he is much more concrete about committing crimes, where "that money is like an addiction," than about getting "involved with something to keep him away from what he was involved with before." The skills he has learned and the education that he is being offered neither kept him out of prison before nor seem to give him much direction now. Apart from keeping him occupied while in prison, it is unclear what "work" programs—even successfully implemented ones—can do for Charles Anthony.

On one level, this is a problem for those interested in successful implementation to be concerned about, but not one for them to solve. Successful implementation is a prerequisite for successful programming, not a guarantee of success. Unless the various vocational, educational, drug education, or other programs offered to Charles Anthony are successfully implemented, they will have no chance of preventing Charles Anthony from becoming a "four-time loser." At another level, Charles Anthony's story raises important questions for implementors. Is it a waste of resources to encourage people to participate in a program—one of the dimensions of successful implementation—when they do not seem motivated to use it?

Such questions touch upon the fundamental question in the study of criminal rehabilitation: what lies at the root of the decision to avoid crime? Is it morality or fear, determination or remorse, skills or opportunities, emotional, social, and financial support or good personal habits, or some combination of the above? Do these factors operate independently, so that repentance and learning a job skill are two separate and unrelated steps? Or do they work through each other, such that having a skill is necessary before people can imagine, and choose, a different life? A study of successful program implementation cannot answer these questions. But it does incur an obligation to consider the ways in which the attributes of successful implementation—in this case, participation in programs as a response to institutional needs—might serve to undercut, or advance, the mission of the programs themselves. In other words, implementation must be evaluated for the way in which it, itself, becomes a part of the treatment.

One of the most important debates in prison policy, indeed much social policy, is implicated in this problem. My model of successful implementation argues that prisoners, and by extension the clients in any type of program implementation, participate in programs because they can satisfy institutional needs by doing so. This flies in the face of an argument advanced by both conservatives and liberals: that voluntary participation in programs is the only way to ensure an efficient and humane use of resources. Voluntary participation is efficient because it directs resources to people who are interested in the program itself rather than in its side-payments or penalties. It is humane because it does not coerce people with few resources and few alternatives into participating in something that they may not believe in or feel they need. While the efficiency argument is more often directed at incentives for participation, and the humane approach more concerned to prevent sanctions, adherents of both groups recognize that incentives and sanctions are in fact not much different. After all, sanctions require resources to administer and enforce, and the withholding of a benefit, even an unexpected one, can be coercive when the client's legitimate needs far outpace his ability to satisfy them.[1]

But while the argument for voluntary participation only is attractive on its face, it conceals some serious problems. The "will + skill" approach to rehabilitation, into which voluntariness is most often translated, allows prison administrators to interpret the lack of prisoner participation as the prisoners' reluctance "to change." They thus miss the ways in which a lack of participation can signal neglected, subverted, or abandoned implementation. In addition, this approach advances a relentlessly optimistic vision of life after release, one that allows prisoners to cherish unrealistic expectations and to avoid learning to cope with disappointment. Its misreading of history can also hobble the serious consideration of alternative programs, programs that might create both the will and the capacity for change.

The Attraction of Voluntary Programs

A drug called Anectine, which causes prisoners "to lose all control of voluntary muscles, including those used for breathing" (Mitford 1974: 139); a prison whose officials had the authority to lock prisoners up for years past their term of sentence until they showed convincing evidence of reform; drug testing and sensory deprivation, administered to prisoners who were paid below-market stipends and had no recourse when the experiments caused physical and psychological damage: here in Jessica Mitford's popular 1974 book, *Kind and Usual Punishment*, was a muckraking account of prisons, graphically depicting these and other abuses in the prison system. High on her list of charges was that compulsory prison rehabilitation both led to immoral abuses such as the ones above, and was illegitimate on its face. For Mitford, "treatment" was a euphemism for breaking prisoners' wills, getting them to accept the rewards and the approval of oppressive administrators rather than the support and friendship of their fellow prisoners. A vast array of services, offered on a voluntary basis both in and out of prison, was the only ethical way to conduct treatment.

Mitford was not the only one to call for such reforms in the 1960s and 1970s. Alarmed by the way in which indeterminate sentencing allowed

---

[1] For an intuitive understanding of this point, think of missionaries during a famine who offer food to anyone willing to convert to their religion. Prospective converts are free to refuse, of course, but there is surely some element of coercion in a choice between starvation and conversion.

prisoners to be kept in prison for years until they could persuade parole boards that they were reformed, a host of prominent legal scholars and criminologists called for the reexamination of the rehabilitative ideal. Francis Allen, dean of the law school at the University of Michigan, suggested that far from making the prison more humane, the expressed purpose of rehabilitation had licensed prison authorities to commit all sorts of abuses in the name of treatment (Allen 1981). The Field Foundation funded a four-year study, led by a prominent committee of academics, politicians, and lawyers, which concluded that the only fair rationale for sentencing was commensurate deserts—sentences based on the severity of the crime, rather than on considerations of rehabilitation. They rejected rehabilitation as a reason for sentencing, they said, because

> in our day-to-day experience, and in our preliminary research findings, it seemed that rehabilitation was far less often achieved than our predecessors would have believed. We could not, therefore, presuppose the validity or desirability of such a rationale. Further, we were not insensitive to the fact that a curious kind of shuffling between rehabilitation and incapacitation often went on within the institutions. Confront an administrator with the fact that his institution is not rehabilitating, and he would tell you he was confining dangerous people; tell him that not everyone inside the walls was dangerous, and he would respond that his was a therapeutic effort designed to rehabilitate the offender.[2]

The concerns of these experts found greater resonance in the politics of the era. Attentive to government actions restricting liberties, to the condemnation of political protesters as criminal, to the overrepresentation of racial minorities and the poor in prison, and to activists who considered some crimes legitimate because directed against a criminal government, supporters of civil liberties and civil rights were more sympathetic to prisoners than at any other time in the history of the country. The American Friends Service Committee argued that "the paternalism implicit in A's assumption that he knows better than B what is for B's benefit is treacherous under any circumstances and becomes an intolerable form of colonialism when invoked by middle-class whites to run the lives of blacks, Chicanos, Indians, and the poor" (American Friends Service Committee 1971:25). The fact that treatment programs were often directed at prisoners, like Black Muslims, whose beliefs challenged the legitimacy of the political system gave credence to accusations that the U.S. was holding political prisoners (Mitford 1971:133–134) And reports of prison riots, culminating in the death of twenty-nine prisoners and ten staff at the hands of police trying to recapture the Attica Correctional Facility,

---

[2] Willard Gaylin and David Rothman, "Introduction," in Von Hirsch (1976: xxxii).

helped to convince activists and even a majority of the public that "prison authorities don't understand the needs of prisoners."[3] Without faith in the benevolence or expertise of wardens, staff, or administrators, it was difficult to have any faith in the conduct of rehabilitation.

These advocates did not call for the abolition of all programs in prisons. Rather, recognizing the need that prisoners had for "good pay, meaningful work, leisure time and the resources to enjoy it, and perhaps counseling on special personal, vocational, or family problems," advocates called for voluntary programs (American Friends Service Committee 1971:98–99). Norval Morris, dean of the University of Chicago Law School, introduced his proposed prison for the repetitively violent criminal by arguing that to "liberate the rehabilitative ideal," the old model of early release in exchange for participation in programs needed to be abandoned. Programs linked to rewards or sanctions, he argued, deprived prisoners of the freedom of choice that is essential to any true decision to reform.

> In one sense they [prisoners] hold the key to their prison, but it is a bogus key. They must present a facade of being involved in their own "rehabilitation" and building that facade may preclude the reality of reformative effort. . . . As a result neither we nor they know whether they genuinely wish to use such retraining for their personal development toward a happier and less criminous life, or whether they merely seek to "con" those who can earlier open the doors to freedom. (Morris 1974:17)

In its place, Morris offered a prison that would give prisoners fixed parole dates upon entry, release within three years to allow for realistic planning by the prisoner while incarcerated, and the development of a series of furloughs, home leaves, and halfway house placements preceding the final parole date, all for the purpose of allowing the prisoner and the prison to test his fitness for freedom (Morris 1974:100–107). Apart from a mandatory assignment to a small discussion group of prisoners and staff, all educational, vocational, and counseling alternatives would be made available on a voluntary basis. "After all, the reason the institution is to be established is not for remedial education . . . if the prisoner is set free to develop his capacity to avoid violent crime in the future, this is likely to come less from the formal treatment programs than from the total milieu of the institution, and from the crucial small group discussions involving other prisoners and the staff" (Morris 1974:113).

Morris's understanding of the principle of voluntariness thus did not mean that every program in the prison had to be voluntary. In addition to

---

[3] Louis Harris, "Public Rejects Force in Quelling Prison Riots," 18, cited in Cullen and Gilbert (1982: 5–6).

the small groups, which he envisioned as a site for discussions about the prisoners' past crimes and their understanding of how to avoid them in the future, he also noted the necessity of sometimes compelling prisoners to "participate in an educational or vocational or psychological training program up to the point where he knows what it is about" (Morris 1974: 19). But voluntariness was the umbrella under which the prison operated: prisoners had to be free to reject programs after learning what they were. Even if a prisoner refused to participate in the mandatory discussion groups, he would face only transfer to another prison. Morris was insistent that noncompliant prisoners should suffer no loss in privileges, conditions, or most importantly, release dates.

Morris's model was thus a compromise between the promise and the abuses of the rehabilitative ideal. And it came at the right historical moment. Norman Carlson, then-director of the Federal Bureau of Prisons, entered the directorship in 1970 with the belief that "Research . . . demonstrated the great difficulty of changing human behavior, particularly in individuals who have little or no desire to help themselves. What we had failed to recognize was the impact of motivation on the part of offenders who have little or no desire to help themselves" ("Interview with Norman Carlson" 1990: 39). Under pressure from opponents of behavioral modification programs, who were particularly critical of a proposed research facility that would study the reformation of criminals, the Federal Bureau of Prisons seized upon Morris's credibility and his model to redesign their approach to correctional programming (McKelvey 1977:39; "Interview with Norman Carlson" 1990). Programs were henceforth to be voluntary, and rehabilitation the responsibility of the prisoner. As Carlson explained, "The Bureau adopted a new model during the early 1970s, which emphasized our obligation to provide for inmates to assist themselves—if they so desired. . . . What we did, in effect, was acknowledge that we could not diagnose or forcibly treat offenders and that change in anyone—including ourselves—must come from within, if it is to have any lasting impact" ("Interview with Norman Carlson" 1990: 39; emphasis in original).

The model adopted by the Bureau with Morris's help, however, lacked some important aspects of Morris's approach. In particular, many of the sentencing reforms were not implemented: most notably, prisoners were not given the furloughs and halfway house placements that Morris considered integral to testing prisoners' fitness for release. The small group discussion sections were despised by staff and prisoners who did not understand their purpose and had little training in how to run them (Bounds 1979:126–35). More subtly, the philosophy behind Morris's approach and the Bureau's voluntary model was different in an important way: while Morris saw individual desire as something to be protected from interference but also guided toward reform, the Bureau's model saw the desire to change as an essentially static condition. Prisoners either had the desire to change, in which case they would take advantage of the opportunities provided; or they were obdurate, in which case the prisons were freed from any obligation toward their reform.

This version of the voluntary approach to programming can be termed "will + skill"—the prisoner provides the will to change, and specific skills are then made available to him. It was soon adopted by numerous state prison systems. In fact, budgets for correctional programming declined little, if at all, in state prisons systems while rehabilitation itself was being attacked by liberals and conservatives alike. John DiIulio writes that even in the face of political hostility toward rehabilitation, "corrections officials, using techniques ranging in bureaucratic sophistication from obvious foot dragging . . . to 'reinvent[ing]' old programs under new names, simply continued to staff and operate institutional programs" (DiIulio 1991:115). Such programs offered prison officials the best of all worlds. Programs, of course, alleviate some of the idleness that threatens institutional peace. They are useful public relations tools, especially with prison reform groups and prisoners' rights advocacy groups, which often influence judges who evaluate prison conditions. They diversify the backgrounds of employees within the prison system, expanding the talent pool for management positions. Yet voluntary programs do not face the chief problem of rehabilitation programs: they do not lead to any expectation that the prison should be responsible for the reform of the prisoners. If a prisoner reforms, the prison can be given some credit for making skills available to him; but when he recidivates, it is his fault, not the prison's, that he had not the will to change.

The reasoning behind this principle is logical, and to the extent that it honors the right of the prisoner to choose only that which he thinks will help him reform, it can be supported by prisoner advocates as well as prison administrators. As we have seen, though, the "will + skill" approach can allow prisons to ignore, or even justify, a host of implementation problems. Under the "will + skill" approach, the lack of prisoner participation in programs is usually considered a sign of lack of motivation. But as this study has shown, a low participation rate is often better characterized as a problem of the programs—particular programs that may not be intensive, well-run, or interesting enough to attract participation. Thus, at Drake, staff were frustrated by pressure to increase enrollments, but there was no institutional pressure to improve teaching or program variety in response. The possibility that the prisoners are motivated, but do not find that the programs in question provide what they need, is easily swept under the rug by a "will + skill" approach to programming.

A corollary to this problem is that the "will + skill" approach admits of no positive way to acknowledge or make use of institutional incentives for participation. Under a pure voluntary system, incentives such as prison privileges corrupt the prisoners' motivation—either because the atmosphere of coercion in a prison means that any incentives are coercive, or because incentives interfere with the development of a prisoner's interior desire for reform. This is plausible in some lights, but it is also odd: it suggests that prisoners, unlike everyone else, must pursue reform apart from any calculation of immediate self-interest, and in fact must sometimes ignore their immediate self-interest to pursue programs. Thus, for instance, prisoners must be willing to accept a lower pay scale or less desirable job to participate in programs at Catawba. To be sure, this would show an admirable dedication,[4] but it also requires that prisoners be less interested in salary or in job quality than most people—surely not an intuitive assumption about human nature.

The "will + skill" approach to programming can also work to marginalize the staff's concern for program quality and participation. Although it would be unreasonable to hold prison officials responsible for the recidivism of prisoners they release, the fact that prison administrators consider themselves obligated only to provide "opportunities" means that there are no obvious reasons for them to evaluate the quality of the opportunities they provide. While prison administrators do not go out of their way to provide bad programs, they tend to assume that if a program exists, it is good enough. Thus at Evergreen, the fact that the college program technically offered a BA trumped the fact that the sponsoring college was hundreds of miles away and did not monitor the curriculum. Even at Drake, where the education administrator wanted to "get his numbers up," there was no interest in discovering the characteristics of programs or of prisoner-staff interaction that kept the numbers down. Administrators cannot produce good programs without staff support, as the example of Catawba shows. But the "will + skill" approach can free administrators from the obligation to try.

"Will + skill" programs certainly avoid the issues of abuse of power that mandatory rehabilitation programs faced in the 1960s and 1970s. And the difficulties that the "will + skill" approach creates for implementation are all surmountable: Antelope Valley and Beaverton surmount them. Nor are "will + skill" programs the only ones that suffer from implementation problems; as I discuss later in this chapter, early rehabilitation programs were often subverted or aborted in implementation,

---

[4] Or it may not; perhaps prisoners who would not be eligible for good prison jobs, because of their lack of willingness to work, are the ones who end up participating in programs, which seem to require less of them than a job.

when "behavioral modification" provided therapeutic legitimacy for the use of sometimes horrendous negative sanctions and staff rejected programs that required them to be group therapists. But while it is not uniquely afflicted with implementation problems, the logic of the "will + skill" approach provides a justification for the failure to worry about, or even consider, the conditions of successful implementation.

Equally dangerous, however, is the understanding of rehabilitation that undergirds the "will + skill" approach. A close look at the circumstances awaiting prisoners upon release shows little reason to assume that motivation, combined with some education or vocational training, could guarantee that ex-prisoners would be successful at finding a job and avoiding crime. Indeed, as the next section shows, in some ways the ideology of "will + skill" actually sets prisoners up for failure, feeding an unrealistic faith in positive thinking rather than a sober preparation for the challenges that await them.

Hitting the Streets

One reason for the popularity of the "will + skill" rehabilitation model is prisoners' evident need for basic skills. To cite just one example, in the interview sample, 31 percent of those interviewed did not have a high school diploma, and another 11 percent had earned their diplomas only after entering prison; nationally, 41 percent of all inmates in state prisons do not have a high school or equivalent diploma. But the jump from this fact to a simple model of rehabilitation—that skills and education lead to jobs, and then jobs to the end of crime—sets up unrealistic and ultimately self-defeating expectations. Having the requisite skills and education is not enough to ensure that a released prisoner will be able to find a job. And it is not clear that having a job, in and of itself, can keep an individual from committing crimes.

Even a quick look at the experiences and attitudes of prisoners themselves suggests that merely increasing skills will not be enough. Leaving aside participants in vocational education, Table 5.1 shows almost no difference between the future plans of participants and nonparticipants in programs: slightly under a third have made no vocational plans for their release, another third expect to return to a previous legitimate line of work, and only 12 percent of the prisoners plan to use the skills or education they received in prison in their future careers. This does not bode well for the argument that rehabilitation programs in prison open up new opportunities for inmates. Of those inmates in vocational education courses, who can point to a specific skill that they acquired or honed in prison, only 39 percent plan to use their newly obtained skills after

TABLE 5.1
Prisoners' Plans to Use Skills Learned While in Prison

	Nonparticipants	Participant (other than voc. ed.)	Vocational Ed. Participant
No vocational plans	34%	28%	31%
Will return to a previous job	26%	32%	23%
Will find a job using skills learned in prison	12%	12%	39%
Plans to go into a new line of work	27%	29%	8%

Note: N = 190. Responses were obtained from the answers to the questions, "What do you plan to do after you leave prison?" and "Would you use any of the skills you learned here in prison?" and from the prisoners' descriptions of their occupational histories. Only those who named the same noncriminal previous job as part of their occupational histories and as their future work are counted in the category, "will return to a previous job."

release. While this group is much larger than the comparable 12 percent figure for other inmates, it leads one to wonder why the other 60 percent would *not* plan to use their skills.

Looking at the breakdown of answers, one gets a hint as to why. Participation in a vocational training program does not lower the number of inmates who say that they have no plans, and it lowers only slightly the number of those who say they would return to a previous line of work. It decreases by 20%, however, the number of people who say they are planning to pursue a new career. Participation, then, might make more realistic the plans of people who had already decided to try something different. But it does not increase the number of people who make plans.

For proponents of rehabilitation, these findings are sobering. It would not be realistic to assume that all participants in programs would use their new skills, even if they all said that they were planning to. If they are not even planning to use their newly acquired skills, or have made no plans at all, the value of those skills can certainly be called into question. Yet opponents of rehabilitation, who might attribute these results to a preference for crime over law-abiding productivity, are misled as well. Seen within the framework of an inmate's realistic expectations upon release, preparation has few concrete benefits, and includes the psychic disadvantage of raising expectations too high. For many prisoners, learning a new skill is, in and of itself, a valuable exercise, which is why they engage in it. But they do not have the luxury of assuming that those skills will give them the ability to go straight.

To understand this, it is important to look first at the circumstances of an inmate's release. Though the lack of training and education is without doubt a handicap in the job market, merely having those skills is not always sufficient. For instance, prisoners face a high barrier in terms of their ability to conduct a job search. An inmate is not able to make phone calls, or interview with employers, until after he leaves prison; thus, he must defer most of his concrete planning until release. Upon release, if he cannot rely upon family support or other types of financial resources, an inmate will normally have only his "gate money"—a sum which averages about $100 in the prisons I visited—along with any money he has managed to save. His financial circumstances thus require him to find a job, any job, as soon as possible. The terms of his release, which normally require verifiable employment, are a further spur to action. The situation is somewhat improved if an inmate can get a halfway house placement at the end of his term, which allows him to find a job, save money for a place to live, and transition slowly back into freedom. But because of legal restrictions as to which inmates are eligible for community custody, most inmates will not be released to a halfway house. Those who do get a halfway house placement usually stay less than six months. And because inmates will be sent back to prison if they do not quickly find and stay in one job, the incentive to take the first job offered, rather than look for something for which they have been trained, is very strong.

The problem of timing is further exacerbated by the fact that inmates reenter the job market with several strikes against them. Employers, of course, are often suspicious of ex-convicts because of their records or out of fear of violence. But it does not take active prejudice for ex-convicts with the same skills as other applicants to be denied jobs; the liabilities inherent in an absence from society are enough to move an ex-prisoner to the "back of the queue" when hiring decisions are made. An ex-prisoner has no experience to cite for the years he was in prison, and the gap on his resume makes it hard for an employer to evaluate his reliability and work habits. Moreover, during the time he is in prison, past employers and other references move away from the area, or no longer remember the prisoner. His absence from social networks apart from his own family means that he has many fewer sources of leads to job opportunities. These problems are exacerbated if, as many federal prisoners, he is released to the sentencing district of his conviction as opposed to an area in which his family lives (Oliveres et al. 1996; Burton et al. 1987; Glaser 1964). As economists Richard Freeman and Harry Holzer have pointed out, the combined impact of these factors could easily mask any positive effects from training programs or other rehabilitative efforts (Holzer and Freeman 1985).

Occupational shifts in the U.S. economy also hurt ex-prisoners more than their competitors on the street. Service jobs, which normally require a great deal of customer contact at the entry level, are the fastest growing sector of the American economy. But former prisoners, struggling to adapt to the outside world, tend to find the social skills needed to deal with customers extremely difficult. In addition, employers, already nervous about hiring ex-convicts, are even more nervous when the job requires customer contact or service. By contrast, many of the blue-collar jobs for which prisons train prisoners, or in which prisoners previously worked, are fast disappearing. Ninety-one percent of the inmates in the sample had some work experience; but their experience was predominantly in construction and manufacturing, farming, or repair and other mechanical work. With the exception of the programs at Beaverton, the vocational training within the prisons in my sample were for similar skills: auto and auto body repair, welding, building trades. Yet these are precisely the types of areas in which unemployment is high. In 1991, to cite just a few examples, the overall unemployment rate for men was 7 percent. But for manufacturing laborers, it was 14.1 percent; for all construction workers, 15.9 percent, and for construction laborers in particular, 22 percent—three times the average unemployment rate.

The problems described above do not "condemn" ex-prisoners to crime. But they do mean that the world to which prisoners return is not a predictable world of work and reward, but an unpredictable world where opportunities, legitimate and illegitimate, come randomly. It is a world in which one prepares oneself, not for a specific job, but "so that if an opportunity presents itself, I will be ready for it" (3FA). Skills certainly help in this world; people who are educated have "resources in their corner" (3FA). But planning does not, because it brings few rewards. "[Some guys] plan to do well," one inmate explained, "but the negativity gets to them" (5NF). Another adds,

> I'm not making plans because when I left last time, I had all these plans—but once I got on the street, I was scared and frustrated and everything went to hell. I'm more toned down this time, and less disappointed. (3FI)

But this inmate—with his determination to be "more toned down this time"—is in the minority. For while most prisoners are quite aware that the world which awaits them is difficult and that their prospects are very uncertain, they invoke their strength of will, their determination to "think positive," to conquer the odds. This produces comments composed of equal parts of defensiveness and bravado.

> I can't really tell [why some people make it]; you shake a guy's hand here and tell him, "Be strong, man," and you think he won't never come back, and next

thing you know he's here. And the ones you're sure will be back, aren't. This is a different environment in here. You just gotta have it in your heart. I know it's gonna be rough, but you know, ain't nothin' can be harder than here. I'm gonna make it; I've got good family ties. They come down to see me once a month, and they believe in me; they're all waiting for me to come home. Lots of guys will tell you straight out, "I'm going out to break the law." But if you're here for twenty years, how can they put you out with nothing—just a bus ticket and $50? Lots has changed out there, and there are people out there who been out there looking for jobs. You go ask for one and they hear you're an ex-con, they'll be skeptical. Like if it's construction, the man will think, hey, I got tools around here, what if this guy goes off? And a person ain't gonna starve. (5MA)

This prisoner wants to distinguish himself from "lots of guys": they intend to keep breaking the law, but he's got people "waiting for me to come home" and he's "gonna make it." But notice the specificity of the comments he has about the difficulties of life after release—the bus ticket, the "gate money," the problems with finding construction work, the overwrought claim about starvation —compared to the almost mystical invocation of "you just gotta have it in your heart." Determination and willpower are simple and straightforward: "If you want to make it, I think you should go out and fight for it—just put your hand out and reach for it" (4JZ). But in the way that prisoners use them, they are closer to an incantation than an aid to reform.

The extent to which willpower substitutes for other strategies of post-prison survival is striking. As Table 5.2 shows, when asked what factors were needed to "make it" on the street, over half of the inmates interviewed volunteered a "willpower" answer—a response that was over two times more likely to be offered than any other response. By contrast, only 14 percent of the inmates cite "preparation in prison" as an important factor in staying out of prison. Only 15 percent mention relying upon family or other support systems, while 21 percent talk about having a job or other resources on the street. There is no difference between program participants, whom one might expect to rate preparation for the outside world more highly, and nonparticipants. Instead, they give essentially the same responses in essentially the same proportions, except that participants are more—not less—likely to cite the importance of determination.

The focus on willpower and optimism persists even in the face of the recognition that most ex-prisoners will face prejudice and other barriers upon their return to society. Just under 90 percent of the prisoners I spoke to believed that prejudice against them does exist and affects most inmates. But about half also believe that they will be the exception to the rule. Some cite their age, or their experience, or the nature of the crime: "Not against me, there won't; I have no reputation of violence. Where I

TABLE 5.2
"What's the Difference between People Who Make It Once They
Get Out of Here, and People Who Come Right Back?"

	Nonparticipant (N)	Participants (N)	All Prisoners (N)
"Willpower, determination and desire."	47% (34)	61% (71)	55% (105)
"Support from family, a job set up, or money waiting for you out there."	27% (20)	17% (20)	21% (40)
"Who your friends are, whether or not you hang with the old crowd."	19% (14)	18% (21)	18% (35)
"Doesn't have anything to do with you; it's if your parole officer has it in for you, or if the feds stay off your back."	14% (10)	16% (19)	15% (29)
"Preparing yourself while you're in prison, like with an education or a skill."	14% (10)	15% (17)	14% (27)
Other	7% (5)	3% (5)	5% (10)
Number of respondents	73	117	190

Note: The Ns in the table are the number of people who gave that particular type of answer. Since some people gave more than one type of response, percentages do not sum up to 100.

come from, though, rape and murder are thought to be wrong; people will look at you rough if you do that" (4JC). Others simply say, "I think there's prejudice but it won't hurt me, because I have goals" (2CB) or, in the words of another, "The possibility [of prejudice] exists, but rejection happens to everyone" (2CG).

The perspective described here is an odd perversion of the work ethic arguments popular in social policy debates. Conservatives like Charles Murray (1984) and Lawrence Mead (1986) commonly argue that the roots of poverty and other social problems are not in the lack of opportunity, but in the lack of will to work, to take unpleasant jobs and strive to make something better out of them. The implication is that if only poor people really wanted to escape poverty, they could certainly do it. The majority of the inmates I interviewed do not disagree. In fact, they take the can-do spirit one step further: that *because* they want to reform, they need be daunted by no obstacles. Will alone will overcome.

But the faith in willpower is often what leads to the greatest disappointments. "When you beg a person for a job and it still don't happen, that really messes you up" (5MA). Getting discouraged makes it very easy for an inmate to justify returning to crime, especially if he tells himself that it is for a good cause. As one inmate explained,

> If you're living comfortable, you won't go to drugs; you'll always try to find a job first. But when you're turned down, and turned down again, you'll go to your friends to be cut in on something. Maybe you start selling to help the family first; then you get hooked on the fast money. It's hard to go back to Burger King after that. (5NL)

For many ex-prisoners, this seesaw between determination and disappointment is the touchstone of recidivism. Recidivists, whether they admit that their previous lifestyle routinely included crimes or swear that they had reformed themselves but for one stupid mistake, describe crime in terms that emphasize the emotional as well as the economic impetuses for breaking the law. Thus one prisoner explained, "I was put away for one robbery for four years and when I got out, I wanted things to happen fast for me. That's what got me sent back here" (2CF). Some prisoners cannot even think of ways to deal with their frustration apart from criminal posturing. This prisoner's story shows how automatic it can be for an ex-offender to take up exactly the kind of behavior that makes others suspicious.

> I called this supermarket in D— —real white town—and they told me to come on over, they had a job for me right away. So I went over—and I was so excited, I told my momma I got a job, and I called my uncle, and he told me that he'd pick me up after work at 11 because I only had bus fare for one way. So I went out there and the manager told me, sorry, I don't have a job for you. I had to walk home in the cold and the dark, and there were horns blowing and people calling me nigger; that hurt, I tell you, that really hurt. I tried to get on a bus— hey man, I said, I don't have the fare, but I'm only going as far as W—(the black section of town)—he got me off his bus. So what was I supposed to do? People were yelling at me from their car windows; finally, I just picked up a piece of wood with some big nails sticking out of it and kept walking. (5MG)

The way in which determination can evaporate in the face of setbacks and frustration illustrates the limits of simply trying harder. But perhaps the most telling detail is that prisoners so easily have recourse to willpower as a strategy because willpower—or more accurately, willfully looking away from obstacles and possible failure—is a strategy familiar to them from their criminal careers. Ironically, "thinking positive" and "being strong"—attitude and willpower—are the attributes which inmates rely upon while committing crimes. When asked whether people weigh the possible sentence against the crime before committing it, prisoners often answer, "No—I don't think negative before I do something" (3GG). Compare this to the prisoner who says, "Determination . . . that and a little luck will help you make it" (5NE).

The similarity between the two statements is astounding—and troubling. Part of the reason that prisoners *are* caught is because they think, "When you're doing something, you don't anticipate getting caught. You think, 'I *can* make it work,' and you don't know the sentences, so you don't focus on the penalties" (5NX). Relying on sheer will is not sufficient to avoid arrest. It is no more sufficient for "making it."

The skills, resources, and values that prison programs provide must be placed in the context of all of these factors. Prisoners do not confront a simple deficit of the skills or the will needed to avoid crime. Instead, they face a situation where being as qualified as their competitors still leaves them in a relatively worse position, and a set of circumstances where self-confidence, willpower, and the determination to "do the right thing" can set them up for failure. One obvious implication is that prisoners need to lower their expectations, giving themselves some room to construct goals that will not leave them disappointed. And, in some senses, prisoners do. Many prisoners find that the experience of incarceration leads them to profess a value for its opposite: the idealized home and family, the virtues of a steady job and a quiet life. Even such modest expectations, however, are difficult for released prisoners to meet. The quotidian attractions of the "straight life" are the hardest ones to attain.

"Success Will Be My Revenge"

> I did want a lot, but now my ambition's shrunk. I used to be kind of wild, but now I'm realistic—just a nice home, two cars, a wife and kids, a small business so no one's telling me what to do, and doing something to help others. Success will be my revenge; my goal is just to be middle class. (2CW)
> (*Convicted Kidnapper*)

In a study of the career paths and aspirations of felons in California, John Irwin (1970) found that prisoners define the successful life after release not as avoiding recidivism, but as "doing good"—entering a social circle in which one can share one's experiences and be respected, finding a good job that will allow some measure of financial security, making up for the lack of sexual relationships in prison. The prisoners in this study, twenty-five years later, share the same sentiments. "I want a family," says one prisoner,

> I want my children to grow up and be people; I want to sit on a porch and hold my woman's hand, if I ever have one; I want to be a positive role model. I want

a nice house, a couple of cars, a vacation now and then; I want to go to the park on Sundays and live like Ozzie and Harriet! (4JD)

What lies behind this type of response? In part, it is the deprivations of prison. The domestic comforts—family, economic security, and making a contribution to the community—are exactly those things most conspicuously absent from prison life. Pleasures that were taken for granted, even scorned earlier, are now seen as particularly precious.

[I want] a house, a wife, a nice job—something I enjoy doing, like inspecting cable or reading blueprints or calligraphy. I want the simple things in life, I want to be away from the city, and I want to stay out in society. (2CA)

This is even more true, however, for prisoners who, whether apart from or due to their crimes, had achieved these goals in the past. Their replies are compounded of equal parts of remorse and bitterness.

[I just want] a good job and kids; I don't want to own a business anymore, just get me a nice paycheck. How can they seize everything I had when I worked for it?—they took everything and left my competitor in fine shape! . . . My kids are with their aunt, and they probably should stay with their aunt now—the change would be too dramatic for them. I won't ever raise them because of my incarceration. I lost my business; now I've lost my kids. (2DC)

But just as compelling as the contrast with imprisonment is the "normalcy" of this ambition. Limited aspirations seem possible, and their possibility makes them more attractive. Sometimes this is expressed pragmatically, as in this comment: "Just to be healthy—now. Before, I guess I wanted the same thing, but I wanted a little more too" (5MJ). For others, the idea of limited ambitions takes on a moral dimension of its own.

I would give half my life now to be near my kids and working a decent job. I don't want to have too much money—just enough to get my kids through school and live a normal life. When you have too much money, you're scared. Money changes your life—you keep getting worried that someone will kidnap you, you get scared it will disappear. (1AN)

I never had everything I wanted so I found a way to get it. With drugs, I got everything I wanted. . . . At first I was greedy, but I got the time and I experienced the aftermath. So now, a job would keep me from coming back. . . . Just the American dream—a family, a home, a dog, a white picket fence—I want my family to be proud of me, so I can say I'm not failing anymore. (4KM)

It is important not to understand these dreams as blueprints. The self-mocking expression of a desire to live like "Ozzie and Harriet" or the invocation of "a family, a home, a dog, a white picket fence" show that prisoners have not really converted these cultural icons of stability and family life into models they can use; they reach for symbolic images rather

TABLE 5.3
Prisoners' Ambitions for the Future

Type of Response	Percentage
"Go back to my wife and kids, get a steady job, have a house and car and a little left over after paying the bills."	67%
"Become wealthy/write a best-selling book/ become a famous musician or TV personality."	11%
"Find peace and quiet; get the government to get off my back and leave me alone!"	8%
Other or no answer	24%

Note: N = 190. Responses were obtained by categorizing the answers to the questions, "What do you want out of life?" and "What do you hope to have achieved, 5 years after you get out of prison?"

than concrete plans. This is particularly evident in the context of other prisoners with different dreams. As Table 5.3 shows, while the vision of a stable family and job is by far the most common hope expressed for the future, the other commonly repeated possibilities—becoming a famous writer or performer, or defending one's home against the government— are even more unrealistic, not less. Thus it makes sense to understand these wishes as a set of expectations, not for particular possessions, but for a type of life in which success, if more modest, will be less costly than crime, and certainly more comforting than prison.

The poignancy of the phrases—"now I'm realistic" and "success will be my revenge"—is that in their phrasing, prisoners concede that even limited goals will be hard to achieve. Even prisoners who use their time in prison to get an education or learn a trade are afraid that they've "let the time do me"; the years away represent family ties that have been broken, money that has not been made, respect that they have not earned. Having the accouterments of the middle class would be revenge on the penal system, in the sense of proving that the sentence could not defeat them, did not deprive them of a "normal" life. But while these "realistic" expectations are not beyond the reach of many people who avoid crimes, they are often beyond the reach of most prisoners.

The first obstacle is the expectation itself. Whether an inmate had a comfortable, secure existence before his incarceration, or whether that security could only be dreamed, regaining or achieving that security after incarceration is the work of months, if not years. But being in prison, which encourages one to think about how different life will be after one is free, does not encourage patience upon release. Businesses lost through forfeiture or sold to pay expenses will not be rebuilt in a matter of weeks;

houses and cars take years to save up for in the normal course of events; even the closest of family members (which most inmates will not have) takes time to get accustomed to once again. If a prisoner has had all these things before, he is apt to be frustrated by the contrast to what he remembers. On the other hand, if a prisoner is pursuing these goals for the first time, the gap between the amount he earns and the amount he needs to lead his vision of "the straight life" is likely to stun him.

Both macro- and micro-evidence bolster these observations. A study conducted by the Federal Bureau of Prisons showed that prisoners who had participated in prison industry work programs while in prison earned an average of $9,863 in the twelve months after their release (Saylor and Gaes 1992:32–36). In 1985, the year of release for most of the ex-prisoners studied, this amount was $18,825 below the median household income ($28,688), and only $4,394 more than the poverty line ($5,469 for one individual).[5] Although sufficient to keep from starvation, this amount is hardly equal to the provision of economic security. Nor is it enough to allow an ex-offender to save money, to go to school for further education, or to make other attempts to stabilize his financial condition.

The problem is even clearer when one looks at prisoners' expectations about what constitutes a "good job," one that would allow them to afford the kind of mainstream lifestyle they crave. When prisoners volunteered a quantitative description of the "good job," the answers, which ranged from $7 to $15 an hour and averaged an hourly wage of $10.45, were modest. These figures can only be suggestive, as prisoners were not systematically asked to state a wage that would satisfy them. But the figures given by people who did mention an amount are surprisingly close to the salary of the average worker in 1990—$10.34 an hour, for a total income of $23,602.[6] This supports the inmates' own protestations that "succeeding just means having a nice stable life, because nothing is perfect."

The problem is that this expectation is at odds with the rewards that they are looking for, and, more to the point, the income which awaits them. At $10.45 an hour, prisoners expect an average salary of $21,736, or 73 percent of the median income ($29,943) in 1990. Although this

---

[5] All statistics come from the *1992 Statistical Abstract of the United States*. A median income figure for one individual was not available; the per capita personal income in 1985, however, was $13,942.

[6] This question was not asked systematically; as a result, numerical estimates came up only when prisoners volunteered them as an example of what they were thinking. Twenty-three inmates out of 190 volunteered estimates. Of these, 3 volunteered only that a job paying the minimum wage was too low. The median hourly wage named was $10. The bulk of the estimates fell between $8 and $13 per hour/hr.

salary would allow them to work toward economic security, it cannot provide them with the house, the car, and the attributes of middle-class living they crave. Yet as we have seen, even this salary is probably unattainable. After recalculating the 1985 figures from the study above, the average ex-prisoner earned $12,476 in 1991 dollars. This is less than 60 percent of the $21,736 that they would consider to be a "good" income. Such a large difference between expectation and reality can only lead to frustration.

Nor is the cost of prison time only economic. In the male prison, where both of these are conspicuous by their absence, a large proportion of a prisoner's dreams center on finding, or reconciling with, a wife and children. "My family's the reason why I will stay off drugs. They deserve more than this. Before prison, I gave them material things, but no love or attention; now I want to. If I didn't have them, I wouldn't care about staying off drugs" (1F). "When I leave, I have to mend my family—my wife never found out about [my mistress], but I owe her anyway. My business is for my family—they're the same" (1AS).

These ties, however, are inherently weakened by the passage of time and the absence of "normal" contact. Even should a prisoner's family visit regularly and keep in frequent, two-way communication, they are always and only visitors to a world that is foreign and frightening to them. For his part, the prisoner's world has stopped while his family's continues; his children forget who he is, his wife learns to cope without him. This, of course, assumes the best of all possible worlds. More commonly, a prisoner's past life has not endeared his family to him; he has not built up a reputation for either trust or dependability; perhaps he has not even been in contact with them. Thus it is not uncommon to find the longing for a family spoken of in mythic, hopelessly unrealistic terms.

> At my age, I want to settle with a nice lady in not a big house—just nice, with a garden and a patio. I just want to sit and think of the bad days. [In five years] I hope I will have met a young lady and we'll start by getting a little house— then we'll comfort each other until the day we're called [the day we die]. (4JV)

> I will be married—I want to be married within six months because I believe as a Christian you must practice abstinence before marriage; and I can't wait any longer than that! I'm getting older, too—I want to make some babies as soon as possible. (1AZ)

The emotional rewards of "going straight" are also less satisfying than the prisoner imagines. Prisoners agree that the pains of imprisonment are overwhelmingly mental and not physical.

> It sets you back—you'll have to start all over again, and you can't get your time back. When you come here, you have the feeling of failure, you feel rejected.

You realize that you'll be under strict rules and regulations, and if you don't abide by them, it just makes it worse. I appreciate freedom on the outside more now. (1BA)

Freedom does bring back the ability to do the "little things" that prisoners crave while within prison. But it does not necessarily bring back the absence of petty constraints or the respect that ex-prisoners long for. To the contrary, an ex-prisoner finds that while he now has the freedom to eat anytime and anywhere he wishes, he may not have the money to do so; while he no longer has to sleep in an open dorm with criminals all around him, he may not be able to find a place where he does want and can afford to stay. More to the point, he will find that very few people respect an ex-felon. His prison "experience" at best embarrasses people, at worst creates suspicion and disapproval. Ironically, the only people who will really be impressed and interested in his tales of prison life are people who are themselves involved in criminal activity. The more he spends time with them, telling and embroidering tales about how tough or how smart he was in prison, the more prison recedes as a threat, and the more likely he is to become involved in crime.[7]

An ex-prisoner always knows that there is another way to get the money, excitement, or feeling of belonging that he craves: to accept the risks, and "return to the game." The feeling that one always has barely enough, and nothing extra to spare, is particularly difficult, because prisoners think of their sentence as a time of enforced deprivation. Subsistence, after all, is available in prisons. When release, contrary to their rosy expectations, offers little more than that, the fear of returning to prison is greatly lessened. The temptation to "run a caper" on the side while maintaining a legitimate front is always present; indeed, with 67 percent of all prisoners working at the time of their arrest, mixing legitimate work with crime is a familiar survival strategy for them.[8] And an ex-prisoner, whose bitterness and disdain of the justice system often leads him to overestimate the hit-and-miss character of law enforcement, can always convince himself that this once, he won't get caught.

---

[7] Spending time with acquaintances who are involved with criminal activity is also dangerous in and of itself. Under some types of supervised release, it is a specified parole violation, for which he can be sent back to prison, even if there is no wrongdoing attached to him. If his associates are arrested for any type of offense while in his company, his past record immediately places him under suspicion of involvement. And while drinking, disturbing the peace, or getting into fights may not make them liable for arrest, any such action in their company is enough to have an ex-prisoner's parole revoked.

[8] In my sample, 69 percent of the prisoners reported that they were working when they were arrested; the 1991 Survey of State Prisoners finds 67 percent working in the month of their arrest. Other sources confirm that the combination of work and crime is common; see Bourgois (1989), Freeman (1991; 1996), Freeman and Holzer (1986), and MacCoun and Reuter (1992).

Ex-prisoners, of course, are not the only ones who must adjust their expectations to a limited reality. Difficult economic times and changing workforce needs affect a large number of Americans. All of them must cope with the disparity between their middle-class dreams and their personal achievements; most of them do not commit crimes as a solution. Similarly, the lack of emotional support and respect experienced by ex-prisoners is not unique to them. What sets ex-prisoners apart as a group, however, is that these pressures are commonly found in conjunction; that their force is exaggerated by the contrast between prerelease expectations and postrelease disillusionment; and that they have a viable alternative to disillusionment. Unlike their peers, they know that they have and therefore can survive prison, and they usually have had some practice in committing crimes. Crime may not be an attractive alternative. But it is a familiar one.

Recent work on criminal careers over the life-course both confirms this problem and suggests some solutions. An influential school of criminological thought suggests that crime, and antisocial behavior more generally, is stable over time for individuals (Gottfredson and Hirschi 1990; Wilson and Herrnstein 1985; Wolfgang et al. 1987). In other words, adults who commit crimes were markedly antisocial children, a pattern that is steady across nations, time periods, and methods of measurement. This would suggest that there is little hope for criminal rehabilitation; instead, crime drops off as people age (Steffensmeier and Harer 1991). But this common wisdom is now being challenged by sociological theory and empirical work reiterating the importance of life-course transitions and social context. As summarized in Sampson and Laub (1993), numerous longitudinal studies have shown that while antisocial adults often have antisocial childhoods, most antisocial children do not become antisocial adults. Moreover, there are substantial differences in the timing and persistence of antisocial behavior in adults, suggesting that life events such as marriage and unemployment can affect the incidence of criminal behavior for the better or worse (Farrington et al. 1986; Gibbens 1984; Sampson and Laub 1993). Sampson and Laub's re-analysis of Sheldon and Eleanor Glueck's decades-long study of 500 matched pairs of delinquents and nondelinquents supports this chapter's claim that being in prison itself is a barrier to future employment: it finds that incarceration has an independent effect upon job stability, even when prior record, alcoholism, unofficial deviance, and exclusion risk are controlled, and that job stability then has an important role in explaining later crime.[9]

[9] Sampson and Laub (1993: 162–71). "Exclusion risk" is the possibility that part of the sample for which adult data were unavailable was absent for theoretically significant reasons—incarceration, for instance, or military service. See also Horney et al. (1995), Paternoster and Brame (1997), Warr (1998). DeJong (1997) has a good discussion of the relative impact of incarceration and social ties.

Rehabilitation programs cannot, of course, marry prisoners off or find them jobs or ensure their job stability after release. But they can, in addition to providing the vocational skills that might help them achieve such goals, help prisoners to harbor realistic expectations and to cope with the disappointments and the obstacles they are likely to face when skill and will are not enough. One way to do this might be to question the assumption that motivation, or "will," admits of only two possibilities—either one has it, or one doesn't. The forced simplicity of this assumption obscures the possibility that a will to change one's behavior might be the *result* of rehabilitation rather than its prerequisite. In other words, the desire to change might need to be developed—through knowledge, through peer support or imitation of role models, through the acquisition of good habits, or through psychological training in self-control and decision-making.

Approaches to rehabilitation that encompassed the development of the will to change could still be voluntary: prisoners could be allowed to opt out of programs, and they could be shielded from links to release dates or "good time." The change would be in the expansion of the paradigm from "will + skill" to the *creation* of both will and skill. Such a paradigm would give prisons some reason to examine both the processes they use and whether they were effective. Existing research provides reason to believe that it would be successful.

Creating the Will and the Tools for Change

As discussed in Chapter 1, the evaluation of rehabilitation programs has moved through several phases, from rejection in the early 1970s to a period of recent reassessment and optimism. The evolution in this field is not just one of results, however; it is an evolution of method. Whereas early reviews such as Lipton, Martinson, and Wilks (1975) categorized studies by the general type of treatment —counseling, education, psychotherapy, and the like—more recent work has assessed the effectiveness of treatment characteristics and conditions. Instead of asking whether studies of counseling have shown positive results, for instance, recent work generally asks about the conditions under which particular types of counseling might be effective. Thus, central themes in this work are the importance of focusing on criminogenic needs—"antisocial attitudes, styles of thinking and behavior, peer associations, chemical dependencies, and self-control issues"—and on matching specific offenders with specific therapies and therapists (Gendreau 1996:122).

The emphasis on criminogenic needs comes from a research tradition in behavioral modification. Behavioral modification, also known as "operant conditioning" or simply as "operant," reinforces particular behaviors through the use of either positive or negative consequences for those behaviors. In prisons, this technique has a long and not-illustrious history, with treatments that ranged from the inappropriate to the ill-designed. The medical treatments described by Jessica Mitford (1973), for instance, were designated behavioral modification programs; so were numerous programs that simply repackaged existing sanctions for antisocial behavior, resulting, in one case, in relabeling a reduced punishment diet for prisoners as "behavior mod. meat loaf" (Ross and McKay 1980:45).

Newer approaches to behavioral modification, however, generally target and reward prosocial behaviors rather than focusing on antisocial activities. Token economies, in which points that can be exchanged for later rewards are given out for positive behavior, are one example of this kind of approach. So are courses that target criminogenic needs by teaching and modeling problem-solving, self-control, and similar cognitive techniques. The focus on criminogenic needs is a move toward targeting behaviors that various studies of recidivism have identified as predictors of criminal activity: in other words, they are characteristics that distinguish recidivists from nonrecidivists. Thus, they do not include factors like low self-esteem, depression, anger, or lack of psychological insight, all of which may characterize many offenders but do not have a consistent relationship to recidivism (Andrews and Bonta 1994; Bonta 1996; Gendreau 1996; Ross and Gendreau 1980).

A second focus of the literature is the emphasis on matching. Sometimes characterized as "responsivity," this principle suggests that offenders with different needs and personalities/maturity be matched to programs that target their needs and program staff who complement their interaction style. While there is general agreement on the importance of matching, there is much less agreement on the appropriate criteria: thus some studies focus on maturity levels, others on characteristics such as verbal hostility or dependence and anxiety, still others on the need for structure or support (Andrews, Bonta, and Hoge 1990a; Gendreau 1996; Palmer 1991; 1995; 1996; Van Voorhis 1987).

Participation in such programs is usually voluntary, and the evaluators of many of these programs stress that they should be created and carried out with meaningful input from the participants in the program. Thus there is no necessary contradiction between these approaches and the principle of voluntary participation. But the focus and the underlying method in these programs are significantly different from "will + skill" approaches. To take just one example, rewarding prisoners for maintaining self-control combines "will" with "skill": it assumes that the skills one needs for self-control and the will to control oneself must be simultaneously developed. "Will" is not a prerequisite for participation, nor is participation maintained by will alone. Instead, such approaches allow the desire to participate in programs to be fragile and elusive, the result of a number of different motivations rather than of a simple determination to change one's life.

The targeting of treatments and treatment staff to prisoners is also an important difference from "will + skill" approaches. Voluntary programs based on a "will + skill" approach normally leave the choice of programs to the prisoner, subject to restrictions based on skill level or security designation. But a targeted program approach suggests that prisoners will not be the best judge of the program that is most appropriate to them; or, at least, that they cannot be the only judges. Instead, programs must target an individual's propensities toward crime, propensities that the individual may not recognize as crime-related. This further complicates the simple "will + skill" understanding of rehabilitation, because it suggests that rehabilitation is not as simple as deciding to go straight. Instead, it suggests that rehabilitation is a matter of learning about what encourages law-breaking behavior in oneself, and building the will and the skill to address those propensities.

One important implication of the reasoning behind such programs is that incentives need not be considered an illegitimate interference with a prisoner's authentic motivation for participating in programs. Instead, in addition to encouraging prisoners to give programs a chance, incentives actually act as part of the treatment regimen, reinforcing prosocial behavior. Because programs targeted on criminogenic needs start from the assumption that the will to change needs to be created, and that the propensities inclining a person to commit crimes are difficult to resist, reacting to an incentive is not a "con" on the part of a prisoner. Instead, it is a way to learn to prefer behaving rightly.

This approach to programs is attractive on both theoretical and practical grounds. Theoretically, it offers an alternative to "will + skill" programs by presenting a more nuanced understanding of psychology; the propositions that it is based on are also clear enough to allow for research into both overall program outcomes and individual aspects of the causal mechanism. There are some early indications of success: in a comprehensive study of thirty-five programs selected for their adherence to needs- and responsivity-based criteria, all but two were found to reduce recidivism. Twenty of the thirty-five lowered recidivism rates by at least 25 percent in comparison with a control group, and the average reduction in recidivism was 50 percent (Andrews, Zinger, et al. 1990b). This study has been subjected to some methodological critiques, most trenchantly because it evaluated both studies designed according to needs/responsivity criteria and studies whose results were interpreted in accordance with needs/responsivity criteria only after the fact (Lab and Whitehead 1990;

Logan et al. 1991). Conclusions about the ultimate effectiveness of such programs will require that more programs be designed around such criteria and then carefully assessed. However, this line of research shows promise precisely because its theoretical presuppositions are coherent, clear, and testable.

Practically, programs which seek to create "will" as well as "skill" are attractive as well. Return to Charles Anthony, whose story opened this chapter, for a moment. Skills alone have not helped him avoid prison, and planning has disappointed him. What he needs is something else—a better understanding of how to avoid the money which "is like an addiction." He needs a set of strategies to "keep him away from what he was involved in before," and a better sense of "what gives you hope" (5MB). He needs, in other words, the self-knowledge and the coping skills whose lack made him susceptible to crime before. And this, precisely, is what programs that focus on "will" as well as "skill" can contribute.

For such programs to take hold in extensive enough ways to provide for a fair evaluation, however, two obstacles must be overcome. The first is a set of historical parallels that reach even farther back than the 1960s medical experiments that gave behavioral modification programs a bad name. Attempts at classifying and treating prisoners individually, according to some notion of their criminogenic needs, were introduced in the 1920s. Systems of classification for prisoners, based on the work of psychologists such as Dr. Bernard Glueck, slowly spread throughout the state systems; coincidentally, this work gained recognition as the mass of American prisons became places of idleness, where schemes to keep prisoners busy through entertainment were the primary response to prison overcrowding and to mounting business and labor opposition to prison factories. Classification schemes gained support among prison administrators from the 1930s to the 1950s, but treatment based on classification never became widespread. Instead, once sorted into categories, prisoners entered prisons in which staff were either too overwhelmed or too ill-trained to establish discipline, prison gang leaders were often entrusted with maintaining order, and idleness and prison brutality encouraged riots. Thus, when classification for the expressed purpose of rehabilitation disappeared in the 1970s, it was not only associated with the more egregious examples of behavior modification but also with the disturbance-prone and dehumanizing prisons of the era (McKelvey 1977; Rotman 1995).

Classification and targeted treatment thus start with a bad name, albeit one not wholly deserved when the historical record is carefully examined. But despite the injustice of blaming classification for the problems of the pre-1970s prison, the historical example does illustrate an important point. Rehabilitation efforts simply cannot proceed without attention to their institutional context. If programs are to have a chance to succeed, they need to give staff and prisoners an immediate reason to participate, by helping to keep order and to alleviate boredom in the prison. Otherwise the programs will be aborted or ignored, even actively opposed, by the staff and prisoners whose participation is required for them to function. This does not mean that programs can be used simply to keep order: making programs available without attentiveness to institutional values easily leads to their subversion. Using the language of behavioral modification to legitimize the prison's existing punishment and sanctioning systems is only one example of the ways in which programs can be misused. Ignoring the role of institutional context is a certain way to make sure that history will discredit rehabilitation again.

A second lesson from this history is also important. Classification was discredited in part because it was never integrated into the daily fabric of prison life. Instead, it served mostly as a diagnostic tool for wardens, useful primarily in the assignment of prisoners to prisons, work camps, lower-security work positions, and later to parole (McKelvey 1977:328–30). Classification without further treatment is information that prisoners have no access to and that does not help them. To compound the problem, prisoners also know that that information allows prison officials to make important decisions about their lives, decisions that they may often disagree with but have no power to challenge. By contrast, "will + skill" programs at least allow participants to feel as if they are "doing" their time, getting something out of it for themselves. For the promise of classification and targeted treatment to succeed, diagnosis must be followed by activity, and activity that prisoners feel they benefit from, both immediately and in the future.

It is from this perspective that the question of voluntary and mandatory participation in programs needs to be reexamined. One way of understanding consent is that individuals have fixed notions of what they believe and want, which programs must respect. Another way of understanding consent is that it is always contingent on circumstances; people change their minds, and thus consent can be earned, withdrawn, and changed. Most types of rehabilitation programs operate exclusively on the first, taking participation as the measure of consent and thus isolating the prisoner's decision to participate from both incentives and sanctions. This standard has the advantage of protecting against the worst abuses that have been performed in the name of rehabilitation. But it has also legitimated the failure to earn prisoners' consent—to question their beliefs about and meet their needs for rehabilitation, in such a way that would persuade prisoners to participate in programs that they might otherwise reject. One advantage of taking seriously the requirements of successful implementation is that it makes the need to attract prisoners' participation a central part of the analysis of a program. As such, thinking about successful implementation can do more than improve the delivery of existing programs; it can lead to a reexamination of their design.

Using Implementation to Improve Programs

Among the most valuable legacies of the rejection of mandatory treatment in the 1960s and 1970s is the attention critics focused upon prisoners' dignity and autonomy. By insisting that it was wrong to coerce prisoners into programs with the threat of indefinite sentences, to subject prisoners to sanctions, physical pain, or psychological suffering as part of "treatment," or to target prisoners' political beliefs as an obstacle to their rehabilitation, activists were able to stem obvious abuses. Equally important, their criticisms serve as an important lesson about the slippery slope of paternalism. As one critic wrote, "To be helpless . . . is not necessarily to be in jeopardy. To be helpless and unloved is the matrix of disaster. . . . It is not benevolence we should abandon, but rather the naive faith that benevolence can mitigate the mischievousness of power" (Gaylin et al. 1978: 122–23).

In the decades since the 1960s, some of these lessons have been lost, or put aside. The public debate over welfare reform has prompted vigorous public defenses of the virtues of paternalism, most of which would have been unthinkable only twenty years earlier (Mead 1997; Kaus 1992). Various mandatory programs have already made their way back into the prison system: not only do many states and the federal system require educational standards for prisoners, but federal sentencing policies now require prisoners convicted of drug or drug-related felonies to undergo 40 hours of drug education. Thus there is ample precedent for a re-introduction of mandatory programming, and seemingly little memory of its abuses.

Nevertheless, attempting to guard against the abuses of mandatory programming should not force prisoner advocates into an unthinking defense of the principle that reform doesn't work unless people want to change. As this chapter has argued, such a claim leads to its own abuses: a lack of commitment to involving prisoners in programs, and a lack of interest in working toward and monitoring rehabilitative program activities. Paying attention to successful implementation reminds both advocates and critics of programming to look at the day-to-day practice of programs, allowing experience rather than abstractions to be their guide. In practice, for instance, mandatory and voluntary programs can be indistinguishable if program requirements on paper are subverted by staff and prisoners for whom the requirements are costly and thus unattractive. And many of the defects of mandatory programming can be miti-gated by taking the definition of successful implementation seriously: providing incentives to ensure the cooperation of staff and prisoners, and ensuring that a match exists between institutional values and the rehabil-itative potential of programs.

Proponents of mandatory programs often argue that a particular skill—for instance, basic literacy—is so important that all prisoners should achieve it whether they wish to or not. Thus, in the federal system, the refusal to participate in GED class can lead to restriction to the lowest prison pay grade, to the refusal of halfway house placement, or even to disciplinary segregation. One can certainly argue that some or all of these sanctions are illegitimate. Yet it is also important to note that these re-strictions are often ignored in implementation. In every prison I visited, mandatory students who refused to take the lessons seriously were al-lowed to sleep or otherwise withdraw their attention from the classroom, as long as they had signed up for class. In prisons where programs were unsuccessfully implemented, these resisters outnumbered the students who were interested in learning, causing classes to resemble babysitting sessions. On the other hand, when programs were successfully imple-mented, students were excited about learning and engaged even though they were assigned to class as mandatory students; these programs of-fered them the chance to do their time in an interesting way, and helped them feel as if they were getting something back. In these prisons, the mandatory learning requirement probably introduced to students who would otherwise have ignored the programs the opportunity to learn.

Without licensing all mandatory programming, therefore, this exam-ple suggests that it is important to think about how mandatory program-ming is implemented. In programs that are successfully implemented, mandatory enrollment can be a tool to compel prisoners to try a program that is challenging and intensive enough to keep prisoners' interest once they start. By contrast, in unsuccessfully implemented programs, prisoner resistance often discourages staff from pushing prisoners to be involved, making the "mandatory" participation actually voluntary in practice. Coercion, too, has to be implemented; and implementing coercion with-out some benefit to prisoners can raise the cost to staff high enough to motivate them to ignore the requirements.

Of course, the incentives that programs can offer to prisoners can be coercive as well. If there is no other way to earn money in prison than by "voluntarily" signing up for AA meetings, the incentive certainly re-sembles coercion. Again, however, the only way to judge whether an in-centive will be coercive is to understand how it will be implemented on the ground. Many are so innocuous as not to be real incentives. Paying prisoners a stipend to enroll in classes, for instance, may look like an incentive. But if classes are scheduled during work hours, so that the choice to attend classes means forgoing an opportunity to earn pocket money or save for restitution and family support payments, then a stipend merely makes the choice between programming and working possible. On the other hand, inducements such as early release for participation in programs are clearly more problematic. In these cases, the value of encouraging prisoners to participate in programs may not outweigh the threat to fair treatment or to the limits of acceptable coercion. But it does not follow that because some kinds of inducements or programs are illegitimate, all should be.

Equally important is the way in which the institutional values of the prison and the rehabilitative potential of programs clash or fit together. The fact that so many early behavioral modification programs were simply fancy names for the sanctions that prisons already had in place suggests that staff considered such programs valuable only insofar as they controlled prisoners' behavior. They were not presented with any reason to value a more thorough approach to programs—an approach that would have required staff to examine their disciplinary practices and to change their interactions with prisoners. This could be because programs were not presented as being consistent with values, like professionalism or prestige, which they already held. It could be because values they held, like staff solidarity, might have clashed with a system that required developing trust and legitimacy with prisoners. Or it could be that the values staff held, for reasons justifiable or not, were values that sanctioned brutality and coercion toward prisoners.[10] Indeed, given the ways in which implementation of these programs was subverted, it is equally plausible that the prisons would have been coercive and sanctions brutal even if rehabilitative programs had not existed. While the programs may have contained unjustifiable restrictions on prisoners' liberty, there is little reason to believe that such restrictions should be blamed on the fact that such programs were mandatory.

The implication here should be clear: for programs to be successfully implemented with respect to rehabilitation, they must fit into their institutional context. Thus programs will look and be justified somewhat differently in different prisons. In some prisons, this justification should be relatively easy; in others, it could be much more difficult to achieve. The less that institutional values sanction interaction between staff and prisoners, the more that such values reject benefits or assistance for prisoners, the less possible it is to successfully implement programs. This does not mean that staff must believe wholeheartedly in rehabilitation for it to be

---

[10] Such values might have included the belief that all prisoners were guilty of heinous crimes and that staff were delegated to punish, rather than merely confine, them.

implemented: staff are not believers in rehabilitation at Antelope Valley or Beaverton, and they will not be at most prisons. But at both those prisons, there were points of contact between institutional values and rehabilitative purposes—communication between staff and prisoners was valued at both prisons, and professionalism and prestige, respectively, sanctioned the program staff's autonomy and expertise. This is the kind of match that must be present for successful implementation to occur.

Implementation is not a panacea for badly designed programs, voluntary or mandatory; nor can it guarantee that participants will avoid crimes or that programs will work. But taking an implementation perspective can force a reexamination of ideological beliefs that limit what programs can do. While it does not broaden the scope of "will + skill" programs, attention to implementation can catch flaws like underenrollment and lack of attention to program quality, which the "will + skill" approach makes particularly likely. Although it does not eliminate the potential for coercion in mandatory programs, attention to implementation can prevent those requirements from being ignored or misused.

Successful implementation may seem like a frail reed on which to hang the avoidance of crime. It is. Much of the evidence suggests that programs alone will not work: skills are of little use if jobs are not available, family relationships are hard to mend from within the prison, and even emotional preparation for dealing with disappointment is different from actually facing disillusionment, day after day after release. If ex-prisoners are to reintegrate into society as full members, as people who have a stake in the society as family members, workers, and citizens, both community expectations and prisoners must be changed. But while succeeding at implementation cannot solve all of these problems, it is an integral part of solving some of them. To overlook its role will not make other reforms easier, and it may make some of them more difficult.

Conclusion _____

Deliberately Successful Implementation

DOING TIME, DOING MY TIME, AND
LETTING THE TIME DO ME

> I'm going to do my time, not let my time do me.
> (*Prisoner [3GO]*)

DOING TIME. It is a phrase that has entered our language, both in its stripped-down version and in the folk warnings of rhyming slang, "You do the crime, you do the time." The very familiarity of the phrase, however, deadens the listener to the violence implicit in both the words and the experience. On the street, to "do" a woman is to rape her. In prison, men speak of "*letting the time do me*"—of allowing the aimlessness of confinement, the isolation from family and friends, the daily strategies of seeking forgetfulness in drugs or alcohol or prison rituals to strip them of initiative and accomplishment. Their frustration and resentment is played out in another phrase, "we're doing *their* time"; even our time is no longer our own, because we have no control over how we spend it.

Prisoners are not the only ones who "do time." Prison staff do so as well, as when they talk about their "sentence" as the time they've got to do until retirement. Less flippantly, doing time for them is the eight-hour shift, where if they do their job well they can be paralyzed by boredom and if they make a mistake, they can be killed. When they are simply guardians of a human warehouse, their work can seem as pointless as the time the prisoners are doing. And the conditions of their work are exacerbated by their own type of isolation. Though they leave the prison daily, they live among a public that often considers prison staff barely a step up from the prisoners they guard: whether their neighbors believe that prisons are too easy on prisoners or too brutal toward them, prison staff are an easy target for their scorn and indignation.

The conditions of confinement—of exclusion from a world of unstructured experience, of isolation from friends and family, of loss of control over the most basic decisions like when one will eat or whom one will associate with—may be fitting punishment for people whose actions have harmed other people and the social order. That is a question outside the scope of this study. Whatever the justification for confinement, however, it has ancillary consequences for staff and prisoner behavior within the prison, and for prisoners' behavior once they leave. "Doing time" turns prisoner and staff attention in toward the prison, making that location and that life their primary reference point. It makes the satisfaction of needs within the prison—and not punishment, deterrence, or rehabilitation—the overriding concern.

Those needs—avoiding violence, battling isolation, making one's time meaningful—require some creative strategizing to meet under the constraints of the prison environment. The implementation of programs within each prison is dependent upon the history of the attempts to meet those needs, the resulting staff and prisoner strategies, and the values that explain, justify, and transmit them. Only accidentally will those strategies and values encourage prisoners to "go straight"; only by chance will they allow staff to act as enforcers, advisors, or role models for prisoners' future lives. This is not to say that those things will not happen: the attempts of prisoners to "do *my* time"—to make the time their own and create an alternative identity, primarily through participation in programs—can lead to the persistence of that identity, that path to self-worth, after release. But such consequences are the byproduct, not the purpose, of prison strategies.

This would not be so bad if prison were in fact a discrete event, unconnected to the future behavior of prisoners or to the various goals—incapacitation, deterrence, rehabilitation, punishment—of a penal system. But with over 1.3 million prisoners incarcerated in the U.S., the vast majority of whom will be released; with the amount of money spent upon maintaining prison systems; with the fact that the time away from jobs, families, and daily functioning is inevitably a barrier to a released prisoner's ability to find and hold a job, nurture a family, or act as a responsible citizen; with all of these consequences, treating prison as if it were unconnected to policy goals or to the future chances of prisoners is a fiction we can ill-afford to indulge. Instead, to combat the inevitable disadvantage of a prison sentence, to make time in prison meaningful in some way, to accomplish any of the multiple goals implicit in the conception of our penal system, those who make policy must find some way to piggyback their goals onto the strategies that staff and prisoners adopt to satisfy their prison-focused needs. To put it another way, they must learn how to accomplish deliberately what now happens accidentally.

This may sound like a drastic reversal of the usual understanding of policy. Certainly much of the focus in public policy is on designing tools to fulfill one's goals; classic works like Herbert Kaufman's *The Forest Ranger* (1960), Martha Derthick's *Agency Under Stress* (1990), and James Q. Wilson's *Bureaucracy* (1989) examine how entire organizations were designed around a particular mission. But these works also make the point, explicitly and implicitly, that tasks falling outside of the organization's central mission are neglected or badly implemented, even when the organization's leadership considers them a priority. The prison studies in this book explain why. It is rare, though not impossible, for programs to immediately mesh with existing institutional values or to immediately satisfy institutional needs. Moreover, because organizational values and needs are mutually reinforcing across an array of situations, aberrant or unfamiliar tasks are likely to be reinterpreted so that they fit into the existing context (Spillane 1998; Vaughan 1996). The possibility that new tasks will quickly change existing practices and beliefs is remote.

Learning how to design tools and organizations directed at achieving particular goals is important. But situations in which it is possible to do this are the exception and not the rule. Learning how to implement policy when it is impractical, unwise, or impossible to redesign an organization—learning to implement within existing contexts instead of hoping or expecting to mandate more appropriate ones—is the missing half of implementation studies. And given the move toward devolution and local control, toward non- and for-profit contracting out of government services, and toward empowering workers, it may be the more important half.

Clearly a study of rehabilitation in prisons can only begin to sketch out the ways in which some of these challenges can be met. But it can be surprisingly helpful. For in the ways that the implementation of rehabilitation programs is accidentally successful, and in the ways in which it unintentionally fails, there is a lesson in the transformation of policy on the ground. By understanding that transformation, we can understand why common attempts to prevent it by limiting discretion, or to harness it through training and increased discretion, so often fail. We can also learn how the alternative—recognizing policy as a joint project of policymakers, staff, and target groups—might succeed.

Policy as a Joint Project

The studies in this book show that implementation failures which might seem the result of incompetence or deliberate resistance are often reasonable responses to the mismatch between programs and their organizational context. When policies are bent to purposes other than those that policymakers anticipated, it is not because staff do not understand their work. Instead, it is precisely because they try to make sense of their work, and thus to understand their jobs as a series of related tasks all bent toward the same purpose. This naturally leads them to refer each new policy to the values that are most salient in their organization. Similarly, when staff or a policy's target group does not participate in a policy as expected, it is not because they are shirking their responsibilities. Rather, they are usually trying to satisfy the needs created by their organizational environment—and the incentives or sanctions attached to a particular policy are useful to them only insofar as they help satisfy those needs.

But the ability of staff and of target groups to shape a policy and a world—to redefine for themselves what policy requires, and thus to subvert, to neglect, or to abandon the intentions of policymakers—creates, of course, an implementation problem. Policymakers have tried to address this problem in two ways. One is to think of the problem as one of incompatible preferences, and then to try to impose their preferences by limiting the discretion of staff and regulating the responses of target groups as much as possible. These limits on discretion can take the form of specifying each action that staff must take, monitoring staff behavior through a variety of checks and balances, or linking uniform incentives and strict sanctions to clear behavioral expectations for the targets of policy. The second is to think of the problem as one of differences in location, so that policymakers have better information about desirable ends, but staff (and perhaps target groups) have better information about the best means to the end. The solution is then to increase the skills and expand the discretion of staff: telling staff what the goals are, providing resources, and letting staff and target groups come to their own decisions about how best to meet those goals.

The first approach can be justified by appealing to the need for accountability and uniformity; the second, by appealing to the efficient division of labor and the enhanced responsibility that comes with "ownership" of a solution. The studies in this book, however, suggest that neither set of ideals fully describes the realities of what staff and target groups do with policy. The requirements used to enforce compliance and limit the discretion of staff and target groups can themselves be subverted when staff re-interpret their meaning in accordance with organizational values. They can be neglected when they impose a set of burdens without immediate offsetting incentives for staff and target groups. They can be abandoned or ignored when they seem neither relevant nor beneficial to staff and target groups. Thus accountability and uniformity do not follow from requirements alone: GED classes for prisoners without a highschool education are mandatory everywhere, but at Evergreen and Drake they amount to little more than busywork and mandatory attendance.

Similarly, giving staff the discretion to reach a policy solution by themselves only works if they "see" the same problem that policymakers do.

If they do not, they may use the discretion to create a solution that they find reasonable, but which does not solve the problem that policymakers had in mind. Training staff, so that they understand the problem as policymakers have defined it and are given some tools with which to solve it, can be more effective. But when it improves the implementation of policy, it does so not only because the staff in question acquire more skills, but because the training or the recruitment process inculcates new values in the staff, alters the needs they perceive, or both. When this does not happen, staff can find themselves in a situation where the skills they have, the directives they are given, are not consistent with the context in which those skills are to be used. As a result, policies are subverted, neglected, or simply abandoned, and the problems underlying the need for a policy solution remain.

Similar problems result when the context of a policy's target population is not considered. Policies that are meant to change the behavior of a particular group are often designed in accordance with some theory about what motivates that group's behavior. Thus companies are given sanctions for polluting, workers given subsidies for retraining, students threatened with disciplinary procedures if they are truant from school, and prisoners promised monetary rewards for passing a GED exam. But such policy instruments are also used within a context: sanctions may be large or small in comparison with the other costs or benefits of a behavior, rewards may differ in meaning from one social class to another. Without an understanding of the context of a policy instrument, the designers of a policy essentially shoot in the dark, unable to do more than guess what might serve as a meaningful inducement to change. As with staff, the target group of a policy has a vital role in implementation: their participation in policy cannot be assumed, and it is always crucial.

This suggests that a different approach is necessary. Certainly, policies can be more clearly explained to staff and target groups, and assistance can be provided to them to change organizational routines and practices that stand in the way of fulfilling particular policy goals. But these explanations and this assistance presuppose an understanding of particular implementation contexts: the explanations will not make sense, and the assistance will not be appropriate, unless those who provide explanations and assistance understand the organizational context they are entering. Getting the values and the problems right requires both that implementation be monitored and that the monitors understand that they are fitting a policy to a particular context—not demanding that established practices and beliefs make way for a policy. Policy thus becomes a joint project, incorporating the aims and instruments specified by policymakers, but incorporating as well the preconceptions and the interests of the world in which staff and target groups must operate.

For monitors, this requires an initial understanding of how staff currently conceive of their work—how they explain their jobs, how they understand requirements and expectations, how they describe the values that guide their interaction with their clients. It then requires the willingness to shape policy instruments in conjunction with these staff: to allow them to explain how a new task will change what they are doing, to alter it so that it will fit in with their other tasks, to tinker with ways in which their new tasks can make their jobs as a whole more rewarding, more integrated, or less complicated. A process like this takes account of the values staff have, and uses them to frame the policy that needs to be implemented. It also builds in incentives for staff participation that make sense given the needs they must meet. It reduces the possibility that a policy will be subverted due to mistranslation, neglected because staff have no incentive to rearrange their work so as to take on another task, or abandoned because staff both misunderstand what they are asked to do and have no reason to do it. (See also Feldman 1989.)

The deliberate creation of successful implementation also requires a clearer understanding of a policy's target group than is normal. Here the context that matters is the context of their lives: the ways in which they manage the demands upon them, and the ways in which any particular set of policy demands will affect their coping strategies. Just as taking on any new or aberrant task has consequences for everything else staff do, responding to the requirements of a particular policy has consequences for people's lives. Therefore, incentives that help people manage their other problems are more likely to motivate participation, while incentives that require them to take on new tasks are likely to be ignored. By making a serious attempt to understand the target group's needs, policymakers can identify the incentives that are likely to be effective. This can prevent the target group from subverting implementation—from paper compliance with requirements so as to gain access to resources that can then be used in other ways.

An approach to implementation that takes context seriously would thus encourage implementors to intervene in the translations and adjustments that staff and target groups now attempt by themselves. In some ways, the role of the monitor would be similar to Eugene Bardach's "fixer"—an intermediary with the job of resolving disputes, keeping implementation on track, pressuring lawmakers for more resources when necessary, and prodding implementors for more action when appropriate (Bardach 1977). But rather than creating a specialized group of coaches for implementation, supervisors at the organizational or regional level could ask the right questions and suggest at least some variation in staff practice or interaction. Supervisors, at least one level up from the routine supervision that line staff face, will be close enough to understand the

idiosyncratic practices and beliefs of the organization, but also distant
enough to understand the broader policy problem. They should also have
the political authority to warn that policy failure is imminent despite
signs of successful implementation: when active participation in activities
that are consistent with some purpose do not produce the results that
policymakers hoped.

Admittedly, this set of suggestions is an extrapolation from the studies
in this book. The cases of successful implementation I discuss are created
not by deliberate attempts to make policy meet the needs and fit the values
of staff and target groups, but rather by the fortunate conjunction of policy purposes with pre-existing needs and values in the context of the particular prisons. It is possible that such conjunctions cannot be created.
For instance, attempts to reframe an aberrant task to fit values available
in the implementation context might not be credible, simply because staff
are smart enough to know that the task was always aberrant before. Attempts to understand the needs faced by staff or target groups can also
backfire if staff and target groups lie to supervisors who indirectly control
those incentives, or discount peer pressure because they do not wish to be
seen as susceptible to others' opinions.

The challenge this points to is that of creating trust between those who
make or monitor policy, and the staff and target groups who feel its effects. Staff and policy targets do not resist policy, or each other, simply
out of natural orneriness. Instead they do so because, directly or indirectly, program mandates or sanctions force them to abandon coping
strategies that at least have the virtues of familiarity and predictability.
Reinterpretations of policy goals are often attempts to bring coherence to
contradictory or ambiguous performance standards. Even the diversion
of resources is often a creative attempt to do more with less. One advantage of making implementation fit a particular context is that it can force
policy monitors, and through them eventually policymakers, to confront
the tradeoffs required to reconcile policies made at different times for
different purposes, or to reconcile contradictory goals embedded in the
same policy.

But given the fact that such contradictions often mask policy conflict at
the level of policymakers, implementation monitors can hardly expect or
promise that such conflicts will easily resolve themselves (Brodkin 1990).
While one of the avowed purposes of the field of implementation studies
is to improve the design of policies, policy design is rarely based on ease
of implementation. Instead, the provisions of policy result from legislative and bureaucratic conflicts over political orientation and constituency
interests, logrolling and symbolism. These conflicts will not disappear.
Thus, programs designed to be easy to implement are unlikely to be very

common. Instead, implementation will continue to be based on process values: open communication between staff, target groups, and implementation monitors; the resolution of organizational problems that seem to have little to do with the implementation of a particular policy; and the willingness to accept a variety of site-based solutions rather than a general, all-purpose approach.

This last point is particularly important because of the wide variety of implementation contexts. Prisons are particularly strong organizations, in which the importance of institutional needs and values dominates both staff and prisoner decisions. But other implementation contexts, in which staff and target groups also have needs and values that do not originate in the implementing organization, are also possible. For instance, in a federal agency with a professional staff that take their values and incentives from professional associations and future job opportunities in the private sector, the implementation context might be a profession rather than an agency (Golden 1992). It is even possible to have a policy whose implementation is left to individual citizens—for instance, store owners who must enforce bans on underage purchases of alcohol—where the implementation context is individual rather than collective. In cases like these, asking what values or needs drive owners, especially with respect to their experience with earlier regulations, still offers useful insights into the possibilities of successful implementation. But these values and needs are less likely to be consistent from individual to individual, and the communication and shared outcomes required for mutually reinforcing behavior are less likely to develop. Similarly, targets of any particular policy can be a homogenous group whose decisions are often interdependent—prisoners, welfare recipients—or a heterogeneous group with different interests and different levels of power in relationship to implementing staff. As with implementors, the more diffuse the target group is, the more difficult it is to discover their values, or judge the "value" that incentives will have for them.

Implementation monitors face different challenges when the context they must understand is an organizational culture, as opposed to when it is more diffuse. An understanding of organizational "sensemaking" explains how new policies can eventually change an organization, paradoxically by their adaptation to the organization in which they are placed (Weick 1995). In organizations like prisons, where the interdependence of staff and the dependence or "nonvoluntariness" of prisoners (Lipsky 1980) create a set of mutually reinforcing beliefs and practices, programs that challenge those beliefs or force revisions to those practices run the risk of quickly being revised or ignored themselves. But the relative coherence of values and needs within an organization, and their relevance to staff and policy targets who otherwise might have little in common, also make it possible for implementation monitors to understand the relevant context more efficiently.

Nor is change in organizations as impossible as it may seem. One of the lessons of this study is that institutional values and needs are continually being reinterpreted. As staff try to make a particular task consistent with the values of the organization, they broaden their understanding of their organization's mission. As prisoners decide whether participating in programs is worth it, they contribute to an environment where participation is valued, or scorned, by the majority. This process of reinterpretation can be harnessed in order to explain new programs and to alter existing practices. And while it always works incrementally, the fact that changes in the culture then go on to change practices and alter beliefs in other areas means that change can eventually be quite far-reaching.

By contrast, attempts to implement within a more diffuse culture, or in a context where no culture binds either implementors or target groups, are likely to have more early success. It is unlikely that policymakers would be so uninformed that the incentives they designed into a policy would be inappropriate for everyone in a diverse group. Moreover, when previous experience with policy or with government agencies is the main source of a citizen's information about how to interpret a new policy, what citizens "know" about policy often matches what policymakers, who design new policies upon the template of older efforts, "know." But the diversity of possible experiences, and thus of the sources of contextual values and needs, can prove a barrier to extending implementation beyond the groups that policymakers best understand. To the extent that policymakers best understand the groups who most resemble them in social background or who have the most resources to write their experience into law, both the design of policy, and its salutary effects when properly implemented, end up benefiting the best-represented.

The difficulties of learning how to use context to implement policy, and the wide variety of implementation contexts that exist, mean that research in this area has much ground to cover. A study that examined change in organizations over time and its effect on policy implementation might, for instance, help to explain how to frame policies more deliberately to assist in implementation on the ground. This would be particularly effective if it could contrast deliberate, leader-centered attempts at changing culture with organic, event- or environment-induced change. Other studies examining the effect of implementation context in different venues—perhaps by looking at a policy that was implemented by strong organizations in some places, by diverse and diffuse citizen groups in another—could explain when and what kinds of context are important. Perhaps most importantly, experiments in treating implementation as a joint project of policymakers, staff, and target groups could discover the likelihood of creating trust among these three groups and the techniques necessary for doing so.

Suggesting that more and better research is needed, however, is not enough to ensure that implementation will or can be more systematically improved. The prospect that such research would ever be put to use is contingent upon a political environment willing to allow particular programs and policy approaches the freedom to improvise and, one hopes, to improve. That freedom is difficult to obtain if programs are continually subjected to outcome evaluations which jeopardize the program's survival and limit the program changes that can be made. A focus on program implementation requires a prior political condition: that a commitment be made to programs that have not been proven to "work."

Successful Implementation and Successful Policy

One of the great "success stories" in the attempt to combine social scientific knowledge with policymaking has been the growing use of experimental design in the evaluation of social programs. This method of program evaluation takes as its model an approach to causation derived from the natural sciences.[1] In this model, the "treatment," or the variable that is hypothesized to cause some effect, operates in isolation. All other possible causes are accounted for, either by isolating the environment in which the experiment takes place, or by averaging out the effects of the environment through randomization. A comparison of the results of some test or examination for those who were treated, and an equivalent group who were not, then determines whether an effect was produced.

Under this model, evaluating a "program" becomes comparable to evaluating a new medicine. To test the effect of a particular medicine on a disease, one would draw from a group of those afflicted, randomly select some but not all for treatment, and then compare the rates of recovery, relapse, or other indicators of illness for the group which was treated and the group which was not. Similarly, to test the effect of a job-training program, one would draw from a group of the unemployed, randomly select some but not all for the training, and then compare the unemployment rate, earnings, dependence on public aid or other indicators of "success" of the two groups. Random selection, in this case, eliminates the possibility that those who were treated or trained are systematically different in ways that could interfere with the evaluation of the treatment. Careful selection of the initial pool from which subjects are drawn can

---

[1] The discussion in this section draws heavily from Cook and Campbell (1979), Chap. 1.

also eliminate, or at least control for, contextual differences such as the unemployment rate in the area.

As a method, an experimental research design is thus very good at answering questions of cause and effect, when they are carefully and specifically tailored. Because the treatment is the only difference between the experimental and the control group, spurious or accidental causes are easily ruled out. When random assignment plausibly accounts for all contextual effects, the independent effect of the treatment can also be isolated.

But while this type of evaluation can be valuable, its assumptions are made questionable by a context-centered understanding of implementation. If treatments are mediated or translated by an implementation context, the nature of the treatment being tested is changed. There is an important difference between a job training program in which the purpose is to keep people enrolled, and one in which the purpose is to train the enrollees. Evaluations which focus primarily on outcome measures, however, may miss the fact that the treatment they are "testing" is in fact something different from what they planned to test. Randomization does not solve this problem, because the effect of the implementation context is on treatment integrity; context is not a variable that operates on the treatment and control group in the same ways, and thus cannot be controlled for.

A second problem has to do with the lessons that a positive evaluation can teach. Assume that an experiment is carefully monitored enough to distinguish both the treatment and the way it has been altered by the implementation context; assume further that it produces successful outcomes. That treatment can now, in theory, be replicated elsewhere. But in fact, implementation contexts will differ from site to site: the variation in prison cultures in this study shows that context can vary even when the organizations are similar. This suggests that the replicable results promised by program evaluation may be of limited utility. Unless organizations can be remade in the image of the one in the successful test, all a successful evaluation gives is an assurance that working to implement a particular treatment is worthwhile. But to be most effective, the values and incentives that will support that treatment in each site need to be drawn from the site, not imported from elsewhere. In practice, then, a description of successful programs will look more like a portfolio of functionally equivalent but dissimilar programs, not a blueprint that can guarantee success across a multitude of sites.

This is not to say that outcome evaluations are of little use; for instance, it is important to be able to identify functionally equivalent programs and any common elements that may contribute to their success.

But without ensuring treatment integrity through successful implementation of a particular program, program evaluations are bound to return disappointing results. For this reason, Donald Campbell, a pioneer in the field of evaluation research, suggested that social scientists "evaluate no program until it is proud." This would avoid "devastating negative or deceptive evaluations taken on programs known by the staffs to be not yet debugged, not yet working," while "par[ing] down our concept of program to that narrow aspect of it which is transportable, transmissible, and borrowable" (Campbell 1987:346–47). Getting implementation right, in other words, is a prerequisite to outcome evaluation. Failing to ensure successful implementation, or assuming that it can be part of the evaluation, means that the research runs the risk of unnecessarily and wrongly condemning programs and the theory behind them.

One clear implication of this book's findings, therefore, is that process evaluation should be taken as seriously as outcome evaluation. Learning what was actually done to implement a policy, why those decisions were made, and what problems those decisions caused is integral to creating successful implementation, and crucial to determining whether outcome evaluations are even advisable. But these kinds of process evaluations are sidestepped or, at the least, made much less useful when legislative requirements mandate early outcome evaluations. Such requirements can prove a straitjacket on changes in policy in midstream, because those changes might confound the validity of outcome evaluations. They may even divert scarce resources away from improving program operations and toward evaluation. They thus cut directly against both the need and the capacity for improving implementation. By contrast, including funding for process evaluations well before outcome evaluations are mandated, and encouraging evaluators to look both at the *process* of implementing a policy and the larger *context* within which staff and target groups interact, can make both policies and eventual outcome assessments more useful.

But Campbell's suggestion also points to another, equally serious problem with the growing dependence on evaluation research to justify programs—the political uses to which experimental design can be put. The quantitative rigor, and thus the scientific reliability, of experimental design allows politicians to relegate the solution of a complicated political problem to a supposedly neutral referee. Maintaining an agnostic stance on social programs—"I'll support it if it works"—allows a politician to claim credit if a program succeeds, but create distance if the program fails. Giving one's commitment to a program, especially if it is directed at a group whose behavior is considered a social problem, is politically hazardous and potentially costly. Conditioning one's commitment upon program success, however, allows a politician to present herself as sympathetic but tough—willing to lend people the bootstraps, but requiring that they pull themselves up.

Unfortunately, however, conditioning support for programs upon their success guarantees that many programs will fail. For programs that are not implemented successfully will not succeed; and implementing programs successfully demands a level of prior commitment to the program. Implementation requires work: work to discover the values and needs that staff and participants bring to a program, and more work to figure out how these can be balanced with the intentions of policymakers. It requires the wise use of flexibility, for that balance will vary with the history and the institutional arrangements present at a particular site. It demands the willingness to address problems that may not be linked to the introduction of programs themselves. All of this takes time, a minimum commitment of resources, and a certain insulation from threats to the program's existence. And political support is what makes that possible.

If this seems like asking policymakers to take a shot in the dark, it should be pointed out that this is, in fact, how most policy is made. There is no guarantee that an expensive weapons prototype will give the military an important strategic advantage, that deregulating the airline industry will increase earnings and hold down prices, that foreign aid will create foreign allies. But based on inference, logic, and practical needs, such policies are adopted—and then followed, amended, and reworked in order to maximize their chances of success. Persistence in the face of initial failure, of course, has a built-in bias toward inefficiency; certainly persistence without monitoring or attempted improvement is inefficient. But persistence with attention to implementation is the only way that policies will eventually succeed.

The recognition that implementation is contextual sets the parameters for this kind of political persistence. It suggests an alternative explanation to incompetence or venality when the stories people hear are those of classrooms in which teachers struggle vainly to keep order, work training programs where idleness rather than skill development is the norm, and drug treatment groups in which self-indulgent whining takes up the counseling hour. It cautions against the overenthusiastic attempt to take a program that has worked in one site and duplicate it in others. It recognizes that staff and that target groups have a role as part of the solution— indeed, as policy *makers* in their own right. And in doing all of these things, it moves the polity a little farther away from the easy promises that some politicians make about ending some social ill, and from the self-righteous attacks that other politicians launch when those promises don't work.

Reform in the Making

Neither prisoners nor prison staff are irretrievably locked into mere acceptance of the conditions of their confinement. Instead, they learn to "do *my* time"—to make the time their own by doing things that they consider worthwhile. Prisoners create an identity around being a college student, or a master woodworker, or a dedicated athlete; prison staff see themselves as proud police, as canny, can't-be-fooled advisors, as educators and ministers. What Erving Goffman observed in 1961 is as true of prisons as other closed societies, and perhaps of many open ones.

> In every social establishment, there are official expectations as to what the participant owes the establishment. . . . [But] whenever we look at a social establishment, we find a counter to this first theme: we find that participants decline in some way to accept the official view of what they should be putting into and getting out of the organization and, behind this, of what sort of self and world they are to accept for themselves. Where enthusiasm is expected, there will be apathy; where loyalty, there will be disaffection; where attendance, absenteeism; where robustness, some kind of illness; where deeds are to be done, varieties of inactivity. We find a multitude of homely little histories, each in its way a movement of liberty. (Goffman 1961:304–5)

In this book, I have recounted these "movements of liberty": the varied ways in which prison staff and prisoners reconstruct the work of the prison, remaking prison programs into vehicles that meet their immediate institutional interests, and translating program purposes in ways that make sense to them. Although they are constrained by the rules governing the prison and the availability of resources, neither prisoners nor staff are passively subject to them. In claiming the time they do as "my" time, they assert some measure of control over a "total institution" whose defining characteristic is its power to control the lives of those it confines. In their actions they construct policy as it actually happens. Reform is theirs, to "make" or "unmake."

The realization that prison staff and prisoners have the power to reconstruct the prison leaves us with a choice. Under some conditions, resistance to official expectations will certainly resemble the kind of purposeful malingering that Goffman described so well. They can "do time" by forming staff cliques and prison gangs, which at times will violently oppose each other and at other times collaborate around smuggling contraband; they can "let the time do me" by resorting to alcoholism or drug abuse, or simple apathy. But under other conditions, staff and prisoners will choose to declare their freedom from official expectations by taking something back from the time that they are forced to spend. While not unaware that participating in programs or working with each other can be interpreted as compliance with prison norms, they recast their compliance as self-assertion. They "do *my* time."

We can take the implementation of rehabilitative programs seriously and deliberately enough to start a dialogue with staff and prisoners about how to do *their* time, to make it more likely that programs will attract active participation and plausibly encourage both prison order and self-improvement. Or we can let it haphazardly occur, finding some prisons in which programs will flourish, letting programs in other places fall by the wayside. The first does not guarantee that prisoners will be able to lead self-sufficient, law-abiding lives upon release. But the second condemns programs that might "work" to political attack and ridicule when they don't. Attention to implementation does not allow us to assume that what we do will always succeed. But it allows us to be sure that we have done what we can.

Research Design Meets Prison Administration: Methodological Notes

A COLLEAGUE of mine, Nancy Burns, says that the most important lesson graduate students can learn in classes on research methods is "all data are evil": anything one finds in a data set is inevitably mismeasured, misspecified, or missing for the purposes of a particular research question. One might add to that the admonition that "all research design is wrong." The best-laid plans of researchers often come to a shuddering halt when the exigencies of the real world loom before them; they slink sheepishly away when it turns out that the really interesting question uncovered by the research is one that they had not prepared to test; and they cower before the realization that the essential pieces of data are always those that have not been collected. But just as the solution for "evil data" is to confront its shortcomings rather than to give up on its analysis, the solution for faulty research design is to concede that every virtue of design comes with a tradeoff. Seen in this way, research design is less a standard to which one must mold the world than it is a tool to help us understand what the world has to tell us.

In this spirit, I offer three sets of thoughts about important tradeoffs in this study: the examination of implementation process instead of policy outcomes; the use of a cross-section rather than an in-depth, one-case design; and the focus on interviews over observation. The first two were intentional, the last accidental, yet all had consequences that I could not fully appreciate until I was long out of the field. Understanding those consequences is an important part of understanding the contribution and the limitations of this study. It is also a lesson—a sometimes humorous one—about how the "real world" influences what researchers do.

Process versus Outcomes—What's Implementation?

When I first started this study, I hoped that I would be able to examine program outcomes as well as program implementation—to look not only at whether staff and prisoners actually participated in programs, and in activities that were plausibly related to a program's purposes, but also at whether participating in those activities led to decreases in recidivism or increases in future earnings. I quickly discovered, however, that measuring recidivism correctly would divert the focus of the work away from assessing implementation.

Because so many factors plausibly influence recidivism, including length of sentence, place of release, age, race, presence of family, and the like, any study of recidivism must come up with some way to control for these factors. One approach is to do a "large n" survey: drawing as many program participants as possible into the sample so that the possible effect of successfully and unsuccessfully implemented programs could be judged while controlling for other factors. The other approach is to use an experimental design, randomly assigning prisoners to participate in successfully and unsuccessfully implemented programs.

Both approaches were simply impossible in terms of time and resources. As a graduate student, I did not have the time, the money, the experience, or the stature to get permission, funding, or help in running studies like these. Even assuming I had the wherewithal to design and administer a survey, no index for "successfully" and "unsuccessfully" implemented programs existed. As for a randomized experiment, assigning prisoners to participate or to refrain from participation would have completely violated the Federal Bureau of Prisons (BOP) policy of letting prisoners volunteer for programs.

Just as importantly, though, neither of these approaches was well-suited to the project I contemplated. I was interested in studying implementation on the ground, looking at the "fit" between policy and practice. Running a "large n" survey focused on the outcomes of practice would be allowing the tail to wag the dog. Similarly, allowing the need for random selection to dictate my study would have kept me from examining what attracts prisoners to participate in programs on their own.

Deciding to focus upon process, however, still left me with some important decisions. One in particular was the question of breadth—studying a variety of programs—versus depth—studying the programs at one prison for a longer period of time. I decided to choose breadth over depth in order to increase the possibility that I would have cases of both successful and unsuccessful implementation in my sample of prisons. This, I hoped, would allow me to differentiate clearly between the two and to make an argument about the conditions under which each occurs. While it was possible that programs within the same prison could be implemented differently, I believed it was more plausible that organizational characteristics would matter enough so that most programs at the same prison would have very similar implementation experiences.

This choice was also rooted in the realization that the prison literature, and to a lesser extent the implementation literature, was largely characterized by studies of one prison or one case. With some notable exceptions, such as DiIulio (1987), researchers had chosen to delve into the culture of one particular prison, creating studies that were rich and specific but also heavily influenced by the peculiarities of the site. Moreover, because prison staff and prisoners have a tendency to attribute their beliefs and behavior to their roles as staff and prisoners rather than to the environment of a particular prison, such researchers often reached general conclusions about "prison culture" that did not, in fact, travel well from prison to prison, or at least from one study to another. I hoped that by including several prisons in my study, I would be better able to distinguish the general from the particular, and in that way provide a fresh perspective on previous work.

Without the benefit of a long period of time in which to meet and observe prisoners informally, and to win their trust, I cannot create the detailed studies of prisoner life or staff culture that some other researchers, with more time in a particular prison, can create. In particular, what I miss is the peer-focused world of the prisoner, with its rituals, its peer pressure, its prisoner-on-prisoner abuse, and its various supportive and exploitative subcultures. I can evaluate the extent of its influence on participation in programs only secondhand, through individual interviews with prisoners. But if prisoners, as is likely, are unwilling to talk about such issues with an outsider, or do not know themselves how the prisoner culture might affect their behavior, then my analysis is incomplete.

While this is an important tradeoff, however, what I gain from the study I designed is equally important. The decision to include five prisons—four federal and one state—in this study, and to interview both staff and prisoners extensively, makes this the largest multisite qualitative study of prisons in the United States. Although I did not become deeply immersed in either staff or prisoner culture, I was able to see enough to discover "both sides" of common, everyday conflicts within the prison. The interviewing of roughly 30 randomly selected staff and 40 randomly selected prisoners in each prison, 354 interviews in all, gave me quick exposure to a variety of perspectives, an exposure I would have gained much more slowly had I started with "key informants." The time I did spend in prison—ten- to twelve-hour days spanning two work shifts—allowed me to balance the interview data with my own observations of events in the prison. The resulting product, I believe, combines some of the systematic breadth characteristic of survey work with some of the "thick description" characteristic of ethnography.

From Theory Validation to Theory Generation

When I began to select sites for this project, I made a few initial decisions. I wanted to focus on medium-security male prisons, because most prisoners are male and medium-security prisons hold the greatest variety and the greatest number of prisoners. I also wanted to select most of my prisons from the BOP, in order to control for differences in program design, staff training, and resource availability that are manifest across states. The one state prison in my sample, Catawba, was chosen because, with the exception of prison industries, it had a menu of program offerings similar to those present at the federal prisons. By eliminating some of the differences in program design, it was easier to focus upon differences in implementation.

But how to choose among the many federal medium-security male prisons available? I wanted to choose sites that would allow me to test and extend a theory of implementation derived from Michael Lipsky's *Street-Level Bureaucracy* (1980). Lipsky described how characteristics of human service work—unclear performance standards and goals, a lack of resources to meet demand, clients who were nonvoluntary and dissatisfied—created staff who routinized their work, rationed resources, and saw clients as problems to be controlled rather than people to be helped. Such staff, I believed, were unlikely to support rehabilitation. By contrast, I expected that in environments where performance standards were clear, where teamwork counteracted the felt scarcity of resources, and where communication between staff and inmates was encouraged, staff would support rehabilitation and implementation would be more successful. Thus, I needed to choose prisons that varied across the presence or absence of the characteristics of street-level bureaucracy.

But how was I to discover the characteristics of the work environment in each prison before entering the prisons themselves? The extraordinarily helpful Office of Research at the Washington, DC, Central Office of the BOP suggested looking at a set of staff surveys that, among other things, measured the staff's evaluation of supervisors, sense of control over the prison's operations, efficacy with prisoners, satisfaction with training, and stress in each prison. Although not perfect indicators of the various characteristics of street-level bureaucracies, these seemed pretty close. For instance, the specific questions about supervisors and about operations seemed to be a pretty good measure of the clarity of performance standards and goal expectations. The questions about relationships with prisoners and about stress provided a rough measure of the extent to which staff rationed the time and effort they provided to prisoners and the kinds of stereotyping they engaged in. And the questions about training were, though not a direct measure of resource availability, at least one indication of whether staff thought they were getting assistance in dealing with demands from prisoners.

Using these scales, I identified a group of eleven prisons that consistently scored either well above or well below the median on these questions. I then narrowed the list to seven prisons based on location in the same administrative regions (to help control for differences in regional office supervision) and on the variety of programming available. From these seven possible sites, I applied for permission to enter four, two prisons that scored above the median and two below. Each of these four prisons had a wide variety of programs, with at least one "special" emphasis—an innovative program or organizational feature that I thought would be interesting to explore.

Here prison administration intervened. For five months I waited while the warden at each of the prisons I had identified decided whether he would allow me to enter. Two (one that scored high on street-level bureaucracy and one that scored low) turned me down outright, citing security concerns. I substituted two prisons, similar to those that refused me entry, from my original group of seven and tried again. Another warden asked for changes in my proposal before rereviewing it. I made the alterations, which mostly concerned issues of tone, and sent it back to him. Meanwhile, the staff in the Office of Research, using their personal contacts, persuaded research staff on-site at the fourth prison in my sample to take responsibility for me. Their willingness persuaded the warden to give me permission, and I entered my first prison in March 1992.

The visit went smoothly, but the lack of problems did not seem to persuade any of the remaining wardens to move more quickly on approving my application. They did not refuse; they simply ignored my inquiries. Then one of my advisors, Norval Morris, invited me to dinner along with the then-director of the BOP, Michael Quinlan. Director Quinlan was intrigued to hear that I had visited one of his prisons and asked me about my observations. At the end of the evening, he kindly invited me back to the BOP. Not one to turn down an opportunity, I mentioned that I had asked for permission to go to several other prisons, but that some wardens seemed to be worried that I would pose a security risk.

"Oh, that's certainly appropriate," he said, "but I'm sure you wouldn't present a problem."

Within two weeks, I had permission to go to the other three prisons.

Did the somewhat haphazard nature of the final narrowing to four sites jeopardize my research design? It is interesting that the wardens who approved my request after Director Quinlan met me were all "fast-track" wardens: each of the three had been recently promoted to his prison as a problem-solver, or was receiving a promotion elsewhere to a higher-profile post. This ended up giving me an unofficial "control" on the quality of the wardens in charge: in other words, I had a sample in which at least three of the four federal wardens were highly regarded by their supervisors. (By chance, this turned out to be true of the warden at the state prison in my sample as well.) This meant that the quality of leadership, and to some extent leadership style, did not vary greatly across three of my federal prisons.

Had all of these prisons then produced the same implementation outcome, I would have worried that the quality of the warden, rather than the way programs fit with institutional needs and values, might account for the outcome. However, as it turns out, I found different outcomes at these three prisons: successful implementation at Beaverton, abandoned implementation at Drake, and subverted implementation at Evergreen. This does not prove that wardens have no effect—in fact, the warden is an important part of my story at Drake—but it does suggest that the warden's impact is mediated through the organizational context. And it strengthens my argument that changing the organizational context requires more than simply changing the leadership at the top.

Despite my inability to investigate all of the four prisons I initially selected, therefore, I am reasonably certain that the final sample showed variation on the indicators I had selected for the independent variable (indicators of street-level bureaucracy) without introducing other variables that could explain the results of the study. However, as it turned out, the variation I had identified through the survey and sought to preserve in my research design was flawed by definition. I had expected, contrary to Lipsky's argument that all human-service organizations displayed the characteristics of street-level bureaucracy, that some organizations would clarify standards, make resource scarcity less salient through teamwork, and reduce stress and stereotyping of prisoners. Instead, I found that the characteristics of street-level bureaucracy and strong organizations co-existed: unclear performance standards did not preclude satisfaction with supervisors or their expectations; staff had concerns about resource scarcity whether or not there was teamwork; and that in some prisons, contact with prisoners reduced stress while in other prisons contact increased it. The continuum that I had imagined, with deeply problematic street-level bureaucracies at one end and flourishing organizations on the other, did not exist.

This negative result, however, led to a much more interesting study. The variation I had identified through the survey and then found in much more interesting detail on the ground proved to be variation in the content of organizational beliefs and practices, not variation in the level of street-level bureaucracy. This in itself provided an interesting question—what factors create different organizational needs and practices at similar prisons?—though, as I explain below, my study was not best equipped to answer it. But in addition, I also found that it was not the beliefs or incentives themselves that controlled the success of implementation. Instead, it is the extent to which program goals can mesh with institutional values, and the ways in which program incentives fit into the incentive structure in the prison, that matters. It is the *match* between context and policy, not merely one particular type of context, that counts. My mistake led to the generation of new theory.

Of course, had I started with this theory rather than ending up with it, I could have designed a study that would have done a better job of testing it. For instance, one way to test the importance of the match between context and policy is to look, not only at the same policy in different contexts, but at different policies in the same context. Had I asked staff about the programs they supported the least and the programs they supported the most, or had I looked at, say, the implementation of furloughs or halfway-house policies as well as the implementation of programs, I would have had some additional tests.

Knowing what I was going to find before I started the study would probably also have led me to create a study with an over-time component. In the story I tell, institutional needs and values are exogenous; they exist as the result of history, seemingly without cause. Yet this cannot be true; the account I give of workers translating policies and telling stories about them, of prisoners and staff changing their practices in response to incentives, implies that their actions update the body of stories and practices in the culture. Values and incentives are thus endogenous, or created by the same actions they cause. But without spending more time in each prison, I cannot trace this process carefully. Similarly, the relatively short period of time I spent in each prison did not allow me to see the effect of "shocks" to the system: to see what might happen when some mandated change in practices, in leadership, or in the environment (an influx of new prisoners, a riot, a workers' strike) disrupts the role of organizational context as the primary provider of values and incentives. Without seeing this, I probably overestimate the extent to which organizational context can influence implementation, and underestimate the ability of mandates to create change.

The limitations of this study clearly suggest avenues for future research. In particular, the need to explore the ways in which context and policy match up and the need to see how context changes over time should send researchers back to single organization case studies with new ideas about what to look for. Yet I should also point out an advantage of the cross-sectional design for the generation of theory. Studies of organizational culture can be so taken by the specifics of how an organization reacts to incremental adjustments over time or to sudden shocks, or so involved in detailing the ways in which the organization handles different tasks, that it is difficult to think about what general lessons can be learned. The advantage of studying five similar organizations at once is that one's attention necessarily turns from the specific—how staff and prisoners in one prison responded to their institutional context—to the general—how the mechanisms of contextual influence can be simplified and organized by abstract concepts like needs and values. This makes future theoretical development easier: researchers can use the concepts of institutional needs and institutional values to make sense of other implementation contexts, whether they are primarily individual, linked to a profession, or well-developed like the prison. The generation of theory ideally leads both to validation and extension in a cumulative process: no one study can answer all questions, but good studies should generate more questions to ask (Glaser and Strauss 1967).

"For Want of a Tape Recorder": Accuracy versus Diversity

Every researcher who does site research has a story about the lost equipment or transportation failure that ends up affecting the course of the study in completely random but wholly significant ways. My story is about the tape recorder that never was. Part of my research proposal to the BOP requested permission to use a miniature tape recorder for interviews and fieldnotes. This part of the proposal passed without comment or complaint, and accordingly I bought a tiny pocket recorder and dropped spare tapes in my shoulder bag. But as I entered my first prison and submitted to the security check, the officer on duty frowned.

"You're not allowed to take this in," he said, pointing to my tape recorder. "Prison regulations say no tape recorders."

I protested that my original agreement with the BOP had included the use of tape recorders. The officer, in turn, showed me the page of visiting regulations that forbade the machines. Realizing that fighting about prison regulations on the first day of my first prison visit was probably not the best way to get myself invited back, I meekly surrendered the tape recorder. Later, talking to the research staff at both the prison and in Washington, I was advised to just go along with the ban.

At the time, I was disconcerted but not greatly distressed. I had had a year of practice doing interviews with homeless teenagers, and had learned to take notes and carry on a conversation at the same time. I had also been worried that the tape recorder might discourage people from talking to me; this problem had just been taken out of my hands. But as the piles of interviews began to grow deeper, I realized that not having the service of a tape recorder not only meant that I had to do all of my own transcribing, but that I had to do it quickly, before I was unable to reconstruct the sound and rhythm of the dialogue from my scribbled notes. I thus followed my days in the prison with nights in the motel room, transcribing. As I quite often did five to six hour-long interviews per day, and on busy days finished as many as eight to ten, the task of transcribing rapidly crowded out anything else.

This had two effects on the data that I collected, one less and one more serious than they might appear at first glance. The obvious question is how accurately I was able to capture the opinions of those I interviewed. I am actually reasonably confident on this point, although there is an unavoidable slippage with paper, compared to tape. Partly because I had a good deal of interviewing experience before I began this project, and partly because I later had the experience of comparing a transcript of a taped interview with a transcript of the same interview from notes, I believe that I accurately represented the majority of what people said to me. My transcripts vary in language and expression, which also gives me reason to believe that I did not impose my own speech patterns on what others said. Still, I am sure that I made people's answers "smoother" as I transcribed, eliminating hesitations, rephrasings, and circumlocutions. Thus, my respondents may sound more definite than they actually were, leading me to draw a picture of each prison that is sharper, more distinct, than is actually the case.

A more important problem, however, is the kind of time management choice that the need for rapid transcription forced upon me. One of the most useful techniques of the participant observer is the daily journal, in which one can put down impressions, recount events that one could not take notes on at the moment, and evaluate one's own behavior at the site. I started such a journal at each site, but was never able to continue it because my evenings so quickly filled up with transcription. Thus, while I do have fieldnotes that I took while observing staff meetings, classes, or other activities where I could scribble unobtrusively, I do not have a daily record of my activities or observations. The lack of this data means that I was a much less efficient participant observer than I could have been; the fact that interview quotes rather than interpreted scenes make up the bulk of the evidence in this book is a direct consequence of this fact.

Knowing what I do now, I might have made different choices. I originally chose to do formal interviews with as many staff and prisoners as I did because I wanted to have a sample large enough to do statistically significant analyses of differences within each prison as well as among the prisons. The 354 interviews I completed represent an exceptionally large number for qualitative work. But across five prisons, this means that I have a little over 70 interviews per prison, subdivided into roughly 40 prisoners and 30 staff. This translates into subgroups of 5 and 10 staff once I subdivide by occupational category—hardly enough for reliable analyses. Similarly, dividing the group of prisoners in each prison by age, length of sentence, time until release, or other possibly relevant factors again creates subgroups too small for quantitative analysis. I was able to

TABLE A1.1
Effect of Demographic Characteristics of Prisoners upon Participation
in Prison Programs

Variable	Chi-square significance	Description
Prior term in prison	.97	No differences in participation between prisoners serving their first term, and those with one, 2-3, or 4+ prison terms.
Prior convictions	.75	People with 2-4 previous convictions participate slightly more than their proportion in the inmate population: 70%, as opposed to an average of 64%.
Offense	.59	69% of those convicted of drug offenses, or 4% more than the average, participate.
Age	.43	71% of those between 35 and 45, as opposed to an average of 67%, participate in programs. By contrast, only 52% of those over 45 participate. Prisoners under 25 are close to the average.
Sentence length	.27	Participation peaks among inmates with a 2- to 5-year sentence; 79%, or 15% above average. It is lowest among those sentenced to less than 2 years; 45%, or 19% below the average.
Time until release	.15	52%, or 12% below average, of those who will leave prison within a year participate. 75% of those who will be released within 2-4 years participate: 11% above average. About 65% of the remaining inmates—those with 5 or more years left in prison—participate.
Race	.14	Only 56% of whites, as opposed to 61% of blacks and 69% of Hispanics, participate.
Education upon arrest	.10	66% of those with a high school diploma or some college/vocational training participate in programs, as opposed to 60% of those without a HSD. Only 27% of those with a BA or more education participate.

Note: This is a summary table of cross-tabulations of each of these factors against participation in programs. For instance, in the table represented by the first row, "prior term in prison," each cell had the number of participants/nonparticipants in programs that were serving their first term, their second term, their 3rd or 4th term, or their 5th term or above. Note that the chi-square statistic does *not* show the strength of the relationship between participation in programs and each of these factors, but only the probability that differences between rows/columns in the cross-tabulation is random. In other words, there is a 97% probability that the relationship between participation and prior terms served is random; there is only a 10% probability that the relationship between education and participation in programs is random.

create Table A1.1 to examine differences in participation across all the prisoners who released background data to me, but cross-tabulations of these factors with specific prison characteristics were inconclusive at best. Thus, given the limitations of data analysis even with the number of interviews I administered, I might have been wiser to do fewer formal interviews and to spend more time observing programs and writing fieldnotes.

Hindsight inevitably creates better studies than the best initial research design. But short of doggedly insisting on listening only to what our studies have to tell us about our original predictions, this will always be the case. Refusing to recognize that the research process is also one of discovery and understanding creates studies that are more about the researcher's preoccupations and limitations than about what the world has to teach us. This is not an excuse for abandoning research design; on the contrary, a careful research design—and careful evaluation of its shortcomings—is one way to verify what we know, and discover what we have yet to know. Used in this way, research designs, which start as blueprints, might best be thought of as diagnostics: an aid to understanding, and not a straitjacket upon it.

Appendix 2

On Being Who You Are:
Credibility, Bias, and Good Research

I AM A Chinese-American woman; when I visited the prisons in this study, I was in my mid-twenties. These facts inevitably cause eyebrows to go up when people identify me with my research. Their immediate instinct, quickly reworded but hard to suppress, is always something like, "But you don't look like you belong in prison!" Of course this is generally an advantage—but in this case, they want to say, it might not be. How can someone who looks like me get people to identify with her enough to trust her with their truth? And more importantly, perhaps, how does someone with my background—resolutely uncriminal, as of yet—know when she is being lied to?

These questions are important, not the least because they should lead the honest questioner to realize that someone who looks more like the staff, or the prisoners, in the average American prison, and thus might be assumed to be more like them, might also have problems of credibility both inside and outside the prison. In fact, the problem is general: researchers who work with people cannot but be part of the interaction, no matter how much they might like to assume that they are invisible observers. And that problem of interference with the research site continues from one's arrival at the site to the selection and analysis of one's data. In the end, the problem of a particular researcher's credibility is less important than the certainty, even under conditions of perfect care and honesty, of a researcher's bias.

Prison researchers have been particularly good at realizing this fact, perhaps because the research site is unique enough to make it impossible to convince oneself that one is simply conducting research as usual. When I first conceived of this project, I benefited tremendously from the lessons in presentation of self offered by the research appendices in Giallombardo (1966), Heffernan (1972), Jacobs (1977), and DiIulio (1987); Fenno's (1978) account of following members of Congress around their districts was also of great use, even though the milieu was somewhat different. In that tradition, I offer the following thoughts on establishing credibility, understanding bias, and doing good research.

Building Confidence

Very few people wake up one morning and say to themselves, "Gee, I'd like to go to prison." I am no exception; my comfort level for taking on this project developed over time and in a haphazard way. Four years before I started this research, I spent six weeks volunteering with a program for female prisoners and their children at Bedford Hills Correctional Center in New York. Going into the prison each day, I got over my initial fears of barbed wire and my initial curiosity about the prisoners' backgrounds. Instead I learned to have normal conversations with the incarcerated women about their everyday activities, about their children, and about current events; I learned, as well, not to use social class as a marker for intelligence or perception. But the prison itself held few charms for me; I was not particularly interested in it.

A year later, I took a leave of absence from graduate school to spend a year doing social work with homeless teenagers at a program in New York City. I had wanted to do something more "real," more "relevant"; my job was real with a vengeance. As intake director of a transitional living program that catered to teens living in a crisis shelter, I controlled a resource that these desperate, street-smart kids badly needed; as the point of contact with staff at the crisis shelter who needed to make space for new arrivals, I was a constant target of pleading, resentment, and back-channel information; and as the gatekeeper for the program, my job was triage. I quickly learned about lies, manipulation, and sincere promises that couldn't be kept; I also learned that while I could get better at telling near-truths from truth, neither I nor anyone else would ever be perfect. But more importantly, the time with the kids, 80 percent of whom were black or Latino, and the time with the staff, whose backgrounds ranged from the high school graduate just off welfare to the Ph.D. psychologist, taught me to be honest about things I did not know or did not understand, and to ask questions with respect and without judgment.

The year gave me an abiding interest in how organizations worked and in how staff and client perceptions did and did not intersect. But more importantly, it cured me of any reflexive fear of the unknown or of my own ignorance. Luckily for me, this was probably the best preparation I could have had for prison. While I never managed to avoid a wave of nerves on my first day in each new prison, I was usually too busy and too interested to be scared after that. Both the staff and the prisoners usually picked that up and responded with some relief: a visitor who treads each step fearfully reminds everyone, uncomfortably, that the prison is abnormal and that their lives are on display. I could also sincerely tell people that I was there to learn from them, and the fact that I did much more listening than talking confirmed it.

Apart from such general perceptions, however, neither staff nor prisoners knew my background or had any particular reason to trust me. I thus tried to establish credibility in a variety of different ways. The most important was the privacy of the interview and the explanation before it began. In each prison, I was given the use of an empty room for my prisoner interviews: sometimes it was a classroom, at other times a small office. The rooms were always private and unmonitored, so that prisoners would not feel that they were under observation. Before each interview, I would shake the prisoner's hand, explain who I was and the purpose of the interview, answer any questions, and give him the chance to refuse the interview. I explained that I had no power over his case and that I would not ask him anything about his conviction, which cut down on the need to lie. I treated anyone who refused with great courtesy, asking for his reason and then thanking him for his time. In these ways, I tried to ensure that the interview subject and anyone he might talk to would have no reason to spread negative stories about his experience, or rumors about who I "really" was.

With staff, I followed exactly the same protocol, with the difference that I usually interviewed the staff member at his or her work location when we could be reasonably private. Thus I climbed up a watchtower to interview one officer and interviewed others while they stood in the yard watching prisoners move toward the dining hall. I gave prisoners and staff the same description of who I was, so that neither group would feel that I was lying; I never pushed anyone to do an interview or answer a specific question if they refused. I also made an effort to introduce myself to as many people as possible, whether or not they were on my random list of interview subjects, and not to spend too much time with any one person, lest I be accused of favoritism.

The interviews themselves were designed so that people started out by giving their general impressions of the prison; moved to a section where staff could talk about prisoners and prisoners about staff; solicited opinions about how to improve the prison; and concluded with a section on social issues. The questions and question ordering thus always placed the interviewee as expert; they also gave people a chance to vent their frustrations and voice their opinions. Some clearly found the process therapeutic: a few staff members told me that the interview helped them relieve stress, and a few prisoners said wistfully that I was the only visitor they had had during their incarceration. Most, however, clearly talked to me primarily because I was a not-unpleasant break in the day's routine, and because most people, in any profession or from any background, seldom have the chance to talk for any length of time to someone who is interested in their opinion of their surroundings.

News travels fast in a prison, and so I was always aware that any instance of disrespect or arrogance on my part would have long-range repercussions. But the staff and prisoners made it very easy to be polite, because with very few exceptions, they treated me with great politeness, and often friendliness and warmth. And usually, I managed one unplanned incident of sheer stupidity per prison, which evoked sympathetic laughter from staff who might otherwise be suspicious: I drove my car into a ditch in full view of a line of cars reporting for shift change at one prison, left my headlights on in the parking lot at another, rasped through the first three days of interviewing while fighting laryngitis at a third, and so on. The moral of the story is one that I heard often in prison, "if you treat a man human, he'll treat you human." The staff and prisoners treated me human, and I tried to do the same.

Race and Gender

Being treated "human," of course, does not eliminate the differences that serve as the foundation for the preconceptions that separate humans from each other. The most obvious of these are race and gender, and my race and gender difference was particularly salient in prisons, where the percentage of female staff averaged about 20 percent and the Asian population, in both the prison and the surrounding towns, was almost nonexistent.

This led to some interesting moments. In one prison town, a slightly inebriated man came up to me on the street and said, "Hi! I haven't seen one of you since Vietnam!" This was not entirely encouraging. But the scarcity of people like me was in one sense very helpful, because it meant that apart from being surprised that I didn't have an accent, neither staff nor prisoners had any reference point for my racial allegiances. In fact, when they liked me, they tended to read their own opinions on to me. Thus, when I asked "Do you think racism has an important effect on people's lives? Does it hurt any one group the most, or is everyone affected by it?," I often found people appealing to the similarities between Asians and their own group. Thus black respondents would make comments like, "Sure, people like you and me know that there's still prejudice out there," and white respondents would give explanations along the lines of, "I really don't think so; look how well Asians like you have done. I think if you want to work, it's out there for you."

This does not mean that no one held back their opinions in ways they wouldn't have with someone of their own race. And in parts of the country where Asians are more common and thus seem more predictable, I am sure I would have gotten different responses. But my sense is that to the extent that answers were biased by my race, the bias was not systematic and not that widespread. By contrast, I think that a white or black interviewer would have confronted more predictable problems, given the different racial mixes of white and black staff and prisoners at each prison.

The way in which gender worked in the research is a little more complicated. Before I started work in the prisons, I was counseled by a female researcher to dress in a businesslike fashion and to remove any jewelry that could be used as a weapon against me. It was good advice, not because I ever felt like I was in physical danger, but because it reminded me to take the possibility seriously and to be on my guard. I never talked about my personal life and politely refused any prisoner's invitation to talk to me more often or to introduce me to other prisoners. This might have deprived me of some contacts, but it also kept me from being seen as a possible target of manipulation. No prisoner ever asked me to mail letters, bring in contraband, or do any other illicit favors for him. For similar reasons, while I did accept some social invitations from staff, I never attended any event that did not include a large gathering of staff, and I did not—as male researchers have done—accept invitations for a beer after the shift or a night out on the town. Again, while this might have cost me the chance to talk to people in more relaxed settings, it also ensured that people would not see me as favoring one group of staff over another, or as someone who was not businesslike and respectful.

There were no questions that explicitly mentioned gender on my questionnaire. But I am sure that people—both staff and prisoners—reacted differently to me than they would have to a male interviewer. For instance, I know my respondents used less casual profanity than they otherwise might have, because they often apologized when profanity slipped out. I also think that prisoners and staff were less likely to be "macho" with me than they might have been with a male interviewer. Books by male researchers often include vignettes of some prisoner recounting his colorful past or staff boasting about how tough they can be. But because I did not ask about criminal history and asked only a few questions about peer relationships, prisoners did not regale me with stories about how they carried off a particular crime or defended their turf in the prison. And while staff did complain to me about restrictions on their use of force, very few people told me about actual uses of force.

For similar reasons, I am sure that prisoners said more to me about missing their families, wanting to be with their mothers or their wives, or hoping to be a good example for their children, than they might have to male researchers. It is not that family is not mentioned in the work that men have done on prisons; in the recidivism literature, in particular, family ties play a large role. But some of the interviewing that men have done also quotes prisoners as talking about the loss of family primarily in terms of sexual deprivation, a theme that tended to be absent from my interviews. Clearly prisoners self-censored in their choices of what to mention to me; but the frequency of their discussion of family ties also suggests that they may self-censor, in the other direction, when they talk to male researchers, or that male researchers give male prisoners more room to talk about sex and less room to talk about family in their interviews.

Are prisoners less family-oriented and more macho than they portrayed themselves to be with me? Were they engaged in deliberate attempts to make me feel more sympathetic toward them? Or are prisoners more family-oriented and less "tough" than most male researchers sense or care to ask about? One can argue this question, but I think the more interesting possibility is that male and female interviewers, especially in a highly gendered environment like the prison, simply "cue" different responses. I would never argue, for instance, that prisoners do not feel deprived of sexual outlets or that they do not take pride in illegality or violence, even though such themes seldom appeared in my interviews. Nor would I argue that their love of family will automatically keep them straight; as I discuss in Chapter 5, many prisoners' images of family are clearly unrealistic fantasies rather than rational descriptions of an available support system. But I do think that interviewing by both sexes allows different themes to emerge, themes that might be absent or less salient if only same-sex interviewing and research were to take place. This means that "lying" should be less our concern than systematic bias, and bias should be evaluated less for how it can be eliminated, than for how it works and what it tells us.

On Lying

When I began this project, the dimension of lying that most concerned me was the possibility that staff or prisoners might think I was a spy for the administration. While delighted that Director Quinlan's intervention helped me to get access to three of the prisons, for instance, I worried that this might lead people to be guarded about what they would say to me. Thus, I told each of my interview subjects about the layers of confidentiality I used—the protection of names, identifying details (for instance, saying that a respondent was a black counselor would, in some prisons, be tantamount to identifying them) and even the names of the prisons themselves. I politely turned down all suggestions to base my work out of the prison's administrative wing.[1] And before beginning the interviews, I spent a lot of time explaining what I was not: not affiliated with the Central or Regional Offices, not a member of the parole board, not anything but a student.

I think that many of these measures did help to inspire confidence. But the problem was also not as severe as I expected. In the time that elapsed between getting permission to do my research and actually arriving at the prison, the wardens barely remembered who I was, much less why I was there or why they had approved my visit in the first place. The staff and prisoners also judged that I looked too young to be well-connected. If the measure of their complaints is any judge, they were willing to be frank: I was freely made the recipient of their dissatisfaction with supervisors (who I did not ask them to name) and colleagues, their opinions of the present and past wardens, suggestions for reorganizing the prison, and the like. The wardens themselves were very good about not asking about my interviews (or, perhaps, just not very interested in the project).

But, of course, there are types of lying that do not involve fear. One is saying things to make oneself look good. This did go on, because I caught people doing it: for instance, I watched one staff member talk about the patience with which he treated prisoners, then hurl insults at prisoners who came to the office to ask for a pass or a favor. Prisoners would sometimes complain that the teachers were not helpful, then recount stories in which it became obvious that the prisoner was the one baiting the staff. Thus, I did my best to use both evidence within the interview and observation outside of it to corroborate the words being said. In general, none of the observations I make about programs or prison operations are based on my perceptions alone, but always upon others' comments and my own investigation; criticism of staff I did not know had to be spontaneously raised by several people before I gave credence to it. In other words, while there is no way to eliminate untruths such as these, one can look to see whether other evidence corroborates it.

Another reason to lie might be to try to influence the results of my research. But this seems less plausible to me, simply because everyone knew that I was interviewing dozens of people within each prison. No one had any reason to believe that I would take them more seriously than anyone else if their comments were not supported by others; in fact, people often prefaced their answers to a particular question by saying something like, "This is what I think, but it would be interesting to know if anyone else felt this way." In the end, I think that my agenda, presented as letting people outside the prison know what the prison was really like,

---

[1] Instead, I was housed in empty offices in a variety of places: the research department, the lieutenant's wing, the education department, and the psychology/counseling wing.

was too vague for most of my respondents to think about what their "position" might be and thus how they could skew my findings.

A different type of interview might have had very different results. For instance, had I asked directly about more controversial topics—prison rape, staff beatings or abuse, corruption or kickbacks, drug use or contraband—I would probably have opened the door to some purposeful exaggeration. The fact that I did not ask, and consequently was not systematically told about any of these incidents, does not indicate that none of these problems exist. Instead, it points to a way in which research can be biased even when no deliberate skewing of the truth occurs. Although I believe that if any of these or similar problems had been widespread, I would have heard about them,[2] what I chose to ask clearly influenced the kind of portrait I created. Asking about everyday practice and rehabilitation brought me answers that focus on those issues, and that in the process deemphasize other aspects of prison life.

To the extent that my research—or anyone's research—is systematically skewed, this is the most important reason. Certainly researchers who are not skilled in interviewing can be deceived by deliberate lies; certainly there will always be respondents who, for their own reasons, decide to lie. But those problems can be caught with some careful thought before one interviews, some care to verify what one hears by using several different sources, and some critical introspection afterwards. More difficult is the way in which one's perspective biases the result, not because one hears or sees selectively, but because one asks and writes selectively. A necessary corollary of a focused look at a problem is that everything surrounding it fades in importance. The end result may be an excellent study of the problem, but a skewed picture of the site in which it occurs.

Some types of research are better suited to avoiding this problem: various kinds of interpretive research, for instance, take as their topic the issues that are most salient to the members of a particular site. The trade-off, of course, is that the issues that are most salient to the participants may not be the issues most salient to observers, to policymakers, or to scholars. And even if one's purpose in research is not to answer a specific question but simply to illuminate a specific phenomenon, culture, or society, one can only minimize the ways in which one's research is partial and skewed. Just as one cannot escape one's physical identity and characteristics as a researcher, one cannot escape one's mental map, the map

---

[2] In fact, I did hear, from a large number of staff at Catawba, complaints about promotions to sergeant and lieutenant being purchased through campaign contributions to state officials. To some extent, the complaints probably reflect sour grapes in a system where having political connections is helpful, but I did hear the complaint often enough to give it some credence. For my work, though, the significance lies primarily in that it was another reason for line staff to withhold their trust from the warden and his administrative team.

that tells the researcher what is interesting, salient, or significant, and what is not.

The only solution is for the researcher to know who she is, not only as someone who affects the research site in particular ways, but also as someone who characterizes it in partial and biased ways. This is less wrong than inevitable, and because of that, suggestions that one can be unbiased should be the most troubling. A good research ethic should allow researchers to discuss how their questions and preoccupations—as well as their personal characteristics and the context of their inter-actions—affected their research. When researchers confront their own bias with honesty and matter-of-factness, rather than with fear and de-nial, they push forth knowledge in the understanding that all knowledge is imperfect.

Bibliography

Allen, Bud and Diane Bosta. 1981. *Games Criminals Play: How You Can Profit by Knowing Them*. Sacramento, CA: Rae John Publishers.

Allen, Francis. 1981. *The Decline of the Rehabilitative Ideal*. New Haven, CT: Yale University Press.

American Friends Service Committee. 1971. *Struggle for Justice*. New York: Hill and Wang.

Andrews, Donald and James Bonta. 1994. *The Psychology of Criminal Conduct*. Cincinnati, OH: Anderson.

Andrews, Donald, James Bonta, and R. D. Hoge. 1990a. "Classification for Effective Rehabilitation: Rediscovering Psychology." *Criminal Justice and Behavior* 17:19–52.

Andrews, Donald, Ivan Zinger, et al. 1990b. "Does Correctional Treatment Work?: A Clinically-Relevant and Psychologically-Informed Meta-Analysis." *Criminology* 28 (August):369–404.

Bardach, Eugene. 1977. *The Implementation Game: What Happens After a Bill Becomes a Law*. Cambridge, MA: MIT Press.

Baumer, Eric. 1997. "Levels and Predictors of Recidivism: The Malta Experience," *Criminology* 35 (November):561–76.

de Beaumont, Gustave and Alexis de Tocqueville. 1833. *On the Penitentiary System in the United States and Its Application in France*. Translated by Francis Lieber. Phildelphia: Carey, Lee, and Blanchard.

Beck, Allan J. and Bernard E. Shipley. 1989. *Recidivism of Prisoners Released in 1983*. Washington, DC: Bureau of Justice Statistics, U.S. Department of Justice. (April, NCJ-116261).

Becker, Gary S. 1988. "Crime and Punishment: An Economic Approach." In George Stigler, ed., *Chicago Studies in Political Economy*. Chicago: University of Chicago Press.

Bonta, James. 1996. "Risk-Needs Assessment and Treatment." In Alan Harland, ed., *Choosing Correctional Options that Work: Defining the Demand and Increasing the Supply*. Thousand Oaks, CA: Sage.

Bounds, V. L. et al. 1979. *Evaluation Study of a Model of Imprisonment Tested at the Butner FCI*. Chapel Hill, NC: Institute for Research in Social Science.

Bourgois, Phillip. 1989. "In Search of Horatio Alger: Culture and Ideology in the Crack Economy." *Contemporary Drug Problems* 16 (winter):619–49.

Brodkin, Evelyn. 1986. *The False Promise of Administrative Reform: Implementing Quality Control in Welfare*. Philadelphia: Temple University Press.

———. 1990. "Implementation as Policy Politics." In D. Palumbo and D. Calista, eds., *Implementation and the Policy Process: Opening Up the Black Box*. New York: Greenwood Press.

Brown, Jodi M., Patrick Langan, and David Levin. 1999. "Felony Sentences in State Courts, 1996." Washington, DC: Bureau of Justice Statistics, U.S. Department of Justice (May, NCJ-173939).

Burton, Velmar, Francis Cullen, and Lawrence Travis. 1987. "The Collateral Consequences of a Felony Conviction: A National Study of State Statutes." *Federal Probation* 51:52–60.

Butterfield, Fox. 1992. "Are American Jails Becoming Shelters from the Storm?" *New York Times*, Sunday, July 19, 1992, Section E, p. 4.

Campbell, Donald T. 1987. "Problems for the Experimenting Society." In Sharon Kagan et al., eds., *America's Family Support Programs*. New Haven: Yale University Press.

Canela-Cacho, Jose, Alfred Blumstein, and Jacqueline Cohen. 1997. "Relationship between the Offending Frequency of Imprisoned and Released Offenders." *Criminology* 35 (February):133–75.

Carter, Robert M., Daniel Glaser, and Leslie T. Wilkins, eds. 1985. *Correctional Institutions, Third Edition*. New York: Harper and Row.

Carroll, Leo. 1974. *Hacks, Blacks, and Cons*. Lexington, MA: D. C. Heath.

Clemmer, Donald. 1958. *The Prison Community*. New York: Rinehart.

Craig, Delores and Robert Rogers. 1993. "Vocational Training in Prison: A Case Study of Maximum Feasible Misunderstanding." *Journal of Offender Rehabilitation* 20 (1/2):1–20.

Cook, Thomas and Donald Campbell. 1979. *Quasi-Experimentation: Design and Analysis Issues for Field Settings*. Boston: Houghton Mifflin.

Cressey, Donald, ed. 1961. *The Prison: Studies in Institutional Organization and Change*. New York: Holt, Rinehart, and Winston.

Cronin, Thomas, Tania Cronin, and Michael Milakovich. 1981. *U.S. v. Crime in the Streets*. Bloomington, IN: Indiana University Press.

Cullen, Francis and Paul Gendreau. 1989. "The Effectiveness of Correctional Rehabilitation: Reconsidering the 'Nothing Works' Debate." In Lynne Goodstein and Doris Layton MacKenzie, eds., *The American Prison: Issues in Research and Policy*. New York: Plenum.

Cullen, Francis and Karen Gilbert. 1982. *Reaffirming Rehabilitation*. Cincinnati, OH: Anderson.

Currie, Elliot. 1985. *Confronting Crime: An American Challenge*. New York: Pantheon Books.

Davidson, Howard S., ed. 1995. *Schooling in a "Total Institution": Critical Perspectives from Education*. Westport, CT: Bergin and Garvey.

DeJong, Christina. 1997. "Survival Analysis and Specific Deterrence: Integrating Theoretic and Empirical Models of Recidivism." *Criminology* 35 (November):561–76.

Derthick, Martha. 1990. *Agency Under Stress*. Washington, DC: The Brookings Institution.

DiIulio, John J., Jr. 1987. *Governing Prisons: A Comparative Study of Prison Management*. New York: Free Press, 1987.

———. 1990a. "Prisons That Work: Management Is the Key." *Federal Prisons Journal* 1:4.

———, ed. 1990b. *Courts, Corrections, and the Constitution: The Impact of Judicial Intervention on Prisons and Jails*. New York: Oxford University Press.

———. 1991. *No Escape: The Future of American Corrections*. New York: Basic Books.

Doig, Jameson. 1983. *Criminal Corrections: Ideals and Realities*. Lexington, MA: D. C. Heath.

Douglas, Mary. 1986. *How Institutions Think*. Syracuse, NY: Syracuse University Press.

Duguid, Stephen. 1989. *Yearbook of Correctional Education 1989*. Burnaby, BC: Institute for the Humanities, Simon Fraser University.

Ellis, Janet. 1993. "Security Officers' Role in Reducing Inmate Problem Behaviors." *Journal of Offender Rehabilitation* 20 (1/2):61–72.

Elmore, Richard. 1979–80. "Backward Mapping: Implementation Research and Policy Decisions." *Political Science Quarterly* 94:601–16.

Fairchild, Erika and Vincent Webb, eds. 1985. *The Politics of Crime and Criminal Justice*. Beverly Hills: Sage Publications.

Farrington, David, Lloyd E. Ohlin, and James Q. Wilson. 1986. *Understanding and Controlling Crime: Toward a New Research Strategy*. New York: Springer-Verlag.

Feldman, Martha S. 1989. *Order without Design: Information Production and Policymaking*. Stanford: Stanford University Press.

Feeley, Malcolm and Jonathan Simon. 1992. "The New Penology: Notes on the Emerging Strategy of Corrections and Its Implications." *Criminology* 30 (November):449–74.

Fenno, Richard F., Jr. 1978. *Home Style: House Members in Their Districts*. Boston: Little, Brown and Co.

Ferman, Barbara. 1990. "When Failure Is Success: Implementation and Madisonian Government." In D. Palumbo and D. Calista, eds., *Implementation and the Policy Process: Opening Up the Black Box*. New York: Greenwood Press.

Flanagan, Timothy J., James W. Marquart, and Kenneth G. Adams, eds. 1998. *Incarcerating Criminals: Prisons and Jails in Social and Organizational Contexts*. New York: Oxford University Press.

Fleisher, Mark. 1989. *Warehousing Violence*. Newbury Park, CA: Sage Publications.

Freeman, Richard. 1991. "Crime and the Unemployment of Disadvantaged Youths." National Bureau of Economic Research Working Paper No. 3875.

———. 1996. "Why Do So Many Young American Men Commit Crimes and What Might We Do About It?" *Journal of Economic Perspectives* 10: 25–42.

Freeman, Richard and Harry Holzer. 1986. *The Black Youth Unemployment Crisis*. Chicago: University of Chicago Press.

Foucault, Michel. 1979. *Discipline and Punish: The Birth of the Prison*. Translated by Alan Sheridan. New York: Vintage Books.

Gaes, Gerald. 1985. "The Effects of Overcrowding in Prisons." In Michael Tonry and Norval Morris, eds., *Crime and Justice: An Annual Review of Research 6*. Chicago: University of Chicago Press.

Garland, David. 1990. *Punishment and Modern Society: A Study in Social Theory*. Chicago: University of Chicago Press.

Gaylin, Willard, Ira Glasser, Steven Marcus, and David Rothman. 1978. *Doing Good: The Limits of Benevolence*. New York: Pantheon Books.

Gendreau, Paul and Robert Ross. 1987. "Revivification of Rehabilitation: Evidence from the 1980s." *Justice Quarterly* 4(3):349–407.

Gendreau, Paul. 1996. "The Principles of Effective Intervention with Offenders." In Alan Harland, ed., *Choosing Correctional Options that Work: Defining the Demand and Increasing the Supply.* Thousand Oaks, CA: Sage.

Gerber, Jurg and Eric J. Fritsch. 1995. "Adult Academic and Vocational Correctional Education Programs: A Review of Recent Research." *Journal of Offender Rehabilitation* 22 (1/2):119–42.

Giallombardo, Rose. 1966. *Society of Women: A Study of a Women's Prison.* New York: John Wiley.

Gibbens, T.C.N. 1984. "Borstal Boys after 25 Years." *British Journal of Criminology* 24:49–62.

Gibbons, Don. 1987. *The Limits of Punishment as Social Policy.* National Council on Crime and Delinquency.

Glaser, Barney and Anselm Strauss. 1967. *The Discovery of Grounded Theory: Strategies for Qualitative Research.* New York: Aldine de Gruyter.

Glaser, Daniel. 1964. *The Effectiveness of a Prison and Parole System.* New York: Bobbs-Merrill.

———. 1995. *Preparing Convicts for Law-Abiding Lives: The Pioneering Penology of Richard A. McGee.* Albany, NY: State University of New York Press.

Golden, Marissa Martino. 1992. "Exit, Voice, Loyalty, and Neglect: Bureaucratic Responses to Presidential Control During the Reagan Administration." *Journal of Public Administration Research and Theory* 2 (1):29–62.

Goffman, Erving. 1961. *Asylums: Essays on the Social Situation of Mental Patients and Other Inmates.* New York: Anchor Books.

Goodstein, Lynne. 1976. "Inmate Adjustment to Prison and Transition to Community Life." *Journal of Research in Crime and Delinquency* 16:246–272.

Goodstein, Lynne and Doris Layton MacKenzie, eds. 1989. *The American Prison: Issues in Research and Policy.* New York: Plenum.

Gottfredson, Michael R. and Travis Hirschi. 1990. *A General Theory of Crime.* Stanford, CA: Stanford University Press.

Gottfredson, Stephen and Sean McConville. 1987. *America's Correctional Crisis: Prison Populations and Public Policy.* New York: Greenwood Press.

Hamm, Mark S. and Jeffrey L. Schrink. 1989. "The Conditions of Effective Implementation: A Guide to Accomplishing Rehabilitative Objectives in Corrections." *Criminal Justice and Behavior* 16:166–82.

Harlow, Caroline Wolf. 1994. *Comparing Federal and State Prison Inmates, 1991.* Washington, DC: Bureau of Justice Statistics, U.S. Department of Justice (September).

Harris, Phillip and Steven Smith. 1996. "Developing Community Corrections: An Implementation Perspective." In Alan Harland, ed., *Choosing Correctional Options that Work: Defining the Demand and Increasing the Supply.* Thousand Oaks, CA: Sage.

Heffernan, Esther. 1972. *Making It in Prison: The Square, the Cool, and the Life.* New York: Wiley-Interscience.

Hepburn, John. 1985. "The Exercise of Power in Coercive Organizations: A Study of Prison Guards." *Criminology* 23 (February):145–64.

Hirschman, Albert O. 1970. *Exit, Voice, and Loyalty: Responses to Decline in Firms, Organizations, and States.* Cambridge, MA: Harvard University Press.

Holzer, Harry and Richard Freeman. 1985. "Young Blacks and Jobs: What We Now Know." *The Public Interest* 78 (winter):18–31.

Horney, Julie et al. 1995. "Criminal Careers in the Short-Term: Intra-Individual Variability in Crime and Its Relation to Local Life Circumstances." *American Sociological Review* 60:655–73.

Hudson, Barbara. 1987. *Justice Through Punishment: A Critique of the Justice Model of Corrections.* Houndmills, Basingstoke, England: Macmillan.

Ignatieff, Michael. 1983. "State, Civil Society, and Total Institutions: A Critique of Recent Social Histories of Punishment." In Stanley Cohen and Andrew Scull, eds., *Social Control and the State.* New York: St. Martin's Press.

——— 1984. *The Needs of Strangers.* New York: Penguin.

Ingram, Helen. 1990. "Implementation: A Review and Suggested Framework." In Naomi Lynn and Aaron Wildavsky, eds., *Public Administration: The State of the Discipline.* Chatham, NJ: Chatham House.

"Interview with Norman Carlson, 11/30/89." 1990. *Federal Prisons Journal* 1 (4) (summer):39.

Irwin, John. 1970. *The Felon.* Englewood Cliffs, NJ: Prentice Hall.

——— 1980. *Prisons In Turmoil.* Boston: Little, Brown.

——— 1985. *The Jail: Managing the Underclass in American Society.* Berkeley: University of California Press.

Irwin, John and Donald Cressy. 1962. "Thieves, Convicts and the Inmate Culture." *Social Problems* 10 (fall):142–55.

Jacobs, James. 1977. *Stateville: The Penitentiary in Mass Society.* Chicago: University of Chicago Press.

——— 1983. *New Perspectives on Prisons and Imprisonment.* Ithaca, NY: Cornell University Press.

Josi, Don A. and Dale K. Sechrest. 1996. "Treatment vs. Security: Adversarial Relationships between Treatment Facilitators and Correctional Officers." *Journal of Offender Rehabilitation* 23 (1/2):167–84.

Kagan, Sharon L., Douglas R. Powell, Bernice Weissbourd, and Edward F. Zigler, eds. 1987. *America's Family Support Programs: Perspectives and Prospects.* New Haven, CT: Yale University Press.

Kassebaum, Gene G., David Ward, and Daniel Wilmer. 1971. *Prison Treatment and Parole Survival: An Empirical Assessment.* New York: Wiley.

Kauffman, Kelsey. 1988. *Prison Officers and Their World.* Cambridge, MA: Harvard University Press.

Kaufman, Herbert. 1960. *The Forest Ranger: A Study in Administrative Behavior.* Washington, DC: Resources for the Future.

Kaus, Mickey. 1992. *The End of Equality.* New York: Basic Books.

Killinger, George, Paul Cromwell, and Jerry Wood, eds. 1979. *Penology: The Evolution of Corrections In America.* St. Paul, MN: West Publishing Company.

King, Roy D. and Rod Morgan. 1980. *The Future of the Prison System.* Westmead, Hants, England: Gower Publishing Company.

King, Roy D. and Kathleen McDermott. 1995. *The State of Our Prisons*. New York: Oxford University Press.

Lab, Stephen P. and John Whitehead. 1990. "From 'Nothing Works' to 'the Appropriate Works': The Latest Stop on the Search for the Secular Grail." *Criminology* 28 (August):405–17.

Latessa, Edmund J., Velmar S. Burton, Sr., and Francis T. Cullen. 1993. "The Correctional Orientation of Prison Wardens: Is the Rehabilitative Deal Supported?" *Criminology* 31 (February):69–92.

Lipsey, Mark W. 1989. "The Efficacy of Intervention for Juvenile Deliquency: Results from 400 Studies." Paper presented at the Annual Meeting of the American Society of Criminology, Reno, NV.

Lipsky, Michael. 1980. *Street-Level Bureaucracy: Dilemmas of the Individual in Public Services*. New York: Russell Sage.

Lipton, Douglas, Robert Martinson, and Judith Wilks. 1975. *The Effectiveness of Correctional Treatment*. New York: Praeger.

Logan, Charles, Gerry Gaes, et al. 1991. "Can Meta-Analysis Save Correctional Rehabilitation?" Unpublished working paper, Federal Bureau of Prisons Office of Research and Evaluation.

Lutz, Faith E., Bruce G. Link, and Francis T. Cullen. 1989. "The Correctional Orientation of Prison Guards: Do Officers Support Rehabilitation?" *Federal Probation* 53:33–42.

MacCoun, Robert J. and Peter Reuter. 1992. "Are the Wages of Sin $30 an Hour?: The Economic Aspects of Street-Level Drug Dealing." *Crime and Delinquency* 38:477–91.

Maguire, Kathleen and Ann L. Pastore, eds. 1998. *Sourcebook of Criminal Justice Statistics 1997*. Washington, DC: Bureau of Justice Statistics, U.S. Department of Justice, USGPO, 1998.

Marquart, James W. and Ben Crouch. 1998. "Judicial Reform and Prisoner Control: The Impact of *Ruiz v. Estelle* on a Texas Penitentiary." In Timothy J. Flanagan, James W. Marquart, and Kenneth G. Adams, eds., *Incarcerating Criminals: Prisons and Jails in Social and Organizational Contexts*. New York: Oxford University Press.

Martin, Susan E., Lee B. Sechrest, and Robin Redner, eds. 1981. *New Directions in the Rehabilitation of Criminal Offenders*. Washington, DC: National Academy Press, 1981.

Martinson, Robert. 1979. "New Findings, New Views: A Note of Caution Regarding Sentencing Reform." *Hofstra Law Review* 7:243–58.

——— 1974. "What Works—Questions and Answers about Prison Reform." *The Public Interest* (spring):22–45.

Marvell, Thomas B. and Carlisle E. Moody. 1994. "Prison Population Growth and Crime Reduction." *Journal of Quantitative Criminology* 10 (4):109–40.

Matland, Richard. 1995. "Synthesizing the Implementation Literature: The Ambiguity-Conflict Model of Policy Implementation." *Journal of Public Administration Research and Theory* 5 (2):145–74.

Mazmanian, Daniel and Paul Sabatier. 1989. *Implementation and Public Policy*. Lanham, MD: University Press of America.

McKee, Gilbert J., Jr. 1985. "Cost-Benefit Analysis of Vocational Training." In Robert M. Carter, Daniel Glaser, and Leslie T. Wilkins, eds., *Correctional Institutions, Third Edition.* New York: Harper and Row.

McKelvey, Blake. 1977. *American Prisons: A History of Good Intentions.* Montclair, NJ: Patterson Smith Publishing Co.

McLaughlin, Milbrey. 1978. "Implementation as Mutual Adaptation: Change in Classroom Organization." In D. Mann, ed., *Making Change Happen.* New York: Teachers College Press.

Mead, Lawrence. 1986. *Beyond Entitlement: The Social Obligations of Citizenship.* New York: Free Press.

———— 1997. *The New Paternalism.* Washington, DC: The Brookings Institution.

Meier, Kenneth J. and Michael Licari. 1997. "Public Policy Design: Combining Policy Instruments." Paper prepared for the Annual Meeting of the American Political Science Association, Washington D.C.

Melnick, R. Shep. 1994. *Between the Lines: Implementing Welfare Rights.* Washington, DC: The Brookings Institution.

Metz, Mary Haywood. 1986. *Different by Design: The Context and Character of Three Magnet Schools.* New York: Routledge.

Meyers, Marcia K. 1997. "Gaining Cooperation at the Front Lines of Service Delivery: Issues for the Implementation of Welfare Reform." Paper prepared for presentation at the 1997 Association for Public Policy Analysis and Management Annual Meetings, Washington, DC.

Mitford, Jessica. 1974. *Kind and Usual Punishment.* New York: Vintage Books.

Mohr, Lawrence B. 1995. *Impact Analysis for Program Evaluation.* Thousand Oaks, CA: Sage Publications.

Morris, Norval. 1974. *The Future of Imprisonment.* Chicago: University of Chicago Press.

Morris, Norval and Michael Tonry. 1990. *Between Prison and Probation: Intermediate Punishments in a Rational Sentencing System.* New York: Oxford University Press.

Morris, Norval and David Rothman. 1995. *The Oxford History of the Prison.* New York: Oxford University Press.

Murphy, Jeffrie. 1985. *Punishment and Rehabilitation.* Belmont, CA: Wadsworth Publishing Company.

Murray, Charles. 1984. *Losing Ground: American Social Policy, 1950–1980.* New York: Basic Books.

Myers, Martha and Suzette Talarico. 1987. *The Social Contexts of Criminal Sentencing.* New York: Springer-Verlag.

Nagel, Stuart, Erika Fairchild, and Anthony Champagne. 1983. *The Political Science of Criminal Justice.* Springfield, IL: Charles C. Thomas.

Nathan, Richard P. 1993. *Turning Promises into Performance: The Management Challenges of Implementing Workfare.* New York: Columbia University Press.

Needels, Karen. 1994. "Go Directly to Jail and Do Not Collect: A Long-Term Study of Recidivism and Employment Patterns Among Prison Releases." Presentation at the SSRC Conference of Fellows: New Perspectives on Urban Poverty Research, June 17, 1994, Ann Arbor, MI.

Oliveres, Katherine, Velmar Burton, Sr., and Francis Cullen. 1996. "The Collateral Consequences of a Felony Conviction: a National Study of State Legal Codes 10 Years Later." *Federal Probation* 60:10–17.

Palmer, Ted. 1991. "The Effectiveness of Intervention: Recent Trends and Current Issues." *Crime and Delinquency* 37 (3):330–46.

——— 1995. "Programmatic and Non-programmatic Aspects of Successful Intervention: New Directions for Research." *Crime and Delinquency* 41:100–31.

——— 1996. "Programmatic and Nonprogammatic Aspects of Successful Intervention." In Alan Harland, ed., *Choosing Correctional Options that Work: Defining the Demand and Increasing the Supply.* Thousand Oaks, CA: Sage.

Palumbo, Dennis J. and Donald Calista, eds. 1990. *Implementation and the Policy Process: Opening Up the Black Box.* Westport, CT: Greenwood Publishing Co.

Paternoster, Raymond and Robert Brame. 1997. "Multiple Routes to Delinquency: A Test of Developmental and General Theories of Crime." *Criminology* 35 (February):49–84.

Petersilia, Joan and Paul Honig. 1980. *The Prison Experience of Career Criminals.* Washington, DC: National Institute of Justice, Department of Justice (November).

Peterson, Paul, Barry Rabe, and Kenneth Wong. 1986. *When Federalism Works.* Washington, DC: The Brookings Institution.

Piehl, Anne Morrison and John J. DiIulio. 1995. "Does Prison Pay? Revisted." *Brookings Review* 13:21–25.

Pressman, Jeffrey and Aaron Wildavsky. 1979. *Implementation: How Great Expectations in Washington Are Dashed in Oakland; or, Why It's Amazing that Federal Programs Work at All, This Being a Saga of the Economic Development Administration, as Told by Two Sympathetic Observers Who Seek to Build Morals on a Foundation of Ruined Hopes.* Berkeley: University of California Press.

Reisig, Michael. 1998. "Rates of Disorder in Higher-Custody State Prisons: A Comparative Analysis of Managerial Practices." *Crime and Delinquency* 44 (2):229–44.

Ross, Robert and Paul Gendreau. 1980. *Effective Correctional Treatment.* Toronto: Butterworths.

Ross, Robert and Bryan McKay. 1980. "Behavioral Approaches to Treatment in Corrections: Requiem for a Panacea." In Robert Ross and Paul Gendreau, eds., *Effective Correctional Treatment.* Toronto: Butterworths.

Rossi, Peter H., Richard A. Berk, and Kenneth J. Lenihan. 1982. *Money, Work, and Crime.* New York: Academic Press.

Rossi, Peter and Howard Freeman. 1993. *Evaluation: A Systematic Approach.* Newbury Park, CA: Sage Publications.

Rothman, David. 1980. *Conscience and Convenience: The Asylum and Its Alternatives in Progressive America.* Boston: Little, Brown.

Rotman, Edgardo. 1990. *Beyond Punishment: A New View on the Rehabilitation of Criminal Offenders.* New York: Greenwood Press.

——— 1995. "The Failure of Reform: United States, 1865–1965." In Norval

Morris and David Rothman. *The Oxford History of the Prison*. New York: Oxford University Press.

Sampson, Robert J. and John H. Laub. 1993. *Crime in the Making: Pathways and Turning Points Through Life*. Cambridge, MA: Harvard University Press.

Saylor, William and Gerald Gaes. 1997. "Training Inmates through Industrial Work Participation and Vocational and Apprenticeship Instruction." *Corrections Management Quarterly* 1 (2):32–43.

———. 1992. "The Post-Release Employment Project." *Federal Prisons Journal* 2 (4):32–36.

———. 1987. "PREP: Post-Release Employment Project: The Effects of Work Skills Acquisition in Prison on Post Release Employment." Paper prepared for presentation at the 1987 Annual Meeting of the American Society of Criminology, Montreal, Quebec, Canada.

Scarpitti, Frank R., James A. Inciardi, and Anne E. Pottieger. 1993. "Process Evaluation Techniques for Corrections-Based Drug Treatment Programs." *Journal of Offender Rehabilitation* 19 (3/4):71–79.

Schlozman, Kay Lehman and Sidney Verba. 1979. *Injury to Insult: Unemployment, Class, and Political Response*. Cambridge, MA: Harvard University Press.

Schneider, Anne and Helen Ingram. 1993. "Social Construction of Target Populations: Implications for Politics and Policy." *American Political Science Review* 87 (2):334–47.

Scott, James. 1985. *Weapons of the Weak: Everyday Forms of Peasant Resistance*. New Haven, CT: Yale University Press.

Sechrest, Lee, Susan White, and Elizabeth Brown. 1979. *The Rehabilitation of Criminal Offenders: Problems and Prospects*. Washington, DC: National Academy of Sciences.

Seiter, Richard. 1990. "Federal Prison Industries." *Federal Prisons Journal* 1 (3):11–15.

Shadish, William R., Jr., Thomas D. Cook, and Laura C. Leviton. 1991. *Foundations of Program Evaluation: Theories and Practice*. Newbury Park, CA: Sage.

Skovran, Sandra Evans, Joseph E. Scott, and Francis T. Cullen. 1990. "Public Support for Correctional Treatment: The Tenacity of Rehabilitative Ideology." *Criminal Justice and Behavior* 17:6–18.

Sparks, Richard, Anthony Bottoms, and Will Hay. 1996. *Prisons and the Problem of Order*. New York: Oxford University Press.

Spillane, James P. 1998. "Cognitive Perspective on the LEA's Role in Implementing Instructional Policy: Accounting for Local Variability." *Educational Administration Quarterly* 34 (February):31–57.

Steadman, Harry J., Joseph P. Morrissey, and Pamela Clark Robbins. 1985. "Reevaluating the Custody-Therapy Conflict Paradigm in Correctional Mental Health Settings." *Criminology* 23 (February):165–79.

Steffensmeier, Darrell and Miles Harer. 1991. "Did Crime Rise or Fall During the Reagan Presidency?: The Effects of an 'Aging' U.S. Population on the Nation's Crime Rate." *Journal of Research on Crime and Delinquency* 28 (3):330–59 (August).

Stephan, James J. 1997. Census of State and Federal Correctional Facilities. Washington, DC: Bureau of Justice Statistics, U.S. Department of Justice. (August, NCJ-164266).

Street, David, Robert D. Vinter, and Charles Perrow. 1966. *Organization for Treatment: A Comparative Study of Institutions for Delinquents.* New York: Free Press.

Sykes, Gresham. 1958. *The Society of Captives: A Study of a Maximum Security Prison.* Princeton: Princeton University Press.

Toch, Hans and Kenneth Adams. 1989. *Coping: Maladaptation in Prisons.* New Brunswick, NJ: Transaction Publishers.

Useem, Bert and Peter Kimball. 1989. *States of Siege: U.S. Prison Riots, 1971–1986.* New York: Oxford University Press.

Van den Haag, Ernest. 1975. *Punishing Criminals: Concerning an Old and Very Painful Question.* New York: Basic Books.

Van Dine, Stephen, John Conrad, and Simon Dimitz. 1979. *Restraining the Wicked: The Incapacitation of the Dangerous Criminal.* Lexington, MA: D. C. Heath.

Van Voorhis, Patricia. 1987. "Correctional Effectiveness: The High Cost of Ignoring Success." *Federal Probation* 51 (1):56–62.

Vaughan, Diane. 1996. *The Challenger Launch Decision: Risky Technology, Culture, and Deviance at NASA.* Chicago: University of Chicago Press.

Von Hirsch, Andrew, ed. 1976. *Doing Justice.* New York: Hill and Wang.

Walton, Hanes, Jr. 1988. *When the Marching Stopped: The Politics of Civil Rights Regulatory Agencies.* Albany: State University of New York Press.

Warr, Mark. 1998. "Life Course Transitions and Desistance from Crime." *Criminology* 36 (May):183–216.

Weick, Karl. 1995. *Sensemaking in Organizations.* Thousand Oaks, CA: Sage Publications.

West, Donald J. and David P. Farrington. 1977. *The Delinquent Way of Life.* London, England: Heinemann.

Wilson, James Q. 1975. *Thinking About Crime.* New York: Basic Books.

———— 1980. " 'What Works' Revisited: New Findings on Criminal Rehabilitation." *The Public Interest* 61:3–17.

————. 1989. *Bureaucracy: What Government Agencies Do and Why They Do It.* New York: Basic Books.

———— 1993. *The Moral Sense.* New York: Free Press.

Wilson, James Q. and Richard J. Herrnstein. 1985. *Crime and Human Nature.* New York: Simon and Schuster.

Wiseman, Michael. 1987. "How Workfare Really Works." *The Public Interest* 89:36–47.

Wolfgang, Marvin, Terence P. Thornberry, and Robert M. Figlio. 1972. *Delinquency in a Birth Cohort.* Chicago: University of Chicago Press.

———— 1987. *From Boy to Man, From Delinquency to Crime.* Chicago: University of Chicago Press.

Wolk, James and Hartmann, David J. 1996. "Process Evaluation in Corrections-Based Substance Abuse Treatment." *Journal of Offender Rehabilitation* 23(1/2):67–78.

Wright, Kevin. 1993. "Prison Environment and Behavioral Outcomes." *Journal of Offender Rehabilitation* 20 (1/2):93–113.

Yanow, Dvora. 1996. *How Does a Policy Mean?: Interpreting Policy and Organizational Actions*. Washington, DC: Georgetown University Press.

Zimmer, Lynn E. 1986. *Women Guarding Men*. Chicago: University of Chicago Press.

Index